TORTURE, INHUMANITY AND DEGRADATION UNDER ARTICLE 3 OF THE ECHR

This book theorises and concretises the idea of 'absolute rights' in human rights law with a focus on Article 3 of the European Convention on Human Rights (ECHR). It unpacks how we might understand what an 'absolute right' is and considers how such a right's delimitation may remain faithful to its absolute character. From these starting points it examines how, as a matter of principle, the right not to be subjected to torture or inhuman or degrading treatment or punishment enshrined in Article 3 ECHR is, and ought to be, substantively delimited by the European Court of Human Rights (ECtHR). Focusing on the wrongs at issue, this analysis touches both on the core of the right and on what some might consider to lie at the right's 'fringes': from the aggravated wrong of torture, to the severity assessment delineating inhumanity and degradation; the justified use of force and its implications for absoluteness; the delimitation of positive obligations to protect from ill-treatment; and the duty not to expel persons to places where they face a real risk of torture, inhumanity or degradation.

Few legal standards are simultaneously so significant and so contested. This book seeks to contribute fruitfully to efforts to counter a proliferation of attempts to dispute, circumvent or dilute the absolute character of the right not to be subjected to torture or inhuman or degrading treatment or punishment, and to offer the groundwork for transparently and coherently (re)interpreting the right's contours in line with its absolute character.

Torture, Inhumanity and Degradation under Article 3 of the ECHR

Absolute Rights and Absolute Wrongs

Natasa Mavronicola

•HART•
OXFORD • LONDON • NEW YORK • NEW DELHI • SYDNEY

HART PUBLISHING
Bloomsbury Publishing Plc
Kemp House, Chawley Park, Cumnor Hill, Oxford, OX2 9PH, UK
1385 Broadway, New York, NY 10018, USA
29 Earlsfort Terrace, Dublin 2, Ireland

First published in Great Britain 2021

A catalogue record for this book is available from the British Library.

Library of Congress Cataloging-in-Publication data

Names: Mavronicola, Natasa, author.

Title: Torture, inhumanity and degradation under Article 3 of the ECHR : absolute rights and absolute wrongs / Natasa Mavronicola.

Description: Oxford, UK ; New York, NY : Hart Publishing, an imprint of Bloomsbury Publishing, 2021. | Includes bibliographical references and index.

Identifiers: LCCN 2020042883 (print) | LCCN 2020042884 (ebook) | ISBN 9781509902996 (hardback) | ISBN 9781509903061 (paperback) | ISBN 9781509903054 (pdf) | ISBN 9781509903061 (Epub)

Subjects: LCSH: Convention for the Protection of Human Rights and Fundamental Freedoms (1950 November 5) | Convention against Torture and Other Cruel, Inhuman, or Degrading Treatment or Punishment (1984 December 10) | International law and human rights. | European Court of Human Rights. | Torture (International law) | United Nations. Committee against Torture. | Refoulement.

Classification: LCC KJC5132 .M384 2021 (print) | LCC KJC5132 (ebook) | DDC 341.4/8094—dc23

LC record available at https://lccn.loc.gov/2020042883

LC ebook record available at https://lccn.loc.gov/2020042884

ISBN: HB: 978-1-50990-299-6
ePDF: 978-1-50990-305-4
ePub: 978-1-50990-306-1

Typeset by Compuscript Ltd, Shannon

To find out more about our authors and books visit www.hartpublishing.co.uk. Here you will find extracts, author information, details of forthcoming events and the option to sign up for our newsletters.

FOREWORD

When I received the manuscript of this book, my first reaction was to anticipate that it would be an additional analysis of absolute rights, which have already received – deservedly, of course – 'substantial attention in both adjudication and academic work', as Natasa Mavronicola rightly observes herself. When I started reading it, I realised that the approach here is truly different and helps to fill an essential gap in the comprehension and interpretation of absolute rights, especially in respect of the right not to be subjected to torture or inhuman and degrading treatment or punishment (Article 3 of the ECHR). 'Rather than questioning whether there *ought to be* any absolute rights', the author's aim is 'to consider what an absolute right *is*'. When we are faced with a sensitive and difficult question, that is exactly what we expect from scholarly work: to frame and address the question from a distinct angle. In this foreword, I wish to touch briefly on some of the book's key dimensions.

What is an absolute right? Strange as it may be, this basic question is very often forgotten not only by doctrine but also by judges. The need for a conceptual approach to absolute rights is all the more urgent in that, at least in the legal order of the European Convention on Human Rights, the absoluteness of the right enshrined in Article 3 is increasingly contested in threatening situations such as terrorism, asylum and migration or security matters. This is a real challenge for the European Court of Human Rights, which must build a robust case-law capable of taking account simultaneously of the necessities or particularities of our time and the inalienable right to human dignity. In agreement with Natasa Mavronicola, I am personally convinced that conceptual clarity could enable 'better reasoning and outcomes across the diverse fields in which the right applies'.

The ideal of integrity. The very rich, learned, and intelligent analysis of the theoretical foundation of the prohibition of torture and inhuman and degrading treatment that the book offers is illuminating. The conceptual framework encompasses two parameters of analysis, applicability and content. With modesty, under the umbrella of Dworkin's *Law's Empire* (1986), the search for consistency and coherence in the interpretation of Article 3 of the Convention is tied to the ideal of integrity that all persons unconditionally deserve in the application of human rights law. Admittedly, such an interpretative endeavour could give rise to objections and such potential objections are addressed by the author in a very systematic manner.

A progressive (re)interpretation. Against this background, the book does not limit itself to being a theoretical study for academic debate or 'classroom discussion'. Having built a strong conceptual foundation, the author revisits, in a very practical and superb way, what she perceives to be both the core and the 'edges (or even fringes)' of Article 3 of the European Convention, under its substantive and its procedural aspect. This encompasses, amongst other things, the following key elements: torture as an aggravated wrong; the famous (and fallacious) threshold of inhumanity that very often leads to the conclusion that the treatment 'falls short of it', particularly in the justified use of force or in the punishment of offenders, which is for me of paramount importance; the delimitation of positive obligations and, accordingly, the scope of the State's wrongful omissions; the inescapable 'non-refoulement' duty and Article 3's obligation against expulsion. Across all the excellent chapters devoted to these matters, the author suggests, with strong arguments, a progressive reinterpretation or reassessment of the right guaranteed under Article 3 of the Convention.

Creative thinking. Throughout the book, Natasa Mavronicola's views and thinking are creative, well-founded, and very stimulating. Taking absolute rights seriously, she can deservedly argue that she is approaching Article 3 of the Convention 'in a way that accommodates contextual sensitivity and dynamism in interpretation'.

The force, genuine interest, and relevance of this book have been made possible – and are served – by a remarkable and profound knowledge of the philosophy and general doctrine of human rights, the rights enshrined in the Convention, and the case-law of the European Court of Human Rights. In this respect, this book is a precious asset and companion for judges, lawyers, scholars, and all those who want to know more on and to better apply the right not to be subjected to torture or inhuman or degrading treatment or punishment, in accordance with its absolute character and the egalitarian commitment to human dignity that underpins it.

Françoise Tulkens
Former judge and vice-president of the
European Court of Human Rights
Professor emeritus *of UCLouvain (Belgium)*

ACKNOWLEDGEMENTS

This is a beloved project, and one that has, at times, been bewilderingly painful to pursue. It takes the idea of an 'absolute right' at human rights law seriously, and endeavours to (re)assess how the wrongs proscribed by the right not to be subjected to torture or to inhuman or degrading treatment or punishment, enshrined in Article 3 ECHR, are (to be) understood in light of its absolute character. This endeavour is all too human, and bound to remain a work in progress. I am profoundly grateful to all those who have helped me strive to 'fail better' at it over the years.

I am singularly indebted to David Feldman for supervising a previous incarnation of this book as a PhD and for so generously sharing his wisdom, insight, and unwavering encouragement, and to Stephanie Palmer for her invaluable advice and support in the pursuit of this project. I am deeply grateful to the examiners of my PhD, Mark Elliott and Liora Lazarus, for engaging so closely with my work and interrogating what needed to be interrogated. I also owe an enormous debt to Fiona de Londras, Laurens Lavrysen, Lydia Morgan and Ben Warwick for their incisive comments on later incarnations of the book, and for helping me see (and say) what I wanted to say, and to Matteo Bianconi for easing the task of doing so with his boundless generosity and care. Thank you to Sophia Ahmed, Barbara Gonzalez-Jaspe, Sumaiyah Kholwadia and Kate Webster for their sterling research assistance, which informed the updating of the study. In writing the book I also benefited tremendously from feedback on my work and from always fruitful discussions with many colleagues, including Gordon Anthony, Meghan Campbell, Brice Dickson, Eithne Dowds, Michelle Farrell, Damian Gonzalez-Salzberg, Alan Greene, Miles Jackson, Kathryn McNeilly, Nils Melzer, Chris McCrudden, Kieran McEvoy, Nigel Rodley, Hannah Russell, Yvette Russell, Alex Schwartz, Henry Shue, Natasha Simonsen, Stijn Smet, Bal Sokhi-Bulley, Ntina Tzouvala, Elaine Webster and Astrid Wiik. I have also benefited greatly from opportunities to present and discuss my work with many other scholars at various conferences, workshops and talks; although they are too many to name here, I am grateful to everyone who shared their thoughts with me in these settings. While completing this book I have been fortunate enough to engage in debates and exchanges with hundreds of brilliant students, and I am grateful to them for having contributed to my thinking on a variety of issues addressed within it.

I owe profound thanks to Tom Adams, Carolyn Fox, Sasha Jawed and Sinead Moloney at Hart Publishing for being so rigorous and professional as well as remarkably encouraging, supportive, and accommodating.

The decision to write this book can probably be traced to the little bookworm of a girl who followed her mum to the bookstore every week for a new adventure, and who, before that, listened attentively to stories read on repeat by a tireless dad.

I am thankful beyond words for my family's unconditional love and support at every step of this journey, and this book is dedicated to them.

Αφιερωμένο στη μάμμα, στον παπά, στη Νίκη, στον παππού, στη γιαγιά και στην Πιτού. Σας αγαπώ πάντα.

CONTENTS

1

Introduction

1.1. The Book's Dual Pursuit

'Absolute rights' receive substantial attention in both adjudication and academic work, but the very concept remains contested. This is especially the case in respect of the right not to be subjected to torture and related ill-treatment.[1] The right not to be subjected to torture or inhuman or degrading treatment or punishment is both intuitively and historically fundamental to the human rights project. It can be said to embody the red line beneath which 'we must not permit ourselves to fall'[2] at the heart of human rights. In spite of all this, contention surrounds every aspect of this right, from its absolute character to its substantive 'essence' and 'fringes'. The significance of and concurrent contestation around this right motivate this book's dual pursuit.

Rather than questioning whether there ought to be any absolute rights,[3] my aim is to consider what an absolute right *is* and what this entails for its interpretation. Moving away from the debate on the existence of absolute moral rights, this book pursues two connected goals that arise when absoluteness is seen as a meaningful concept in respect of legally protected human rights. First, I unpack how we might understand what is an 'absolute right' in human rights law and draw out what a right's absolute character entails for its interpretation. Second, and without purporting to offer a comprehensive legal analysis of the right, I concretise that framework by investigating how, as a matter of substance, the right not to be

[1] See, for example, S Greer, 'Is the Prohibition against Torture, Cruel, Inhuman and Degrading Treatment Really "Absolute" in International Human Rights Law?' (2015) 15 *Human Rights Law Review* 101; S Smet, 'The "Absolute" Prohibition of Torture and Inhuman or Degrading Treatment in Article 3 ECHR: Truly a Question of Scope Only?' in E Brems and J Gerards (eds), *Shaping Rights in the ECHR: The Role of the European Court of Human Rights in Determining the Scope of Human Rights* (Cambridge University Press 2013); MK Addo and N Grief, 'Does Article 3 of the European Convention on Human Rights Enshrine Absolute Rights?' (1998) 9 *European Journal of International Law* 510.

[2] J Donnelly, *Universal Human Rights in Theory and Practice* (Cornell University Press 2003) 14.

[3] See, for example, the discussion between Alan Gewirth and Jerrold Levinson: A Gewirth, 'Are There Any Absolute Rights?' (1981) 31 *The Philosophical Quarterly* 1; J Levinson, 'Gewirth on Absolute Rights' (1982) 32 *The Philosophical Quarterly* 73; and A Gewirth, 'There Are Absolute Rights' (1982) 32 *The Philosophical Quarterly* 348. On the moral philosophical debate surrounding the prohibition of torture see, for example, three distinct accounts: M Farrell, *The Prohibition of Torture in Exceptional Circumstances* (Cambridge University Press 2013); M Kramer, *Torture and Moral Integrity: A Philosophical Enquiry* (Oxford University Press 2014); H Shue, *Fighting Hurt: Rule and Exception in Torture and War* (Oxford University Press 2016) chs 3 and 6.

subjected to torture or inhuman or degrading treatment or punishment enshrined in Article 3 of the European Convention on Human Rights (ECHR)[4] is and ought to be interpreted by the European Court of Human Rights (ECtHR).[5]

Article 3 ECHR has been described as encapsulating an 'absolute right',[6] and its absolute character has often played a decisive part in addressing the issues arising in cases before the ECtHR. However, the seemingly cemented doctrinal description of the right enshrined in Article 3 ECHR as 'absolute' is increasingly contested. There is a growing tendency to criticise or dismiss this characterisation of the right, such characterisation being cast as an inapposite or indeed as an inaccurate account of the right at law.[7] This disputation is often tied to the interpretation of the right, the contestation surrounding the right's content, and the complex, context-sensitive reasoning employed in concretising it.[8]

In this book, I outline and defend a coherent way of conceptualising an absolute right and the implications of its absolute character in delimiting its (contested) demands, concretising this by an examination of the substantive reasoning shaping the delimitation of Article 3 ECHR by the ECtHR. In this process, I explore various aspects of the right that are both widely and less commonly discussed. In doing so, I take seriously the importance of and challenges inhering in the interpretive task with which the ECtHR is faced in respect of Article 3. I proceed on the premise that not only are the hardest cases capable of 'making' bad law, they are also often where legal norms are best illuminated and concretised and, accordingly, where the law and its arbiters ought to be especially robust. When it comes to absolute rights such as the right enshrined in Article 3 ECHR, much may be illuminated by focusing not only on the most obviously egregious violations of the right, but also on what are sometimes perceived to be its edges (or even fringes). Accordingly, particular attention is warranted not only in respect of the way that 'torture' is understood and delimited, but also on how the ECtHR reasons through the 'threshold' of inhumanity and degradation;[9] the justified use of force and its implications for absoluteness; the particularities of punishment; the delimitation of positive obligations; and the character and scope of the *non-refoulement* duty under Article 3. Much of the book is therefore dedicated to considering the

[4] Convention for the Protection of Human Rights and Fundamental Freedoms (1950) 213 UNTS 222 (hereafter 'ECHR' or 'the Convention').

[5] The European Court of Human Rights will be referred to hereafter as 'the ECtHR', 'the Strasbourg Court' or 'the Court'.

[6] See, for example, *Gäfgen v Germany* (2011) 52 EHRR 1, para 176; *Derman v Turkey* (2015) 61 EHRR 27, para 27.

[7] See, notably, Greer (n 1).

[8] See, for instance, Addo and Grief (n 1) 515–16; Greer, ibid 111–12.

[9] Jeremy Waldron, writing on the subject, lamented the dearth of research on inhuman and degrading treatment in J Waldron, *Torture, Terror and Trade-offs: Philosophy for the White House* (Oxford University Press 2012) ch 9. Subsequently, degrading treatment has been the focus of an important monograph by Elaine Webster: E Webster, *Dignity, Degrading Treatment and Torture in Human Rights Law: The Ends of Article 3 of the European Convention on Human Rights* (Routledge 2018).

principled parameters within which these elements of the right are (best) specified in light of (and in line with) its absolute character.[10]

The significance of this book's dual pursuit is multifaceted. The subject matter is ubiquitous in academic commentary, debate and classroom discussion, and has considerable political and legal significance. The right not to be subjected to torture or inhuman or degrading treatment or punishment is at the centre of a vast range of areas of law and policy. By offering a coherent picture of the concept of an absolute right and its implications for the delimitation of the right not to be subjected to torture or inhuman or degrading treatment or punishment enshrined in Article 3 ECHR, this study seeks to provide conceptual and doctrinal clarity so as to enable better reasoning and outcomes across the diverse fields in which the right applies.

1.2. The Approach Taken

The study establishes and employs a conceptual framework to unpack the concept of absolute rights and engage in a critical examination of the interpretation of the right not to be subjected to torture or to inhuman or degrading treatment or punishment under Article 3 ECHR. Following the setting of conceptual foundations in Chapters 2–3, doctrinal analysis in Chapters 4–7 is interwoven with elements of the theoretical groundwork and conceptual analysis that form the starting point of the study. The examination, in Chapters 4–7, of the ECtHR's substantive reasoning on various aspects of Article 3 ECHR – from the wrong of torture, to the Article 3 'threshold' of inhuman or degrading treatment or punishment, to positive obligations and finally to the *non-refoulement* duty – seeks to provide conceptual and doctrinal depth on certain key issues of contention within the doctrine, in pursuit of principled coherence within the ECtHR's interpretation of Article 3.

My pursuit of coherence in the interpretation of Article 3 may be tied broadly to the idea(l) of 'integrity', of seeking to speak with one voice in delineating this right.[11] The labour of this study, however, is humble rather than 'Herculean':[12] my analysis and critique are premised on a search for conceptual and doctrinal coherence within the delimitation of Article 3 ECHR, which is proclaimed to be

[10] This exercise is based on examining relevant ECtHR case law on Art 3 ECHR up to December 2019. My focus here is substantive, and does not seek to address jurisdictional, procedural or remedial matters. Moreover, I confine my analysis to Article 3 ECHR, and do not claim to capture the delimitation of the anti-torture standard in general international law, or the nature and demands of related *jus cogens* and *erga omnes* norms.

[11] See R Dworkin, *Law's Empire* (first published 1986, Hart Publishing 1998). My efforts are by no means as all-encompassing as Dworkin's theory entails, nor do they seek to transpose all of Dworkin's substantive positions to the endeavour pursued in this study.

[12] This is a reference to Dworkin's imaginary judge, ibid.

an absolute right at law. Thus, I take the Court's absoluteness starting point seriously, and endeavour to tell a 'coherent and defensible'[13] story of the character and substance of Article 3 ECHR.[14] This approach accommodates the constructive (re)interpretation of the right,[15] on the understanding that such interpretation can strive to better articulate, coherently and defensibly, the demands of the absolute right enshrined in Article 3 ECHR.[16]

Such an interpretive endeavour may face critique from opposing fronts. On the one hand, some may view it as carrying too much dynamic potential, enabling as it does the emergence of new answers to old questions,[17] and may instead support variations of originalism or other less dynamic approaches on the basis of the importance of State consent in international law.[18] These misgivings are addressed persuasively, in relation to the ECHR, by George Letsas in his account of his own – chiefly theoretical – project in *A Theory of Interpretation of the European Convention on Human Rights*;[19] I consider some of their variations, with specific focus on Article 3 ECHR, in Chapter 3. For present purposes, it is sufficient to say that I regard embracing the prospect of, and striving towards, progressive evolution in our (and the ECtHR's) understanding of the wrongs of torture, inhumanity and degradation and their manifold concrete manifestations as vital in the context of our (and the ECtHR's) all-too-human, inevitably flawed interpretive endeavour in delineating human rights.

Perhaps a more forceful critique, however, relates to how the pursuit of coherence in interpretation relies on and holds the capacity to perpetuate (at least different shades of) the status quo.[20] One response to this would be to highlight that seeking principled coherence within the human rights context is anchored in

[13] S Hershovitz, 'Integrity and Stare Decisis' in S Hershovitz (ed), *Exploring Law's Empire: The Jurisprudence of Ronald Dworkin* (Oxford University Press 2008) 114.

[14] In this sense, the endeavour is very much pursuing 'local' coherence rather than 'global' coherence: see J Dickson, 'Interpretation and Coherence in Legal Reasoning', *Stanford Encyclopedia of Philosophy* (2010).

[15] See Webster (n 9) 11–12, citing Dworkin (n 11) 46–48, 52–53.

[16] Indeed, this is arguably embodied in the ECtHR's dynamic, 'living instrument' approach to the interpretation of Art 3 ECHR. See *Tyrer v UK* (1979–80) 2 EHRR 1, para 31; *Selmouni v France* (2000) 29 EHRR 403, para 101.

[17] For a critique of 'new answers to old questions' see J Finnis, 'Judicial Law-Making and the "Living" Instrumentalisation of the ECHR' in NW Barber, R Ekins and P Yowell (eds), *Lord Sumption and the Limits of Law* (Hart Publishing 2016).

[18] See, for example, the Separate Opinion of Judge Fitzmaurice in *Golder v UK* (1979–80) 1 EHRR 524. But see G Letsas, *A Theory of Interpretation of the ECHR* (Oxford University Press 2007) ch 3.

[19] See especially Letsas, *A Theory of Interpretation of the ECHR*, ibid 29–36 and chs 2–3. For a historical account of the 'constitutionalisation' of the ECHR and (its interpretation by) the ECtHR, see E Bates, *The Evolution of the European Convention on Human Rights: From Its Inception to the Creation of a Permanent Court of Human Rights* (Oxford University Press 2010).

[20] Feminist critique of the status quo is significant in this regard. See, for example, A Edwards, *Violence Against Women under International Human Rights Law* (Cambridge University Press 2011) 36. See, too, the critique of integrity in S Levinson, 'Hercules, Abraham Lincoln, the United States Constitution, and the Problem of Slavery' in A Ripstein (ed), *Ronald Dworkin* (Cambridge University Press 2007).

the egalitarian idea that we hold certain basic rights by virtue of being human.[21] And while a healthy degree of scepticism, given the concrete failings of the human rights project and its realisation of its egalitarian premise or promise, is always warranted,[22] I take the commitment that 'no one shall be subjected to torture or to inhuman or degrading treatment or punishment' to be one worth upholding and sustaining. I also proceed on the premise that interpreting the ECHR in a way that coheres with its principled underpinnings[23] is both a normatively worthwhile pursuit and one that is sustainable without having to rewrite it.[24] Moreover, understanding, elucidating and coherently improving ECtHR doctrine is significant both to the rule of law and to the ECtHR's effective pursuit of its ever-challenging task of overseeing the interpretation and application of the ECHR,[25] and vital with a view to safeguarding a right whose violation we seek to eradicate.[26] This study is pursued with these points in mind.

The aim of this study has been to probe both theoretical thought and legal doctrine towards addressing the conceptual issues and puzzles that arise under the rubric of the book's dual pursuit. Thus, although books outlining the doctrine relating to Article 3 of the ECHR[27] form a useful starting point, my analysis zooms in on particular puzzles of principle raised by the topics explored in each chapter. These are addressed both by unpacking ECtHR doctrine and by reference to relevant academic perspectives, in light of the conceptual foundations set up in Chapters 2–3.

[21] G Letsas, 'Two Concepts of the Margin of Appreciation' (2006) 26 *Oxford Journal of Legal Studies* 705, 707.

[22] As Upendra Baxi has highlighted, over the course of the twentieth century and the growth of the human rights project, 'large masses of colonized peoples were not regarded as sufficiently human or even as potentially human' – U Baxi, *The Future of Human Rights* (3rd edn, Oxford University Press 2008) 48. See, for a distinct set of critiques, D Kennedy, 'The International Human Rights Movement: Part of the Problem?' in D Kennedy, *The Dark Sides of Virtue: Reassessing International Humanitarianism* (Princeton University Press 2005).

[23] The constitutionalising potential of such an approach is highlighted in S Greer, 'Constitutionalizing Adjudication Under the European Convention on Human Rights' (2003) 23 *Oxford Journal of Legal Studies* 405.

[24] See, on this, B Hale, 'Common Law and Convention Law: The Limits to Interpretation' (2011) 5 *European Human Rights Law Review* 534.

[25] The significance of this is attested in the Court's continuing efforts to promote coherence, not least with a view to alleviating its considerable backlog – see, for example, E Myjer, 'Why Much of the Criticism of the European Court of Human Rights is Unfounded' in S Flogaitis, T Zwart and J Fraser (eds), *The European Court of Human Rights and its Discontents: Turning Criticism into Strength* (Edward Elgar 2013).

[26] As Kanstantsin Dzehtsiarou and Alan Greene suggest, cases concerning a breach of Art 3 possess a 'constitutional' quality: see K Dzehtsiarou and A Greene, 'Restructuring the European Court of Human Rights: Preserving the Right of Individual Petition and Promoting Constitutionalism' [2013] *Public Law* 710, 714, specifically footnote 23.

[27] See, for example, J Cooper, *Cruelty – An Analysis of Article 3* (Sweet & Maxwell 2003); U Erdal and H Bakirci, *Article 3 of the European Convention on Human Rights: A Practitioner's Handbook* (OMCT Handbook Series 2006); A Morawa, N Bürli, P Coenen and L Ausserladscheider Jonas, *Article 3 of the European Convention on Human Rights: A Practitioner's Handbook* (2nd edn, OMCT Handbook Series 2014); A Reidy, *A Guide to the Implementation of Article 3 of the European Convention on Human Rights* (Council of Europe 2002).

1.3. The Book's Structure

Following this introductory chapter, Chapter 2 offers the conceptual framework that underpins the book's dual pursuit. This framework introduces two parameters of analysis that help elucidate the character of absolute rights: the 'applicability' parameter, which concerns whether and when the standard referred to as absolute can be displaced, in other words whether extraneous considerations can justify its infringement; and the 'specification' parameter, which concerns the way the content of the standard characterised as absolute is delimited. This framework is key to understanding the concept of an absolute right and how it may be interpreted in a way that coheres with its absolute character. As an examination of the concept through this framework establishes, an absolute right is non-displaceable. Given that any infringement of an absolute right is conclusively unlawful, the right's specification – that is, the delimitation of its substantive scope – takes centre stage. In light of the applicability parameter and the significance of specification, I identify three requirements for the legitimate specification of absolute rights: (1) that it has the capacity to guide; (2) that it consists of relevant, and not extraneous, reasoning; and (3) that it does not amount to (disguised) displacement of the right. These form the starting points for critically examining the delimitation of the absolute right not to be subjected to torture or inhuman or degrading treatment or punishment enshrined in Article 3 ECHR.

Chapter 3 provides the conceptual starting points for the legitimate specification of the right enshrined in Article 3 ECHR, and broadly addresses the interpretive stance that the ECtHR ought to take in this regard in the face of key challenges and pitfalls surrounding this endeavour. The chapter advances an understanding of the 'torture continuum' that sees torture as a radical renunciation of human dignity: of the elevated and equal status ascribed to the human person within the human rights edifice. Inhumanity and degradation lie on this continuum and may be understood as wrongs that attack that equal and elevated status in particular ways, though not necessarily in the deliberate and often elaborate way found in torture. These ideas form a groundwork for understanding the way the ECtHR may distinguish between relevant and extraneous reasoning in the specification of the wrongs proscribed by Article 3 ECHR. As argued in this chapter, while the ECtHR must set a 'red line', it is appropriate for the Court to employ sensitivity to relevant contextual factors, and imperative for the Court to avoid complacency and heed good faith critical engagement. There is scope, therefore, in the legitimate specification of Article 3 ECHR, for a progressive (re-)interpretation of the right and its corresponding wrongs.

Chapters 4–7 are dedicated to key elements of the ECtHR's interpretation of Article 3 in light of the starting points set up in previous chapters. Chapter 4 considers the specification of torture, which is seen as lying at the apex of the spectrum of wrongs proscribed by Article 3. It unpacks and assesses the distinguishing characteristics of torture under Article 3 ECHR, focusing on the aggravated *wrongfulness* of torture and the aggravating elements that make it up. As argued in this chapter, what makes torture stand out from inhuman and degrading treatment and punishment pertains to the character of the conduct rather than solely or largely to its consequences. It is the augmented severity of the treatment, rather than the intensity of suffering or other consequences it brings about, that is key to the aggravated wrong of torture. This entails that the elements of control, intentionality and purposiveness, which emerge implicitly or explicitly in the ECtHR's case law, should take centre stage in delineating what is appropriately to be understood as torture.

Chapter 5, which should be read alongside Chapter 4, explores the Article 3 'threshold', focusing on the specification of treatment or punishment that is often described as falling 'short' of torture but that is also absolutely proscribed by Article 3, and thus on the criteria that shape the Court's determination of whether treatment or punishment is inhuman or degrading. Chapter 5 examines under-discussed aspects of the Article 3 'threshold', including the justified use of force against persons, and the reasoning involved in the delimitation of inhuman and degrading *punishment*, which raises particular challenges and conundrums. As I argue, it is possible, in the specification of inhumanity and degradation, to reconcile attention to a range of relevant contextual factors as well as some forms of justificatory reasoning with the absoluteness starting point. A fundamental aspect of such reconciling is an appreciation of the relational and qualitative nature of the 'minimum level of severity' that delineates the Article 3 'threshold', which is not attached solely to a 'quantum' of suffering.

Chapter 6 examines the specification of one of the most challenging aspects of Article 3's substantive scope: positive obligations. The delimitation of positive obligations under Article 3 is probed by appraising the circumstances giving rise to positive obligations under Article 3, and the considerations and constraints shaping the positive obligations arising. As argued in the chapter, applying criteria of reasonableness and adequacy to delimit the scope of positive obligations is an appropriate approach to determining the wrongfulness of State omissions under Article 3. While the criteria shaping the Court's delimitation of positive obligations do not in principle contradict the absoluteness starting point, troubling elements in the ECtHR's doctrine call for elucidation or reassessment. In particular, integrity demands that the ECtHR elucidates its doctrine in relation to suffering of which no particular human agency can be said to be the immediate cause, and that it rethinks, in the spirit of integrity, the often coercive and carceral slant of its positive obligations doctrine under Article 3.

Chapter 7 scrutinises the specification of the *non-refoulement* duty under Article 3. As the chapter argues, the obligation against expulsion (understood as encompassing extradition) under Article 3 ECHR can be understood as corresponding to the broader wrong(s) of subjecting or knowingly exposing someone to (a real risk of) torture or inhuman or degrading treatment or punishment. As observed in this chapter, while the Court sets up robust starting points that tend to cohere with the requirements of non-displacement and relevant reasoning in the delineation of this obligation, it sometimes unduly deviates from these. Moreover, the prospective assessment involved in the application of the *non-refoulement* duty should compel the Court to offer more generalisable guidance and, at the same time, err on the side of caution where doubt persists in respect of the nature of the treatment faced or the degree of risk involved.

Finally, the book's conclusion offers a brief reflection on the implications of taking absoluteness seriously, and approaching the absoluteness of the right enshrined in Article 3 ECHR in a way that accommodates contextual sensitivity and dynamism in interpretation. Looking to the future, it invites further engagement towards (re)interpreting – and even reimagining – the right not to be subjected to torture or inhuman or degrading treatment or punishment in line with its absolute character and the egalitarian commitment to human dignity that underpins it.

2

What Is an 'Absolute Right'? A Conceptual Framework on Applicability and Specification

2.1. Introduction: Interrogating the Concept of an 'Absolute Right'

What is an 'absolute right'? The answer to this question is often assumed or elided, even while the existence of 'absolute rights' is contested. This chapter briefly outlines the controversy surrounding the idea of an 'absolute right', and unpacks what we ought to understand by 'absolute right' by means of a framework encompassing two parameters: applicability and specification. The analysis provided in this chapter aims to set the conceptual foundations for exploring elements of Article 3's substantive scope in light of its absolute character, and to provide the groundwork for interpreting absolute rights more generally.

Although the label 'absolute' is used frequently in legal commentary and adjudication, the concept of an absolute right remains fraught with uncertainty or scepticism. For instance, while David Feldman states that State obligations under Article 3 are 'absolute, non-derogable and unqualified',[1] he proceeds to caution: 'Nevertheless … a degree of relativism cannot, in practice, be entirely excluded from the application of the notions of inhuman or degrading treatment'.[2] While Alastair Mowbray remarks that Article 3 is 'the most absolute right guaranteed by the Convention',[3] Helen Fenwick suggests that the standard of treatment that

[1] D Feldman, *Civil Liberties and Human Rights in England and Wales* (2nd edn, Oxford University Press 2002) 242.

[2] ibid. See also O Ze'ev Bekerman, 'Torture – The Absolute Prohibition of a Relative Term: Does Everyone Know What Is in Room 101?' (2005) 53 *American Journal of Comparative Law* 743.

[3] A Mowbray, 'A Study of the Principle of Fair Balance in the Jurisprudence of the European Court of Human Rights' (2010) 10 *Human Rights Law Review* 289, 307. *Cf* S Greer, 'Is the Prohibition against Torture, Cruel, Inhuman and Degrading Treatment Really "Absolute" in International Human Rights Law?' (2015) 15 *Human Rights Law Review* 101; H Battjes, 'In Search of a Fair Balance: The Absolute Character of the Prohibition of *Refoulement* under Article 3 ECHR Reassessed' (2009) 22 *Leiden Journal of International Law* 583.

qualifies as Article 3 ill-treatment 'does not connote an absolute standard and, in its application, it allows for a measure of discretion'.[4] Such commentary raises the question of what an absolute right is (and what it is not), and what its absolute character entails. Furthermore, it necessitates an examination of how 'relativism' and other warranted or unwarranted aspects of the interpretation of a right relate to its absolute character. This provides the impetus for the investigation undertaken in this chapter.

Attaining conceptual clarity on the questions raised above requires us to distinguish between two parameters of absoluteness. The first, which concerns whether and when a standard can be lawfully 'displaced', can be labelled the *applicability* parameter. The second, which concerns the delimitation and concretisation of the standard,[5] can be labelled the *specification* parameter. This allows us to understand the two different planes on which analysis of the concept of an absolute right can operate. The distinction does not, however, negate the possibility of interplay between these two parameters. Indeed, specification, which 'fleshes out' the standard, is decisive of its application to a given set of facts. The applicability parameter determines whether the standard, *as specified*, can be lawfully displaced or not. As will be illustrated, distinguishing between these two parameters can serve to elucidate the relationship between the absolute character of the right enshrined in Article 3 ECHR and its delimitation. It also helps illuminate problematic aspects of the Court's case law, as well as rationalise aspects that attract unwarranted or misplaced critique.

2.2. The Applicability Parameter: Absolute Rights as Non-displaceable Entitlements

The applicability parameter of an absolute right is captured by Alan Gewirth as follows: 'A right is *absolute* when it cannot be overridden in any circumstances, so that it can never be justifiably infringed and it must be fulfilled without any exceptions'.[6] Following the Hohfeldian model of rights,[7] absoluteness pertains to claim-rights, that is, justified entitlements to the performance of correlative duties. Applying this to human rights law, the entitlements at play are entitlements to the performance of correlative duties by the State. The right is fulfilled when its correlative duty is performed (including a duty to refrain from a particular act) and the

[4] H Fenwick, *Civil Liberties and Human Rights* (3rd edn, Cavendish Publishing 2004) 44–45.

[5] The term 'specification' is here taken to refer to specifying, in the sense of identifying content, and not to any other technical or legal term.

[6] A Gewirth, 'Are There Any Absolute Rights?' (1981) 31 *The Philosophical Quarterly* 1, 2.

[7] See W Hohfeld, *Fundamental Legal Conceptions as Applied in Judicial Reasoning* (Yale University Press 1919).

right is infringed when its correlative duty is not carried out. The right is *violated* when it is unjustifiably infringed. Lastly, the right is *overridden* when it is justifiably infringed. Absolute rights can never be overridden, according to Gewirth. In other words, no considerations can displace absolute rights; infringement automatically amounts to a *violation*,[8] which is conclusively unlawful.

To give a fictitious example, an absolute human right not to be killed would encompass an obligation on State agents not to kill anyone in any circumstances; no consideration, not even self-defence, could operate to override the right; any killing by State agents would amount to a violation of the right and would therefore be unlawful. A consequentialist approach – broadly looking at the (undesirable) consequences of fulfilling the right or the (desirable) consequences of infringing it – would have no place in determining the lawfulness of infringing the right. On the other hand, if, say, the human right to freedom of expression provides that it can be lawfully interfered with in pursuit of the protection of reputation or derogated from in particular circumstances, this means that certain considerations can operate to override the right; not all restrictions on freedom of expression would amount to violations and therefore be unlawful. Laws restricting certain defamatory speech could therefore justifiably infringe the right.

This understanding of the applicability parameter of absolute rights is adopted by many other theorists. For instance, it is taken for granted by Jerrold Levinson,[9] who embraces rather than disputes Gewirth's conceptual understanding of the applicability parameter of absoluteness, but considers there are no absolute (moral) rights. Alan Dershowitz, prominent in his critique of the absolute prohibition of torture, appears to take it as legally non-displaceable and to condemn this state of affairs.[10] Similar approaches are taken across legal texts, where absolute rights tend to be treated as 'those rights that cannot be interfered with whatever the justification'.[11]

[8] The analysis here adopts Gewirth's approach but places it strictly within a legal conceptual framework, so that 'infringement' means interfering with or acting contrary to a right and 'violation' means doing so unlawfully. Thus, if one looks at Judith Jarvis Thomson's analysis, for the purposes of the legal framework outlined here, it is necessary to recast her perspective on infringement and violation by substituting the adverb 'unlawfully' for the adverb 'wrongly': 'Suppose that someone has a right that such and such shall not be the case. I shall say that we infringe a right of his if and only if we bring about that it is the case. I shall say that we violate a right of his if and only if both we bring about that it is the case and we act wrongly in doing so'. J Jarvis Thomson, 'Some Ruminations on Rights' in W Parent (ed), *Rights, Restitution, and Risk* (Harvard University Press 1986) 51. See also J Jarvis Thomson, *The Realm of Rights* (Harvard University Press 1990) 122. For a critique of the moral implications of the infringement/violation distinction in rights theory, see J Oberdiek, 'Lost in Moral Space: On the Infringing/Violating Distinction and its Place in the Theory of Rights' (2004) 23 *Law and Philosophy* 325.

[9] J Levinson, 'Gewirth on Absolute Rights' (1982) 32 *The Philosophical Quarterly* 73.

[10] A Dershowitz, 'Tortured Reasoning' in S Levinson (ed), *Torture: A Collection* (Oxford University Press 2004) 257.

[11] S Foster, *Human Rights & Civil Liberties* (2nd edn, Pearson Education 2008) 27. See also P Sieghart, *The International Law of Human Rights* (Clarendon Press 1983) 161: 'All that is therefore required to establish a violation … is a finding that the state concerned has failed to comply with its obligation in respect of any one of these modes of conduct: no question of justification can ever arise'. See, too, J Cooper, *Cruelty – An Analysis of Article 3* (Sweet & Maxwell 2003) 29.

The absolute character of a right entails that it cannot be displaced by extraneous considerations. This, however, gives rise to the following question: what if the conflicting considerations are also rights? Those who argue against absolute rights tend to frame circumstances supposedly compelling infringement, such as the widely invoked 'ticking bomb' scenario, as a conflict of rights.[12] The debate is relevant in determining where the applicability parameter of absoluteness stands in such (alleged) conflict.

To address this question of conflict, Gewirth contemplated a hypothetical scenario whereby a group of political extremists announce that they will use an arsenal of nuclear weapons against a distant city unless Abrams, a politically active lawyer in the city, tortures his mother to death in public. Gewirth recognised this might be presented as a conflict of rights:

> [I]t may be argued that the morally correct description of the alternative confronting Abrams is not simply that it is one of not violating or violating an innocent person's right to life, but rather not violating one innocent person's right to life and thereby violating the right to life of thousands of other innocent persons through being partly responsible for their deaths, or violating one innocent person's right to life and thereby protecting or fulfilling the right to life of thousands of other innocent persons.[13]

Gewirth rejected this analysis of the situation by putting forward the doctrine of *novus actus interveniens*:

> According to this principle, when there is a causal connection between some person A's performing some action (or inaction) X and some other person C's incurring a certain harm Z, A's moral responsibility for Z is removed if, between X and Z, there intervenes some other action Y of some person B who knows the relevant circumstances of his action and who intends to produce Z or who produces Z through recklessness. The reason for this removal is that B's intervening action Y is the more direct or proximate cause of Z and, unlike A's action (or inaction), Y is the sufficient condition of Z as it actually occurs.[14]

The problem with using this argument is that it stands at odds with Gewirth's recognition that a right can encompass both positive and negative obligations. It eliminates positive obligations insofar as there is an intervention by a human agent with intent or recklessness. Human rights generally encompass both negative and positive obligations, including obligations to protect persons from various intentional acts of non-State actors.[15] Henry Shue has classified the correlative duties of rights into three groups: duties of restraint, duties to protect and duties to provide.[16]

[12] See, for example, Greer (n 3) 103. See, further, S Greer, 'Should Police Threats to Torture Suspects Always be Severely Punished? Reflections on the Gäfgen Case' (2011) 11 *Human Rights Law Review* 67.

[13] Gewirth (n 6) 9.

[14] ibid 12.

[15] S Fredman, 'Human Rights Transformed: Positive Duties and Positive Rights' [2006] *Public Law* 498.

[16] H Shue, *Basic Rights: Subsistence, Affluence and U.S. Foreign Policy* (2nd edn, Princeton University Press 1996) 35.

As Sandra Fredman has explained, these consist of 'the primary duty whereby the state should not interfere; the secondary duty whereby the state should protect individuals *against other individuals*; and the tertiary duty to facilitate or provide for individuals' (emphasis added).[17] The ECtHR itself boasts a rich body of case law on positive obligations,[18] which have been described as 'the hallmark of the European Convention on Human Rights'.[19]

Positive obligations expose a fundamental flaw in Gewirth's response to the conflict of rights challenge, and raise an apparent conundrum for absolute rights: what if negative and positive obligations that pertain to the same absolute right conflict? The way to salvage the absolute rights thesis is by refuting the idea of a clash of absolute rights. The response is as follows. While an absolute right gives rise to a whole host of positive obligations, there is *no* positive obligation under an absolute right to act in a way that constitutes a violation of the negative obligation encompassed by an absolute right.[20]

Let us take something closer to a realistic scenario concerning the right not to be subjected to torture or inhuman or degrading treatment as an example: the police have arrested a person they know to have been involved in the kidnap of a 10-year-old child. The whereabouts of the child are unknown and the child may be facing ill-treatment or risk of death at the hands of accomplices, or significant suffering or risk of death in the absence of adequate food or shelter. In such a scenario, it would be wrong to argue that, because of the kidnapper's intervention, there is *no* positive duty on the State to take action to avert the risk of suffering or death and accordingly no State responsibility for the State's failure to take protective action. In fact, a number of duties, including duties of effective investigation and deployment of search parties, obviously arise. Yet recognising that positive duties are generated in this situation does not preclude delimiting such duties in a way that excludes taking action that amounts to a violation of the negative duty under an absolute right. This is a matter of specification of positive duties rather than of certain considerations *displacing* positive duties under an absolute right: that is, while positive duties to take a host of measures arise in such a kidnap

[17] Fredman (n 15) 500.

[18] See A Mowbray, *The Development of Positive Obligations Under the European Convention on Human Rights by the European Court of Human Rights* (Hart Publishing 2004); L Lavrysen, *Human Rights in a Positive State: Rethinking the Relationship between Positive and Negative Obligations under the European Convention on Human Rights* (Intersentia 2016).

[19] K Starmer, 'Positive Obligations Under the Convention' in J Jowell and J Cooper (eds), *Understanding Human Rights Principles* (Hart Publishing 2001) 159.

[20] I propose this perspective in N Mavronicola, 'What Is an "Absolute Right"? Deciphering Absoluteness in the Context of Article 3 of the European Convention on Human Rights' (2012) 12 *Human Rights Law Review* 723, 732. It has subsequently been argued in somewhat distinct terms by Stijn Smet – see S Smet, 'Conflicts between Absolute Rights: A Reply to Steven Greer' (2013) 13 *Human Rights Law Review* 469, 469–77. See, too, N Mavronicola, 'Is the Prohibition against Torture and Cruel, Inhuman and Degrading Treatment Absolute in International Human Rights Law? A Reply to Steven Greer' (2017) 17 *Human Rights Law Review* 479, 483–85.

scenario, there is no positive duty to torture or ill-treat the kidnapper in order to discover the child's whereabouts.[21]

Positive duties are not boundless, nor could they sensibly be, unless we are prepared to countenance that every act of ill-treatment in its jurisdiction should automatically entail the State's liability,[22] or that the State should be compelled to install surveillance cameras in every street or home.[23] The idea that positive obligations are not boundless, in that 'not any [or every] action that amounts to or causes protection … is obligated',[24] does not mean that positive obligations are displaceable – that is, it does not follow that the overarching duty to take protective action is capable of being overridden entirely. That there is no positive duty to torture or inflict inhuman or degrading treatment on a child's kidnapper in order to discover a kidnapped child's whereabouts is a matter of the *specification* of positive duties rather than of certain considerations *displacing* the right of an individual in peril to protective action by the State.[25]

Another issue sometimes raised in relation to absolute rights in general and the right not to be subjected to torture or inhuman or degrading treatment in particular is the often considerable gap between the right as a matter of law and its enjoyment in practice. The issue is broadly as follows: in theory, rights labelled as absolute can never be overridden; but in practice, for all sorts of reasons including brazenly unlawful State action, lack of goodwill, poor implementation, failure to investigate effectively, apathy, or 'failure' by the victims to assert their rights or to take legal action in respect of a violation of their rights, the right is frequently flouted, without redress. An article by Nicholas Grief and Michael Addo broadly exemplifies this challenge.[26]

Certainly, the frequent flouting of an absolute right in general, and of the right not to be subjected to torture or related ill-treatment in particular, is a major cause for concern. At the same time, an argument to the effect that the (unredressed) violation of an absolute right in practice vitiates its absolute character *in law* is misplaced. It is crucial not to equate legal inviolability with actual inviolability.

[21] Indeed, this appears to be the approach taken by the ECtHR in *Gäfgen v Germany* (2011) 52 EHRR 1, examined below. *Cf* Greer (n 3).

[22] George Rainbolt has addressed this with reference to the distinction between 'perfect' and 'imperfect' obligations, drawn by Kant: see I Kant, *The Moral Law: Kant's Groundwork of the Metaphysics of Morals* (HJ Paton trans, Routledge 1976) 84; and in I Kant, *The Metaphysics of Morals* (M Gregor trans, Cambridge University Press 1996) 153. Rainbolt interprets this as a distinction between obligations with latitude (imperfect) and obligations without latitude (perfect); he argues that most positive obligations are 'imperfect'. See G Rainbolt, 'Perfect and Imperfect Obligations' (2000) 98 *Philosophical Studies* 233.

[23] Report of the Special Rapporteur on Torture and Other Cruel, Inhuman or Degrading Treatment or Punishment, UN Doc A/74/148, 12 July 2019, para 23.

[24] M Klatt, 'Positive Obligations under the European Convention on Human Rights' (2011) 71 *Heidelberg Journal of International Law* 691, 694.

[25] See further analysis in Chs 3 and 6.

[26] N Grief and M Addo, 'Some Practical Issues Affecting the Notion of Absolute Right in Article 3 ECHR' (1998) 23 *European Law Review* 17.

While 'can' and 'cannot' may be used interchangeably to signify both permission/prohibition and possibility/impossibility, these two connotations are evidently distinct. When it is said of a legally enshrined human right that it cannot be (lawfully) interfered with, this is not – at least not within the conceptual framework developed here – a reference to actual impossibility. It is therefore inapposite to argue, without more, that the possibility of violation or of a violation being left without redress refutes an absolute legal prohibition. That the right 'is not *always*' respected or fulfilled cannot appropriately be equated with 'ought not always' to be respected or fulfilled.

This is not to suggest that frequent violation or limited realisation and enjoyment of a legally absolute right in practice is somehow unproblematic. The gravity of what is at stake is the reason for rendering a right absolute and it is also a reason for seeking its effective implementation and enjoyment. The above account simply clarifies that the applicability parameter is not conceptually affected by the fact that the right is frequently violated in practice.

2.3. The Applicability Parameter Affirmed in ECtHR Doctrine

The applicability parameter of absoluteness emerges clearly in ECtHR doctrine on Article 3 ECHR. In unpacking Article 3's absolute character, the ECtHR focuses on a juxtaposition, contrasting absoluteness with the potential for lawful derogations, exceptions or interferences. As the ECtHR frequently reiterates:

> The Convention prohibits in absolute terms torture and inhuman or degrading treatment or punishment, irrespective of the victim's conduct. Unlike most of the substantive clauses of the Convention and of Protocols 1 and 4, Article 3 makes no provision for exceptions and, under Article 15(2), there can be no derogation therefrom even in the event of a public emergency threatening the life of the nation.[27]

Elsewhere, the Court puts it as follows:

> Within the Convention system it has long been recognised that the right under Article 3 not to be subjected to torture or to inhuman or degrading treatment or punishment enshrines one of the fundamental values of democratic society. It is an absolute right, permitting of no exception in any circumstances ...[28]

These statements reflect the idea, embodied in the applicability parameter, that an absolute right cannot be justifiably infringed. The Court contrasts Article 3 with 'most of the substantive clauses of the Convention', which make provision for

[27] *Ireland v UK* (1979–80) 2 EHRR 25, para 163.
[28] *Derman v Turkey* (2015) 61 EHRR 27, para 27.

proportionate interference in pursuit of a legitimate aim and/or for derogation in time of war or other public emergency.[29]

The ECtHR's response to arguments relating to Article 3's demands coming into conflict with States' allegedly overwhelming need to protect themselves and their citizens from the threat of terrorism has been firm:

> The Court is well aware of the immense difficulties faced by States in modern times in protecting their communities from terrorist violence. However, even in these circumstances, the Convention prohibits in absolute terms torture or inhuman or degrading treatment or punishment, irrespective of the victim's conduct.[30]

In *Gäfgen v Germany*, which concerned the use of threats of torture by police against a child's kidnapper for the purpose of extracting information on the whereabouts of the child, the ECtHR maintained its stance and underlined the unconditional nature of Article 3's protection:

> The Court has confirmed that even in the most difficult circumstances, such as the fight against terrorism and organised crime, the Convention prohibits in absolute terms torture and inhuman or degrading treatment or punishment, irrespective of the conduct of the person concerned. The nature of the offence allegedly committed by the applicant is therefore irrelevant for the purposes of art.3.[31]

The ECtHR proceeded to find that the threats of torture to which Magnus Gäfgen, the kidnapper of Jakob von Metzler, had been subjected amounted to inhuman treatment in violation of Article 3 ECHR.[32]

The ECtHR's approach in respect of the applicability parameter of absoluteness can be distilled to three main elements. First, Article 3 makes no provision for lawful exceptions. In contrast to other provisions within the ECHR, there is no possibility of lawful interference that is 'necessary in a democratic society' for the fulfilment of a legitimate aim.[33] Second, Article 15 ECHR, which governs derogation from obligations under the ECHR in exceptional and restricted circumstances, does not allow for any derogation from Article 3 even in the event of war or other public emergency threatening the life of the nation (including the threat of terrorist violence).[34] Lastly, Article 3 ECHR protects everyone unconditionally, irrespective of their conduct. Whether the victim or potential victim

[29] Rights which contain an in-built qualification that allows for infringements in the pursuit of a legitimate aim include Arts 8–11 ECHR; rights which allow for derogation under Art 15 ECHR include Arts 5 and 6 ECHR (as well as the qualified rights set out above).

[30] *Chahal v UK* (1997) 23 EHRR 413, para 79. See also *Saadi v Italy* (2009) 49 EHRR 30, para 127. This can be contrasted with the position under Art 8 – see, for example, *Üner v Netherlands* (2007) 45 EHRR 14, para 57.

[31] *Gäfgen* (n 21) para 87.

[32] ibid para 108.

[33] See, for example, Arts 8(2), 9(2), 10(2), 11(2) ECHR. For an interesting critical take on the ECtHR's – and legal commentators' – approach to such rights vis-à-vis absolute rights, see G Webber, 'Proportionality and Absolute Rights' in V Jackson and M Tushnet (eds), *Proportionality: New Frontiers, New Challenges* (Cambridge University Press 2017).

[34] Art 15(2) ECHR provides: 'No derogation from Article 2, except in respect of deaths resulting from lawful acts of war, or from Articles 3, 4(1) and 7 shall be made under this provision'.

is an innocent child or a cold-blooded murderer[35] or 'terrorist',[36] they enjoy the protection of Article 3 alike.

The unqualified terms of Article 3 and the ECtHR's categorical statements indicate that Article 3's absoluteness is understood consistently with the applicability parameter unpacked above. Given that the Convention, as the ECtHR affirms, leaves no scope for Article 3 to be justifiably infringed or overridden, failure by the State to abide by its obligations under Article 3 is conclusively unlawful. Moreover, the protection conferred by Article 3 ECHR is not conditional on the 'good' behaviour of the victim or potential victim – such considerations can never displace its application. It is in these two senses that the right is, as described by Stephanie Palmer, 'unqualified'[37] and 'unconditional'.[38]

The three elements of absoluteness outlined by the Court – no exceptions, no derogations, and the unconditional protection of all individuals within ECHR States' jurisdiction – form part of what I will refer to as the absoluteness starting point. Yet these reasonably straightforward starting points necessarily lead to the much more complex question which forms the subject of this book: how is the content of an absolute right to be delimited? The specification of its content is, after all, what determines what amounts to a (conclusively unlawful) breach of an absolute right. The remainder of this chapter explores how the specification of an absolute right can conceptually cohere with its absolute character.

2.4. The Specification Parameter: Significance and Implications

2.4.1. The Significance of Specification

Absoluteness, on the applicability parameter, entails an either-or approach: either there is a breach of Article 3, which is conclusively unlawful, or there is not; there is no second step, such as that involved in the case of qualified rights, of establishing whether an infringement of the right is justified. Specification – which delimits the content of what is non-displaceable – therefore takes centre stage,[39] and its significance cannot be overstated.

[35] See *Gäfgen* (n 21).

[36] See *Chahal* (n 30).

[37] S Palmer, 'A Wrong Turning: Article 3 ECHR and Proportionality' (2006) 65 *Cambridge Law Journal* 438, 447.

[38] ibid 450.

[39] For a critical take on this point, see S Smet, 'The "Absolute" Prohibition of Torture and Inhuman or Degrading Treatment in Article 3 ECHR: Truly a Question of Scope Only?' in E Brems and J Gerards (eds), *Shaping Rights in the ECHR – The Role of the European Court of Human Rights in Determining the Scope of Human Rights* (Cambridge University Press 2014).

I propose to zoom in on two key elements of significance, which will run through the rest of the study: first, the level of specificity – or abstraction – of the obligations encompassed in the right; and second, the substance of the specification of said obligations. Building on a number of observations in relation to these two elements, I propose a theory of legitimate specification of absolute rights. Chapter 3 then considers how these starting points may be transposed to the specification of the right not to be subjected to torture or to inhuman or degrading treatment or punishment.

Gewirth was conscious that the structural implications – that is, what I label the applicability parameter – of absoluteness are only the beginning of the story, and that the substantive delimitation of the standard discussed is also key to its absolute character. Pondering the significance of specificity/abstraction, Gewirth distinguished between three different levels of abstraction/specification of non-displaceable standards.[40] These three levels may be unpacked (and refined) as follows.

(1) 'Principle Absolutism' maintains that the non-displaceable standard is a very general moral principle, like Immanuel Kant's Categorical Imperative.[41] Such a principle usually presents the subjects (beneficiaries), respondents (duty-bearers) and objects (the actual entitlement) of the right in a 'relatively undifferentiated way, present[ing] a general formula for all the diverse duties of all respondents … toward all subjects'.[42] The problem is that principles of a high degree of generality are not sufficiently specified to constitute precise entitlements and obligations or to address the resolution of moral dilemmas (including apparent conflicts between rights). Accordingly, even if a principle at this level of generality is non-displaceable, it is difficult – and in legal practice it may be a substantial judicial undertaking – to distil Hohfeldian claim-rights from it.

(2) 'Individual Absolutism' describes a highly specified absolute right, which Gewirth placed on the other end of the generality–specificity spectrum. 'Individual absolutism' refers to a particular person's non-displaceable entitlement to a particular object or action in a particular geographic and chronological context and, as Gewirth saw it, when all reasons for overriding the right in the particular case have been overcome.[43] In essence, on Gewirth's understanding, individual absolutism tells us what someone is entitled to after external considerations have displaced any other potential entitlements and were either irrelevant to, or incapable of displacing, the remainder. Such a highly specified right is therefore, for Gewirth, a post-consequentialist residual entitlement. Russ Shafer-Landau appeared to accept this in his article 'Specifying Absolute Rights', where he posited that sufficient 'specification' can render all moral rights absolute.[44] Achieving this involves the

[40] See Gewirth (n 6) 3–5.

[41] Kant's Categorical Imperative is here taken to be: 'Act only in accordance with that maxim through which you can at the same time will that it become a universal law'. See Kant, *Groundwork* (n 22) 84.

[42] Gewirth (n 6) 4.

[43] ibid.

[44] R Shafer-Landau, 'Specifying Absolute Rights' (1995) 37 *Arizona Law Review* 209. See also J Oberdiek, 'Specifying Rights out of Necessity' (2008) 28 *Oxford Journal of Legal Studies* 127.

'narrowing' of all rights to encompass a number of exceptive clauses, which Shafer-Landau called, following Judith Jarvis Thomson,[45] 'full factual specification':

> On this view, there is no right to life *simpliciter*, but rather a right not to be killed except in circumstances A, B, C, etc. On this theory, rights are always absolute, i.e., are of the utmost stringency and can never be morally overridden. Any situation that appears to call for infringement is instead subsumed under one of the exceptive clauses.[46]

Yet this interpretation of absoluteness reduces the applicability parameter to something which, in the context of human rights law, would be virtually meaningless, relating only to a post-displacement residue. It does not present specification as something distinct from displacement.

To salvage the compatibility of this category with the applicability parameter of absoluteness, Gewirth's individual absolutism is best reframed as simply lying at the most individually concretised end of a spectrum of specificity – *not*, however, as a post-consequentialist residue. Even so, to tie absoluteness only to fully concretised rights, for instance the right of X to be free from the application of treatment Φ in y circumstances at the hands of Z, distances the concept of 'absolute right' from any notion of a general standard applicable to all.[47] As RM Hare has argued, high degrees of specificity can remove the capacity of legal standards to guide behaviour.[48] Lacking a capacity to guide is problematic in light of the particularly compelling imperative of securing *ex ante* fulfilment of a right which is so important as to be non-displaceable.

(3) 'Rule Absolutism' is identified by Gewirth as the intermediate level of specification. At this level what is non-displaceable is a specific rule which describes the content of the entitlement and the correlative duty (or duties) in both specific and generalisable terms:

> At this level, the rights whose absoluteness is in question are characterized in terms of specific objects with possible specification also of subjects and respondents, so that a specific rule can be stated describing the content of the right and the correlative duty. The description will not use proper names and other individual referring expressions, as in the case of Individual Absolutism, nor will it consist only in a general formula applicable to many specifically different kinds of rights and duties and hence of objects, subjects and respondents.[49]

As Gewirth put it, 'It is at this level that one asks whether the right to life of all persons or of all innocent persons is absolute, whether the rights to freedom of

[45] J Jarvis Thomson, 'Self-Defense and Rights' in Parent (ed), *Rights, Restitution, and Risk* (n 8) 37.

[46] Shafer-Landau (n 44) 210.

[47] For a similar point made specifically in relation to the definitions of torture and cruel, inhuman and degrading treatment and punishment, see J Waldron, *Torture, Terror and Trade-offs: Philosophy for the White House* (Oxford University Press 2012) at 190, 202, 289–90.

[48] RM Hare, 'The Presidential Address: Principles' (1972–73) 73 *Proceedings of the Aristotelian Society, New Series* 1, 3.

[49] Gewirth (n 6) 4.

speech and of religion are absolute, and so forth'.[50] For Gewirth, therefore, this encapsulates where any discussion on the absolute character of legally enshrined human rights mainly lies.[51]

Gewirth's three-level analysis provides a useful illustration of the significance of the *level* of specification – how abstract or how specific the right is – as regards an absolute right. Specification is significant, therefore, not only because it delimits what is non-displaceable – setting the substantive limits of the 'absolute' – but also because it carries implications for the absolute right's Hohfeldian claim-right status, and its capacity to guide behaviour. Generality and specificity are ultimately matters of degree,[52] and Gewirth's grid is best understood as a spectrum. At the same time, the range within the spectrum occupied by what Gewirth would label 'rule absolutism' carries some significance in relation to a legally recognised human right. The capacity to guide behaviour is arguably a *sine qua non* of any conception of the (rule of) law.[53] Certainly, this quality is also a matter of degree, but it may be said that it is not sufficiently fulfilled at either of the two ends of the generality/specificity spectrum: a very general principle suffers from too much uncertainty and disagreement in relation to its concrete application, while a highly specified standard provides minimal *ex ante* guidance and is not, in Hare's terms, 'teachable and usable'.[54]

This issue is reflected in two of the eight elements which, according to Lon Fuller, are components of the rule of law: generality and clarity.[55] Fuller considered that 'the requirement of generality rests on the truism that to subject human conduct to the control of rules, there must be rules'.[56] At the same time, the requirement of clarity pulls towards a degree of specificity. Fuller stated that 'The desideratum of clarity represents one of the most essential ingredients of legality'.[57] Although his arguments were largely set in the legislative context, Fuller sought clear standards by both legislators and adjudicators. Addressing legal provisions conveyed in very general, abstract, terms, he called for an assessment of the 'prospect that *fairly clear standards of decision* will emerge from a case-by-case treatment of controversies as they arise' (emphasis added).[58] These are requirements that may be appropriately transposed to a legal order conferring

[50] ibid.

[51] See also the somewhat distinct principle/rule taxonomisation of ECHR rights in A Green, 'A Philosophical Taxonomy of European Human Rights Law' (2012) 1 *European Human Rights Law Review* 71.

[52] Hare (n 48) 3.

[53] See J Raz, 'The Identity of Legal Systems' (1971) 59 *California Law Review* 795, 802. See further J Jowell, 'The Rule of Law and its Underlying Values' in J Jowell and D Oliver (eds), *The Changing Constitution* (6th edn, Oxford University Press 2007), where he draws on the value of certainty. Certainty also plays an important part in Fuller's account of legality in L Fuller, *The Morality of Law* (2nd edn, Yale University Press 1969); it underlies the analysis of principles by Hare (n 48).

[54] Hare (n 48) 15.

[55] See Fuller (n 53) ch 2.

[56] ibid 49.

[57] ibid 63.

[58] ibid 65.

rights to individuals and imposing correlative obligations on the State: general and clear standards are needed to guide both individuals and State officials. This is so especially in the context of a legal right so fundamental as to be absolute.

George Letsas has made a forceful argument, pursued in the context of defending the dynamic interpretation of the ECHR against originalist views, that the State is not an actor whose autonomy requires protection through legal certainty.[59] Nonetheless, his stance should not be taken to contradict the value of a degree of certainty and a capacity to guide in the specification of human rights.[60] Certainty in the sense of clarity as well as generalisability remains an important quality in human rights law, particularly in the operation of absolute rights, and in this context it is important for several reasons. First, guidance as to the standards binding State officials can militate against unlawful conduct by boosting norm-awareness and accountability processes. Secondly, certainty is important in light of the concrete possibility that persons within State machinery or outside of it may ultimately be held individually to account, including by means of criminal law,[61] for engaging in behaviour contrary to human rights such as Article 3 ECHR.[62] There is, moreover, both instrumental and intrinsic value in knowing one's rights. A court adjudicating on and specifying human rights, notably a right that must be fulfilled without exceptions, must therefore carefully tread the line between over-generality and over-specificity to ensure a sufficient level of both generality and clarity.

A key significance of specification therefore relates to the norm's capacity to guide behaviour.[63] Turning to specification's significance as a matter of *substance*, the obvious starting point is to highlight that specification determines the substantive scope of the right – the breadth and the substance of what is conclusively unlawful.

As part of what is perhaps one of the most famous theories of the specification of rights – although this is not the term employed – Ronald Dworkin criticised the idea of a broad right to liberty corresponding to Isaiah Berlin's influential idea of

[59] G Letsas, *A Theory of Interpretation of the European Convention on Human Rights* (Oxford University Press 2007) 73.

[60] See his more nuanced position in G Letsas, 'Lord Sumption's Attack on Strasbourg: More Than Political Rhetoric?', *UK Constitutional Law Blog*, 9 December 2013, available at https://ukconstitutionallaw.org/2013/12/09/george-letsas-lord-sumptions-attack-on-strasbourg-more-than-political-rhetoric/ (accessed 3 January 2020).

[61] See L Lazarus, 'Positive Obligations and Criminal Justice: Duties to Protect or Coerce?' in L Zedner and J Roberts (eds), *Principles and Values in Criminal Law and Criminal Justice* (Oxford University Press 2012). See also the study of coercive duties under the ECHR in L Lavrysen and N Mavronicola (eds), *Coercive Human Rights: Positive Duties to Mobilise the Criminal Law under the ECHR* (Hart Publishing 2020).

[62] A clear example of this possibility is the Grand Chamber's judgment in *Gäfgen* (n 21), in which the Court indicated that police officers involved in the inhuman treatment suffered by the applicant ought to be more severely punished in order for the requirements of Art 3 to be fulfilled. The coercive edge of Art 3 ECHR is further touched on in Ch 6.

[63] See also J Feinberg, 'Voluntary Euthanasia and the Inalienable Right to Life' in J Feinberg, *Rights, Justice and the Bounds of Liberty: Essays in Social Philosophy* (Princeton University Press 1980) 221, 228–29.

negative liberty[64] as the absence of constraints placed by a government on what someone might do. Dworkin considered the idea of such a right to be not only inapposite, but absurd: 'Indeed it seems to me absurd to suppose that men and women have any general right to liberty at all, at least as liberty has traditionally been conceived by its champions'.[65] Dworkin meant to *narrow* what we conceive to be our right to liberty in a way that would cohere with his view of rights as 'trumps' and his broader thesis that liberty and equality are not competing entitlements. Letsas interprets this in an instructive way. After setting out that we have a fundamental right not to be deprived of liberty or opportunity 'on the basis of certain considerations' (it is unnecessary to set out these considerations at this point), Letsas states:

> Rights thus understood are *absolute*: it can never become justified for the government to restrict my liberty for the reasons just mentioned … [When justified restrictions operate,] we should not say that we have a right which is not absolute and whose limitation is justified. Rather, we should say that we had no right in the first place.[66]

Specification's significance therefore goes beyond the capacity to guide, in that specification can operate to *narrow* the substantive scope of the right and its correlative duty or duties, so that what is in fact an 'absolute right' may ultimately only be a 'fraction' of what might at first sight be perceived as such. If the specification of a right considered to be absolute fails to deliver *ex ante* guidance but also appears to load the perceived 'absolute right' with qualifiers, the specification process carries the risk of uncertainty, as well as of an indefinite narrowing of what might be thought to be an absolute entitlement. This could be a critique launched in respect of the specification of the First Amendment to the United States Constitution, for example, which admits of no qualifications on its face but has been 'loaded' with qualifications through relevant judicial pronouncements.[67]

There is an additional and crucial risk, however. This is the possibility that specification may bring extraneous considerations into delineating the content of the right and thereby undermine the applicability parameter. In other words, specification may operate as (disguised) displacement. This is a critical issue to address in relation to the right not to be subjected to torture or inhuman or degrading treatment or punishment under Article 3 ECHR, and appears to be at the forefront of concern for academic commentators citing 'relativism' as being in tension with Article 3's absoluteness.[68]

[64] See I Berlin, *Liberty* (first published 1969, Henry Hardy ed, Oxford University Press 2002).

[65] R Dworkin, *Taking Rights Seriously* (Harvard University Press 1977) 267. See also ibid 261, where he posits that 'The more limited the range of a principle, the more plausibly it may be said to be absolute'.

[66] Letsas (n 59) 117.

[67] Mavronicola, 'What Is an "Absolute Right"?' (n 20) 745. For a nuanced perspective on this, see F Schauer, 'Freedom of Expression Adjudication in Europe and the United States: A Case Study in Comparative Constitutional Architecture' in G Nolte (ed), *European and US Constitutionalism* (Cambridge University Press 2005). But see the more critical account in J Greene, 'Rights as Trumps?' (2018) 132 *Harvard Law Review* 28.

[68] See Feldman, text to n 2 above.

The rest of this chapter contemplates how best to address these risks. It unpacks how specification can delimit an absolute right in a way that appropriately navigates the abstraction–specificity spectrum and that delimits its substantive scope without unduly narrowing or distorting the right and, crucially, without undermining its absolute character. These ideas are considered concretely in relation to the right not to be subjected to torture or inhuman or degrading treatment or punishment in the remainder of the book.

2.4.2. A Theory of Legitimate Specification of Absolute Rights

Gewirth recognised that, even at the level of what he labelled 'rule absolutism', a right might come with layers of specification: from the right of all persons to life, to 'the right of all innocent persons to an economically secure life',[69] and so on. He acknowledged that the specifications he outlined could be seen as *exceptions* to the more general right in a way that would challenge what I have labelled the applicability parameter of absoluteness. Yet he posited that 'not all specifications of the subjects, objects or respondents of moral rights constitute the kinds of exception whose applicability to a right debars it from being absolute'.[70] This broadly offers the starting point for drawing a distinction between legitimate and illegitimate specification of an absolute right. The label 'legitimate', for these purposes, pertains to the soundness of the substantive specification of an absolute right. It characterises specification which coheres with the right's absolute character. It does not concern the legitimacy of particular actors.

Gewirth suggested that for specifications to cohere with the right's absolute character, they must fulfil three requirements: they must amount to concepts that are recognisable in ordinary practical thinking; they must be justifiable through a valid moral principle; and they must exclude reference to the consequences of fulfilling the right.[71] Refining and adjusting Gewirth's requirements, I would suggest that the specification of an absolute right must have the following three characteristics:

(1) it must have the capacity to guide;
(2) it must be premised on reasoning which relates to the wrongs that the right proscribes; and
(3) it must not amount to displacement of the right.

Gewirth's first requirement, that specifications be made up of concepts recognisable in ordinary practical thinking, is meant, as far as Gewirth is concerned, to exclude rights that are 'overloaded with exceptions' or based on intricate utilitarian

[69] Gewirth (n 6) 4.
[70] ibid 5.
[71] ibid.

considerations.[72] I take this requirement to pertain primarily to certainty, rather than to exceptions or extraneous considerations, and would therefore refine it into a requirement that the formulation of the right should have the capacity to guide. The capacity to guide, or 'teachability', to paraphrase Hare,[73] is undermined by over-generality and over-specificity, as discussed above. More broadly, the requirement highlights the duty of the authoritative judicial body adjudicating on the matter to provide some guidance through meaningful, clear and generalisable specification of the right's substance.

Gewirth's second requirement, of justifiability through a valid moral principle, may at first sight appear inapposite in the context of legally enshrined entitlements. For Gewirth, whose thesis lies in moral philosophy, the criterion is indissolubly linked with, and meant to be a prerequisite for, the moral justifiability of absoluteness. For example, Gewirth considers that there is 'a good moral justification for incorporating the restriction of innocence on the subjects of the right not to be killed',[74] but no such similarly sound moral justification for incorporating racial or religious specifications. Yet Gewirth's moral reasoning takes place in a legal and textual vacuum, and forms the sole basis of determining the content of the right. This is not the case with regard to an absolute right located in a legal instrument. In the context of such a right, I propose that the essence of the second requirement – which is intertwined, as I will show, with the third requirement analysed directly below – is that the specification of an absolute right must be based on relevant reasoning.

The requirement of relevant reasoning demands that the right be *interpreted* through relevant reasoning rather than distorted by irrelevant considerations. The legitimate specification of the wrongs of torture, inhuman or degrading treatment or punishment should, on this requirement, be based on criteria determining whether a treatment or punishment is inhuman or not; degrading or not; torturous or not. That this is not mere tautology is shown by considering the irrelevance of criteria such as the colour of the victim's hair, what the perpetrators had for breakfast, or the popularity or unpopularity of the victim. Employing such criteria, which do not relate to the attributes of treatment or punishment proscribed in the right,[75] would distort the right and contradict its absolute character. On the other hand, taking into account nuanced considerations such as whether a particular act would deeply injure one person's religious sensibilities but leave someone with no religious sentiments indifferent would amount to relevant reasoning. More broadly, navigating the requirement of

[72] ibid.

[73] See Hare, text to n 54 above.

[74] Gewirth (n 6) 5.

[75] This distinction differentiates my analysis from Alexy's idea of 'subsumption' in R Alexy, 'Balancing and Subsumption' (2003) 16 *Ratio Juris* 433.

relevant reasoning fundamentally demands that the specification of the right and its correlative duties remains loyal to the fundamental underpinnings of the right and its absolute character – that it stays true to what the right is there to protect and safeguard.[76]

Gewirth's last requirement is that the specification of an absolute right 'must exclude any reference to the possibly disastrous consequences of fulfilling the right'.[77] Through this requirement, Gewirth was essentially pointing out that specification of an absolute right should not displace the right through the back door. Thus, the reasons why inhuman treatment may be seen as desirable by some – for instance, to elicit useful information – should not be inserted into the specification of what amounts to inhuman treatment with a view to excluding treatment with such perceived positive consequences from what is understood to be inhuman treatment. Whether this is done expressly or covertly, this would amount to displacement; and it would also amount to irrelevant reasoning. The third requirement therefore intertwines closely with the second requirement.

Underpinning these requirements is also the implied requirement of good faith.[78] This requirement militates against bad-faith efforts to circumvent a legal norm by seeking to interpret one's desired behaviour out of what it proscribes. A classic example of this are the infamous US Torture Memos, which sought to circumvent the prohibition of torture by interpreting it in an extraordinarily narrow fashion.[79] Good faith does not, of course, pertain solely to absolute rights, but it is an important imperative for all norm-appliers engaging in the process of specification in line with the requirements outlined above.

The line of legitimate specification becomes particularly difficult to tread in relation to positive obligations under an absolute right. As indicated above, positive obligations cannot logically be without limit, and States should not be expected to commit absolute wrongs in order to protect persons from a general or concrete risk of harm. The specification of positive obligations is discussed further in Chapter 3, while Chapter 6 examines the ECtHR's reasoning on positive obligations and considers it in light of the legitimate specification requirements.

[76] This animates much of the analysis in Ch 3 of this book.

[77] Gewirth (n 6) 5.

[78] This is reflected in Art 31(1) of the Vienna Convention on the Law of Treaties (1969) 1155 UNTS 331 (VCLT) and may also be taken to be inherent in the ECHR – see *Rooman v Belgium* App no 18052/11 (ECtHR, 31 January 2019), Partly Dissenting Opinion of Judge Serghides, para 6. On good faith in international law and interpretation, see S Reinhold, 'Good Faith in International Law' (2013) 2 *UCL Journal of Law and Jurisprudence* 40.

[79] See D Cole (ed), *The Torture Memos: Rationalising the Unthinkable* (The New Press 2009). David Luban refers to the Torture Memos as representing 'moral failure': D Luban, *Legal Ethics and Human Dignity* (Cambridge University Press 2009) 163. Rebecca Sanders examines the legal 'reframing' of torture techniques as the construction of 'plausible legality': R Sanders, *Plausible Legality: Legal Culture and Political Imperative in the Global War on Terror* (Oxford University Press 2018) ch 3. On the Torture Memos and the demands of good faith and legality, see W Bradley Wendel, 'The Torture Memos and the Demands of Legality' (2009) 12 *Legal Ethics* 107.

2.5. Conclusion

This chapter distinguishes between the applicability and specification parameters of an absolute right with a view to elucidating the concept of an absolute right and providing a coherent framework for its delimitation. Addressing the key structural implication of a right's absolute character, I suggest that the applicability parameter of absoluteness offers the primary answer: absolute rights amount to entitlements that are non-displaceable. The non-displaceability of absolute rights is reflected in ECtHR doctrine on Article 3 ECHR. It is the crux of what it means for a right to be absolute. Specification, which interprets and concretises the right and thereby determines the substantive scope of what is conclusively unlawful, therefore takes centre stage. The specification of a right in light of its absolute character must be capable of providing guidance, must employ reasoning that relates to the wrongs at issue, and must not (overtly or implicitly, in bad faith or otherwise) amount to displacement of the right. These parameters constitute the absoluteness starting point and set the foundations for contemplating how the right enshrined in Article 3 ECHR should be specified, and for assessing the ECtHR's undertaking of this arduous task.

3

Delimiting the Absolute: How Should the ECtHR Approach the Specification of Article 3 ECHR?

3.1. Introduction

The purpose of this chapter is to elaborate some general starting points that ought to shape the ECtHR's significant and complex endeavour of specifying the right enshrined in Article 3 ECHR in line with its absolute character. The chapter considers the way in which the Court should navigate the legitimate specification criteria in light of the uncertainty and contestation that surrounds the wrongs encapsulated by Article 3 ECHR. I argue that the uncertainty and contestation which surround Article 3's content and Strasbourg's broader interpretive endeavour should not lead to an abdication by the ECtHR of its morally loaded interpretive task in specifying Article 3, nor an abandonment or undermining of the imperatives of guidance, non-distortion and non-displacement that emanate from Article 3's absoluteness. The Court should therefore specify Article 3 authoritatively and without undue concessions to majoritarian or other extraneous pressures. At the same time, the boldness that the ECtHR is called upon to demonstrate in its specification of Article 3 ECHR should entail not complacency, but rather care and rigour in its reasoning as well as a readiness to refine prevailing understandings of the wrongs at issue.

In view of the legitimate specification criteria, particularly those of relevant reasoning and non-displacement, the chapter proceeds to contemplate the wrongs encapsulated by Article 3 ECHR, and provides some ideas for reasoning through the substantive parameters of torture, inhumanity and degradation, as well as of States' positive obligations in securing protection therefrom. I argue that torture, inhumanity and degradation may be viewed as being fundamentally at odds with human dignity, understood as the equal and elevated status ascribed within the human rights edifice to all human persons, and the basic respect and concern that it demands. Identifying these wrongs in a set of particular circumstances requires attention to the way *relevant* contextual factors shape the character of a particular (in)action or situation. Turning to positive obligations under Article 3 ECHR, I consider what can amount to relevant reasoning in their delimitation, underlining both the imperative of effective protection and the constraints that duly operate in delineating what constitutes a wrongful omission by the State in securing this absolute right.

3.2. Specifying Article 3 ECHR: The ECtHR's Task

3.2.1. Neither Paralysis Nor Complacency

As outlined in Chapter 2, to cohere with its absolute character, the specification of the right not to be subjected to torture or to inhuman or degrading treatment or punishment enshrined in Article 3 ECHR:

(1) must have the capacity to guide;
(2) must consist of relevant reasoning (that is, reasoning that relates to, rather than distorts, the wrongs at issue); and
(3) must not amount to displacement of the right.

Underpinning these principles is also the implied requirement of good faith.[1] The right is accordingly to be interpreted and applied in a way that coheres with, and does not seek to circumvent, its letter and spirit.[2]

The specification of the right enshrined in Article 3 ECHR involves pronouncing on the concrete obligations distilled out of the stipulation that 'No one shall be subjected to torture or inhuman or degrading treatment or punishment'. As with all of the Convention, the ECtHR is the final arbiter on what Article 3 demands[3] and is the entity from which the authoritative specification of the right emerges.[4] The legitimate specification criteria require that in specifying the contours of Article 3 ECHR, the ECtHR must engage in relevant reasoning and not displace the right through its very interpretation. It must also, in mediating between the general terms of Article 3 ECHR and the concrete findings arrived at, elaborate the right's substance in a way that is capable of guiding State authorities and individuals. How should the Court navigate these requirements?

[1] See the good faith requirement in Art 31(1) of the Vienna Convention on the Law of Treaties (1969) 1155 UNTS 331 (VCLT). Note *Rooman v Belgium* App no 18052/11 (ECtHR, 31 January 2019), Partly Dissenting Opinion of Judge Serghides, para 6. On good faith in international law and interpretation, see S Reinhold, 'Good Faith in International Law' (2013) 2 *UCL Journal of Law and Jurisprudence* 40.

[2] On interpreting the ECHR in line with its 'spirit', see the Article 3 case of *Svinarenko and Slyadnev v Russia* App nos 32541/08 and 43441/08 (ECtHR, 17 July 2014), para 118. See also the point made in two reports of the Special Rapporteur on Torture and Other Cruel, Inhuman or Degrading Treatment or Punishment, UN Doc A/HRC/37/50, 23 November 2018, para 14; and UN Doc A/72/178, 20 July 2017, para 77.

[3] Art 32 ECHR.

[4] On the challenges of this task, including in dealing with 'unprecedented' practices, see the interesting account in J Waldron, *Torture, Terror and Trade-offs: Philosophy for the White House* (Oxford University Press 2012) ch 9.

The first step in delineating the legitimate specification of the absolute right enshrined in Article 3 is to appreciate that what Article 3 demands is both morally loaded and contestable.[5] Whether one considers morality to be an essential aspect of law and legal interpretation or not – and it is impossible to exhaust or resolve the debate here – it is difficult to deny that some legal provisions are imbued with moral content. The right not to be subjected to torture or inhuman or degrading treatment or punishment is a quintessential example of this.[6] This is evident even if one takes what might be called a more 'formalist' approach and turns to Article 31 of the Vienna Convention on the Law of Treaties (VCLT). Article 31 calls for an interpretation that relies on the 'ordinary meaning' of treaty terms, and follows the treaty's object and purpose.[7] Both the 'ordinary meaning' starting point, in the sense of our preliminary understanding of the nature of torture and inhuman and degrading treatment and punishment, and the ECHR's object and purpose, which is to secure the protection of human rights such as Article 3 ECHR, invite evaluative moral judgement. The terms of Article 3 are not so much 'ambiguous'[8] as unambiguously moral.[9] Article 3 ECHR therefore 'cannot be properly interpreted without sound moral reasoning'.[10] Its specification calls for an evaluative interpretive exercise which seeks to identify the best understanding of the (obligations corresponding to the) right not to be subjected to torture or to inhuman or degrading treatment or punishment.[11] Such an evaluative endeavour requires grappling with the wrongs at issue and employing evaluative judgement in determining how they manifest themselves in an array of circumstances and (in)actions.

Even though a moral reading of the right not to be subjected to torture or to inhuman or degrading treatment or punishment is in principle not only apposite but necessary, more questions emerge. These questions relate chiefly to the uncertainty and disagreement surrounding terms such as those found in Article 3 ECHR. Are there really right answers to what is (and what is not) 'torture or inhuman or degrading treatment or punishment'? Even if there are,

[5] See ibid ch 9.

[6] S Fredman, 'Foreign Fads or Fashions? The Role of Comparativism in Human Rights Law' (2015) 64 *International & Comparative Law Quarterly* 631, 646.

[7] See Art 31(1) VCLT.

[8] This is a loose reference to Art 32 VCLT.

[9] On Art 3 ECHR as encapsulating a moral imperative, see R Spano, 'The Future of the European Court of Human Rights – Subsidiarity, Process-based Review and the Rule of Law' (2018) 18 *Human Rights Law Review* 473, 483.

[10] DO Brink, 'Legal Interpretation, Objectivity, and Morality' in B Leiter (ed), *Objectivity in Law and Morals* (Cambridge University Press 2007) 55; see also Waldron (n 4) 289, 313–19. See generally R Dworkin, *Freedom's Law: The Moral Reading of the American Constitution* (Harvard University Press 1997) especially at 2–3 and 7–12. On the interpretive judgement necessitated by international legal texts, seeB Çalı, *The Authority of International Law: Obedience, Respect, and Rebuttal* (Oxford University Press 2015) 122.

[11] See the analysis below on the particular issues arising in the delimitation of positive obligations under Art 3.

can we trust judges to find them? Those who would provide negative answers to these questions may cite the 'indeterminacy'[12] of such or similar terms in light of their morally loaded character, and the disagreement generated as to their specific demands, to suggest there is no right answer, and that it is inapposite to speak of right and wrong answers in this context.[13]

The objection which equates fundamental and pervasive uncertainty and/or disagreement with indeterminacy – that is, the 'no right answer' thesis – is addressed by Ronald Dworkin in his discussion of objectivity and truth in morality, in which he argues that uncertainty, disagreement and the absence of verification mechanisms immune to rational contestation do not entail, in a particular case or situation, the absence of a right answer or a futility in seeking it.[14] For the purposes of this study, I assume that Article 3 ECHR invites us to 'make particular, rather than all-purpose, evaluations'[15] – that torture, inhumanity or degradation, as Jeremy Waldron puts it, 'don't just mean "bad"'[16] – and that there are right and wrong (and certainly better and worse) ways of specifying what Article 3 ECHR proscribes and demands, but I accept that what these are can attract significant and even profound uncertainty and contestation.

Those of us engaged in, or cast with the responsibility of, interpreting such rights as Article 3 ECHR may be uncertain as to the contours of the wrongs of torture or inhuman or degrading treatment or punishment and consider these not to be automatically or easily within our grasp. We may – quite rightly – expect that our efforts to establish whether something amounts to torture or to inhuman or degrading treatment or punishment will often yield flawed, perhaps deeply flawed, reasoning and answers. These difficulties can lead to paralysis. While a person with no institutional duty to interpret and apply the right not to be subjected to torture or inhuman or degrading treatment can absolve themselves of this arduous task, officials who operate under such a duty and, in the ECHR context, the ECtHR especially cannot legitimately do so.[17] Deliberations and judgements on

[12] See Waldron (n 4) ch 9. See also M Koskenniemi, *From Apology to Utopia: The Structure of International Legal Argument* (2nd edn, Cambridge University Press 2005) 39; but see the nuanced account in S Besson, *The Morality of Conflict: Reasonable Disagreement and the Law* (Hart Publishing 2005) 59–65. On legal indeterminacy see, for instance, B Leiter, 'Legal Indeterminacy' (1995) 1 *Legal Theory* 481; see also Brink (n 10) 17–19.

[13] See, generally, E Voyiakis, 'International Law and the Objectivity of Value' (2009) 22 *Leiden Journal of International Law* 51, 53 and 63. See, further, J Mackie, *Ethics: Inventing Right and Wrong* (Penguin 1977) 38–39.

[14] R Dworkin, 'Objectivity and Truth: You'd Better Believe It' (1996) 25 *Philosophy & Public Affairs* 87; R Dworkin, *Justice for Hedgehogs* (Harvard University Press 2011) chs 1 and 2. See also Brink (n 10) 44–57; and J Tasioulas, 'The Legal Relevance of Ethical Objectivity' (2002) 47 *American Journal of Jurisprudence* 211. But for a sceptical perspective on the relevance of moral objectivity in shaping judicial decision making, see J Waldron, *Law and Disagreement* (Oxford University Press 1999) 186–87. See, too, the analysis in B Tripkovic, *The Metaethics of Constitutional Adjudication* (Cambridge University Press 2017) ch 4.

[15] Waldron (n 4) 295.

[16] ibid.

[17] ibid 314.

the substantive scope of Article 3 ECHR must be made by the appropriate actors and ultimately and authoritatively by the Strasbourg Court.[18]

Paralysis, therefore, is not an option in the specification of Article 3 ECHR; the Strasbourg court, and indeed Contracting States' authorities, must earnestly grapple with the contestable, evaluative standards that they must do their best to interpret and apply. This is not to suggest that officials, and notably the ECtHR, should be indifferent to the uncertainty and potential pitfalls surrounding this endeavour. Rather, these should compel the actors tasked with interpreting Article 3 to abandon complacency and instead remain alert to new insights and vigilant as to any shortcomings in the prevailing understanding of the wrongs at issue, and remedy those shortcomings when they are recognised. The proposition that there are right and wrong, or better and worse, answers does not mean that the answer provided at any given time *is* the right one or best one; or that it may not be improved upon through deliberation, disagreement,[19] and engagement with new information, new arguments and new perspectives. A deliberative, multilateral, constructive and plural engagement with varied actors and institutions that allows information, arguments, experiences and perspectives to be exchanged and evaluated is key to ensuring that those tasked with Article 3's interpretation can reconsider and improve upon established (pre-)conceptions of what amounts to torture or inhuman or degrading treatment or punishment.[20] Constant questioning is vital in maintaining the rigour of this endeavour. It follows, of course, that bodies such as the ECtHR should be open to the progressive (*re*-)interpretation of Article 3 and what it proscribes.[21]

While complacency should be avoided, this does not mean that the ECtHR ought to shy away from the authoritative pronouncements that it is called upon

[18] See R Spano, 'Universality or Diversity of Human Rights?' (2014) 14 *Human Rights Law Review* 487, 494.

[19] For a constructive account of disagreement in law and politics, see Besson (n 12).

[20] On the multiple interpreters of a right such as Art 3 ECHR, see E Webster, *Dignity, Degrading Treatment and Torture in Human Rights Law: The Ends of Article 3 of the European Convention on Human Rights* (Routledge 2017) 11–12. On 'looking outward' in the specification of Art 3 ECHR, see N Mavronicola, 'The Mythology and the Reality of Common Law Constitutional Rights to Bodily Integrity' in M Elliott and K Hughes (eds), *Common Law Constitutional Rights* (Hart Publishing 2020) 45–46. For a distinct and important argument on the reflective model of according value to 'foreign law' in particular, and its limits, see B Tripkovic, 'The Morality of Foreign Law' (2019) 17 *International Journal of Constitutional Law* 732.

[21] On the capacity within legal interpretation to 'refine unexamined moral beliefs and challenge embedded assumptions', see C O'Cinneide, 'Rights under Pressure' (2017) 1 *European Human Rights Law Review* 43, 47. See also N Bratza, 'Living Instrument or Dead Letter: The Future of the ECHR' (2014) 2 *European Human Rights Law Review* 116, 120–21. For an interesting reflection on the progressive (re)interpretation of Article 3, see E Yildiz, 'A Norm in Flux: The Development of the Norm Against Torture under the European Convention from a Macro Perspective', iCourts Working Paper Series, No 45, 2016. On the ECtHR's 'living instrument' doctrine more generally, see G Letsas, 'The ECHR as a Living Instrument: Its Meaning and Legitimacy' in G Ulfstein, A Follesdal and B Peters (eds), *Constituting Europe: The European Court of Human Rights in a National, European and Global Context* (Cambridge University Press 2013).

to make. If the Court were to avoid undertaking the authoritative specification of Article 3 when it is called upon to do so, this would entail *enshrining* uncertainty into the right's delimitation and affirmatively blurring the red lines meant to mark the difference between conclusively unlawful and potentially lawful State conduct. This would fundamentally undermine the demands of absoluteness.[22] In sum, the Court must do its best, without complacency, and without shirking its duty to delimit the wrongs at issue.

3.2.2. Navigating Contention and Discontent

Although the ECHR formally tasks the ECtHR with determining the Convention's substantive scope,[23] the question of who should have the 'final say' on what the Convention demands endures, particularly in areas of significant contestation.[24] The way in which this issue is approached by the Court in the specification of Article 3 can have significant implications in respect of Article 3's absolute character and the legitimate specification criteria. In light of this, three key positions which seek to *qualify* the Court's authoritative specification of the substantive scope of Convention rights warrant assessment, in relation to Article 3 ECHR, in light of the absoluteness starting point. These three positions may be sketched out as follows:

(a) The Strasbourg Court should interpret contested terms in an originalist and/or minimalist fashion and allow any substantive 'extension' of the terms to take place through redrafting of the ECHR,[25] and for more extensive protections to be afforded domestically by Contracting States.
(b) The final say on the substantive scope of rights should, on (certain) contested matters, lie with those domestic institutions which bear the greatest extent of procedurally democratic credentials in Contracting States (usually parliaments).[26]

[22] This is supported by Robert Spano: see Spano (n 9) 483.

[23] Art 32 ECHR. See Y Roznai, 'The Theory and Practice of "Supra-constitutional" Limits on Constitutional Amendments' (2013) 62 *International & Comparative Law Quarterly* 557, 579.

[24] Many of the relevant writings on this issue are outlined excellently in Spano (n 18); see also the broad debate on subsidiarity and the ECtHR, summarised in M Iglesias Vila, 'Subsidiarity, Margin of Appreciation and International Adjudication within a Cooperative Conception of Human Rights' (2017) 15 *International Journal of Constitutional Law* 393. But see, on the limits of subsidiarity in relation to absolute rights, S Cassese, 'Ruling Indirectly: Judicial Subsidiarity in the ECtHR', Paper for the Seminar on 'Subsidiarity: a double sided coin?', Strasbourg, 30 January 2015; Spano (n 9) 483–84.

[25] See Lord Sumption, 'The Limits of Law', 27th Sultan Azlan Shah Lecture, Kuala Lumpur, 20 November 2013, available at: www.supremecourt.uk/docs/speech-131120.pdf (accessed 3 January 2020) 7; but see G Letsas, 'Lord Sumption's Attack on Strasbourg: More than Political Rhetoric?', *UK Constitutional Law Blog*, 9 December 2013, available at: https://ukconstitutionallaw.org/2013/12/09/george-letsas-lord-sumptions-attack-on-strasbourg-more-than-political-rhetoric/ (accessed 3 January 2020). For a critique of an 'expansive' approach and praise of a minimalist/originalist approach, see also M Bossuyt, 'Is the European Court of Human Rights on a Slippery Slope?' in S Flogaitis, T Zwart and J Fraser (eds), *The European Court of Human Rights and its Discontents: Turning Criticism into Strength* (Edward Elgar 2013).

[26] See, for example, Lord Sumption (n 25) 14–15.

(c) The final say should, on (certain) contested matters, lie with domestic *courts*, which are more finely attuned to the context and constitutional imperatives of their particular State than the distant Strasbourg Court.[27]

These positions, of course, go beyond Article 3 and its specification, but in this section I address them only as they might apply specifically to Article 3 and its absolute character. Let me take them in turn.

The approach in (a), applied to Article 3 ECHR, may be broadly presented as an argument which suggests that focusing on the original intention of the drafters would entail that Article 3 captures only the 'special' kind of brutality envisaged at the Convention's inception – and arguably tied to the atrocities witnessed during the Second World War. The problems with an originalist approach to interpreting the ECHR have been persuasively addressed.[28] Trying to pin down the drafters' specific intentions on the substantive contours of ECHR rights, as George Letsas argues, elides the most provable intention of the drafters, namely to enshrine these morally loaded rights into law,[29] an intention which broadly encapsulates the 'object and purpose' of treaties such as the ECHR.[30] Turning specifically to Article 3 ECHR, the very uncertainty and contestation surrounding the wrongs at issue compels a dynamic rather than a static approach to ascertaining the right's proper contours, including by 'refin[ing] unexamined moral beliefs and challeng[ing] embedded assumptions', as Colm O'Cinneide puts it.[31]

The argument has frequently been made that the terms of Article 3 were originally intended to capture only a very high degree of brutality or cruelty[32] *and* that

[27] See, for example, P Mahoney, 'The Relationship Between the Strasbourg Court and National Courts', Inner Temple Lecture, 7 October 2013, 10, available at: https://d17g388r7gqnd8.cloudfront.net/2017/08/lecture_mahoney_2013.pdf (accessed 3 January 2020); Lord Justice Laws, 'Lecture III: The Common Law and Europe', Hamlyn Lectures 2013, 27 November 2013, 13, available at: www.judiciary.uk/wp-content/uploads/JCO/Documents/Speeches/laws-lj-speech-hamlyn-lecture-2013.pdf (accessed 3 January 2020). See also Lord Hoffmann, 'The Universality of Human Rights' (2009) 125 *Law Quarterly Review* 416, 429. But note the nuanced response in R Spano, 'The European Court of Human Rights and National Courts: A Constructive Conversation or a Dialogue of Disrespect?' (2015) 33 *Nordic Journal of Human Rights* 1.

[28] See G Letsas, *A Theory of Interpretation of the European Convention on Human Rights* (Oxford University Press 2007) ch 3; and Letsas (n 21).

[29] See Letsas (n 28) ch 3. Eirik Bjorge argues that dynamic interpretation is in line with the principled intention of treaty drafters: see E Bjorge, *The Evolutionary Interpretation of Treaties* (Oxford University Press 2014) 62.

[30] See also Bratza (n 21) 120. But see the argument that Letsas' stance, building on Dworkin's opus, amounts to 'originalism of principle' in D Brink, 'Originalism and Constructive Interpretation' in W Waluchow and S Sciaraffa (eds), *The Legacy of Ronald Dworkin* (Oxford University Press 2016) 274.

[31] O'Cinneide (n 21) 47.

[32] A notable assertion of this may be found in the Separate Opinion of Judge Fitzmaurice in *Ireland v UK* (1979–80) 2 EHRR 25. See also J Finnis, 'Absolute Rights: Some Problems Illustrated' (2016) 61 *American Journal of Jurisprudence* 195. See, too, the 'mission creep' thesis in the Conservative Party's attitude to the EC(t)HR: Conservative Party, 'Protecting Human Rights in the UK: The Conservatives' Plans for Changing Britain's Human Rights Laws' (2014), available at: http://news.bbc.co.uk/1/shared/bsp/hi/pdfs/03_10_14_humanrights.pdf (accessed 3 January 2020).

interpreting Article 3 in a way which captures a vast array of wrongs entails the dilution of its moral force.[33] Yet advocating minimalism as the better approach to interpreting torture or inhuman or degrading treatment or punishment is unpersuasive insofar as it is grounded not on substantive reasoning about the proper substantive scope of Article 3, but rather on an originalism that envisages a 'closed list' of ill-treatment frozen in time, or indeed that is blind to the moral connections between the atrocities of the Second World War and the manifold ways in which persons are abused and dehumanised today.[34] It is also unpersuasive if it simply pursues minimalism for minimalism's sake – that is, purely so that Article 3 may capture the smaller number *x*, and not the greater number *y*, of instances of ill-treatment – rather than genuinely grappling with the wrongs proscribed by Article 3 ECHR. A minimalist approach would be more insidious still if it were premised on prudential, extraneous policy considerations, such as making ECtHR doctrine on Article 3 more palatable to Contracting States. None of these positions genuinely grapples with the wrongs encapsulated by Article 3. On the other hand, an approach grounded in relevant substantive reasoning on the content of Article 3 which adopts what some might identify as a narrow understanding of the wrongs it proscribes should be taken seriously – just as any other good faith, coherently reasoned argument concerning the content of Article 3 should be.

As regards the redirection of the authoritative specification of Article 3 to domestic bodies, broadly encompassed in positions (b) and (c), the implications of such an approach for absoluteness are evident. First, such an approach would validate a range of potentially disparate conceptions of torture and of inhuman or degrading treatment or punishment across the Council of Europe. Were the ECtHR to refuse to offer authoritative interpretation of the red line represented by Article 3, it would be abdicating its interpretive task, countering the absolute character of the right, and recasting it as a fundamentally variable, open-ended, negotiable construct. Such leeway could pave the way to the sort of 'cynical opportunism'[35] displayed in the US after 9/11, which saw officials specify desired conduct *out of* the right,[36] and Member States of the Council of Europe being implicated in extraordinary rendition practices.[37] Cynical opportunists may also view the

[33] See, for instance, M Bossuyt, 'Belgium Condemned for Inhuman or Degrading Treatment Due to Violations by Greece of EU Asylum Law' (2011) 5 *European Human Rights Law Review* 582, 589–91. See further *Bouyid v Belgium* (2016) 62 EHRR 32, Dissenting Opinion of Judges De Gaetano, Lemmens and Mahoney; *cf* N Mavronicola, '*Bouyid v Belgium*: The "Minimum Level of Severity" and Human Dignity's Role in Article 3 ECHR' (2020) 1 *The European Convention on Human Rights Law Review* 105.

[34] See the discussion in Section 3.3 below. For an incisive account of continuities in practices of torture across history, see D Rejali, *Torture and Democracy* (Princeton University Press 2007).

[35] Waldron (n 4) 318.

[36] See, on this, Waldron's discussion of US policy in Waldron (n 4) ch 7. See also Letsas (n 21) 139.

[37] See, for instance, two relevant cases at the ECtHR: *El-Masri v Former Yugoslav Republic of Macedonia* (2013) 57 EHRR 25; *Al Nashiri v Poland* (2015) 60 EHRR 16.

wrongs' 'contestedness as a chance to muddy the waters and undermine the operation of any standards at all in this area'.[38]

Even absent bad faith, a redirection of the authoritative specification of the relevant wrongs to politically representative bodies may subject this specification to an all-things-considered deliberation, rather than deliberation focused on determining the contours of the relevant wrongs and whether certain (in)action amounts to torture or inhuman or degrading treatment or punishment. An all-things-considered deliberation – encompassing, for example, majority preferences regarding how certain 'categories' of persons should be treated, or determining a particular practice as far too useful or popular to be prohibited – can distort or displace the right, contrary to the requirements of legitimate specification, by incorporating extraneous considerations into the specification of the wrongs at issue. Therefore, if the ECtHR were to leave the authoritative specification of Article 3 to domestic parliaments, it would no doubt open up the spectre of illegitimate specification, thereby contradicting the absolute character of the right.

Pragmatic supporters of human rights and of the ECHR and the ECtHR in particular may still insist that even if the ECtHR *should* have the 'final say' on the substantive contours of Article 3 ECHR the Court would do well, in specifying those contours, to heed the 'mood' of (certain) Contracting States, notably those whose attitude towards the Court is seen to carry particular weight or contamination potential within the Council of Europe. In other words, the argument broadly goes, the ECtHR should specify Article 3 in ways that appease relevant Contracting States (and their 'publics') where this is deemed necessary or desirable to secure its continued survival.[39] Exemplifying this approach is Joshua Rozenberg's response to the ECtHR's judgment in *Ahmad v UK*[40] in 2012, in which the ECtHR found the extradition of a number of terrorist suspects to the US to face trial and likely long-term or whole life imprisonment in supermax-security prisons to be Article 3-compatible. Rozenberg observed that 'No human rights court *would last very long if* it took the view that mass murderers and other convicted terrorists should not be locked up for a very long time indeed' (emphasis added).[41] (It is worth noting that the finding in *Ahmad* has now been overtaken by the Grand Chamber judgment on whole life imprisonment

[38] Waldron (n 4) 318.

[39] See Spano (n 18) 490. Note the general study on the adoption of such tactics in S Dothan, *Reputation and Judicial Tactics: A Theory of National and International Courts* (Cambridge University Press 2015), especially ch 6 (on the ECtHR).

[40] *Ahmad v UK* (2013) 56 EHRR 1; see the criticism of the judgment in N Mavronicola and F Messineo, 'Relatively Absolute? The Undermining of Article 3 ECHR in *Ahmad v UK*' (2013) 76 *Modern Law Review* 589.

[41] J Rozenberg, 'European court makes the right call on Abu Hamza', *The Guardian*, 10 April 2012.

in *Vinter v UK*,[42] and a subsequent judgment on expulsion to face whole life imprisonment in *Trabelsi v Belgium*.[43])

Adopting such a pragmatic approach to the specification of Article 3 is not in line with the legitimate specification requirements. Waldron illustrates – and emphatically condemns – the problematic nature of such an approach in considering how to interpret the term 'inhuman':

> We are certainly not permitted to follow … a realist logic proceeding on the basis of *modus tollens*:
>
> (1) If X is inhuman then X is prohibited;
>
> (2) But because X is [seen as] necessary, it is unthinkable that X should be prohibited;
>
> therefore,
>
> (3) X cannot be regarded as inhuman.[44]

Waldron makes this point to underline that the interpretation of the absolutely proscribed wrong of inhuman treatment demands good faith interpretation that employs relevant reasoning. The legitimate specification criteria therefore militate against the specification of Article 3 by the ECtHR being captured by the multifarious interests and considerations at play in the politics of institutional self-preservation.[45]

These arguments are equally relevant insofar as a variant of this argument may support wholly deferring to Council of Europe-wide consensus or, rather, convergence on the interpretation of the wrongs at issue, while opting for options (a)–(c) outlined above where consensus or convergence is lacking.[46] There are several issues with such a stance vis-à-vis the legitimate specification requirements. Convergence 'does not guarantee that we have got the right answer; all it means is that we have the same answer'.[47] It is possible that the legal approaches adopted in certain or even most States may have arisen out of deliberations irrelevant to, or tending towards displacement of, the right, such as the view that some persons do not merit protection from inhumanity or degradation. It is interesting in this

[42] *Vinter v UK* (2016) 63 EHRR 1. But see the ECtHR's finding in *Hutchinson v UK* App no 57592/08 (ECtHR, 17 January 2017), ultimately finding UK law on whole life imprisonment to be compatible with Art 3 ECHR, and Judge Pinto de Albuquerque's scathing criticism of what he saw as the Court's pragmatic approach in his dissent in this judgment. See, too, the commentary on *Hutchinson* in B Çalı, 'Coping with Crisis: Whither the Variable Geometry in the Jurisprudence of the European Court of Human Rights' (2018) 35 *Wisconsin International Law Journal* 237.

[43] *Trabelsi v Belgium* (2015) 60 EHRR 21.

[44] Waldron (n 4) 297.

[45] See, in this respect, *Hutchinson* (n 42), Dissenting Opinion of Judge Pinto de Albuquerque, criticising what he saw as the Court's pragmatic approach. See, too, the commentary on *Hutchinson* in Çalı (n 42).

[46] On how the ECtHR's references to European 'consensus' tend more towards a particular degree of convergence than complete unanimity, see K Dzehtsiarou, *European Consensus and the Legitimacy of the European Court of Human Rights* (Cambridge University Press 2015) 2. Dzehtsiarou's account in the aforementioned book offers a nuanced perspective on how consensus reasoning operates.

[47] J Waldron, *'Partly Laws Common to All Mankind': Foreign Law in American Courts* (Yale University Press 2012) 117–18. See also Dzehtsiarou (n 46) 201.

respect that in *Tyrer v UK*, where the ECtHR embraced the idea of the Convention being a 'living instrument'[48] and found judicial corporal punishment to be degrading after being 'influenced by the developments and commonly accepted standards in the penal policy of the member States of the Council of Europe in this field',[49] it also stated:

> [E]ven assuming that local public opinion can have an incidence on the interpretation of the concept of 'degrading punishment' appearing in Article 3 (art. 3), the Court does not regard it as established that judicial corporal punishment is not considered degrading by those members of the Manx population who favour its retention: it might well be that one of the reasons why they view the penalty as an effective deterrent is precisely the element of degradation which it involves. As regards their belief that judicial corporal punishment deters criminals, it must be pointed out that a punishment does not lose its degrading character just because it is believed to be, or actually is, an effective deterrent or aid to crime control.[50]

As the Court recognised, the popularity or unpopularity of a particular treatment in a given jurisdiction is not indicative – and certainly not conclusive – of whether it amounts to torture or inhuman or degrading treatment or punishment. The Court in *Tyrer* made it clear that consensus in favour of what is in fact degrading punishment, precisely *because* its degrading character makes it appealing to some of the public, must not be used in the Court's determination of whether the treatment falls within the Article 3 prohibition. What the Court did not acknowledge, however, is that the same can be true of transnational convergence, which aggregates the outcomes of such domestic deliberations.

Ultimately, an approach of undue restraint, pragmatic concession and/or deference to consensus or dissensus in determining the acceptability of a particular treatment under Article 3 can distort the right in a potentially drastic manner, especially where those most vulnerable to unpopularity and to the heavy hand or cruel indifference of the State are concerned. As elaborated further below, othering is central to the wrongs captured by Article 3 ECHR.[51] Insofar as such approaches may transform the specification of Article 3 into a process of (explicitly or implicitly) demarcating those that particular publics think deserving of cruelty or inhumanity, they stand at odds with the substantive essence and unconditional character of the right.[52]

[48] *Tyrer v UK* (1979–80) 2 EHRR 1, para 31.
[49] ibid para 31.
[50] ibid.
[51] See also N Mavronicola, 'Torture and Othering' in B Goold and L Lazarus (eds), *Security and Human Rights* (2nd edn, Hart Publishing 2019).
[52] For broader critical reflection on consensus reasoning in particular and the interpretation of (minority) rights under the ECHR, see Letsas (n 28) 74; D Kagiaros, 'When to Use European Consensus: Assessing the Differential Treatment of Minority Groups by the European Court of Human Rights' in P Kapotas and VP Tzevelekos (eds), *Building Consensus on European Consensus: Judicial Interpretation of Human Rights in Europe and Beyond* (Cambridge University Press 2019).

The absolute character of the right enshrined in Article 3 ECHR therefore entails that the Court should engage in an evaluative interpretive endeavour that seeks to specify the wrongs at issue in accordance with the legitimate specification criteria and without undue concessions to extraneous majoritarian concerns or the politics of institutional self-preservation. Before proceeding, in subsequent chapters, to assess how far the Court's substantive reasoning on Article 3 ECHR aligns with the legitimate specification requirements of guidance, non-distortion and non-displacement, the remainder of this chapter offers some substantive starting points on reasoning through the wrongs proscribed by Article 3 ECHR.

3.3. The Words, and Wrongs, Themselves

3.3.1. Specification and Abstraction

Article 3 ECHR requires norm-appliers – culminating in the ECtHR – to specify, through relevant reasoning, the wrongs of torture or inhuman or degrading treatment or punishment and of failure to protect therefrom. Accordingly, in this section I briefly consider 'the words themselves',[53] as Waldron encourages in his study of torture, and the *wrongs* encapsulated therein. A key starting point in this regard is that the wrongs of torture, inhumanity and degradation are distinct from more basic – though deeply contestable – notions such as 'bad' or 'evil'.[54] Article 3's text and the remaining provisions in the Convention in which Article 3 is located convey particular concepts and do not simply embody broadly conceived notions of moral right and wrong.[55] The Court and other norm-appliers are called upon to interpret and apply morally loaded concepts rather than to impose an unconstrained moral vision.[56]

Identifying the 'wrongs themselves' arguably necessitates an exercise in specification that involves elements of abstraction: contemplating the wrongs at issue in general or paradigmatic terms, in light of underlying values or ideas, and concretising them in particular contexts through relevant reasoning. I proceed on the understanding that grasping the central wrong of torture in the abstract can help inform the legitimate specification of the ill-treatment proscribed by Article 3

[53] Waldron (n 4) ch 9.

[54] ibid 306. For the – contested – distinction between 'thick' and 'thin' evaluative concepts, the former category seen to be capturing concepts such as 'inhuman' and the latter seen to capture concepts such as 'good' and 'evil', see M Eklund, 'What Are Thick Concepts?' (2011) 41 *Canadian Journal of Philosophy* 25.

[55] See Waldron (n 4) 295; N Mavronicola, 'Is the Prohibition against Torture and Cruel, Inhuman and Degrading Treatment Absolute in International Human Rights Law? A Reply to Steven Greer' (2017) 17 *Human Rights Law Review* 479, 493–94.

[56] A focus on text should not be equated to originalism, particularly 'intended-application originalism': see Waldron (n 4) 294.

ECHR in line with its underpinning ideas and values, so that the delimitation of the right and its correlative duties 'stays true' to what the right is there to protect and safeguard. Grasping the central wrong of torture, that is, can enable us better to understand and distinguish between relevant and extraneous reasoning and ensure that the specification of Article 3 does not allow displacement through the back door.

Waldron offers a starting point on how the right not to be subjected to torture or related ill-treatment may be specified through abstraction. He argues that the prohibition of torture is a legal archetype of the commitment to non-brutality in law.[57] Waldron describes the idea of a legal archetype as

> a particular provision in a system of norms which has a significance going beyond its immediate normative content, a significance stemming from the fact that it sums up or makes vivid to us the point, purpose, principle, or policy of a whole area of law ... a rule or positive law provision that operates not just on its own account, and does not just stand simply in a cumulative relation to other provisions, but that also operates in a way that expresses or epitomizes the spirit of a whole structured area of doctrine, and does so vividly, effectively, publicly ...[58]

While Waldron confines his argument to a single liberal democratic polity (as he conceives it), the right not to be subjected to torture or inhuman or degrading treatment or punishment can be understood as an archetype of human rights law, epitomising respect for human dignity. In the context of the ECHR, the ECtHR has explicitly affirmed that 'respect for human dignity forms part of the very essence of the Convention'[59] and that Article 3 represents a commitment that is 'closely bound up with respect for human dignity'.[60] Although there is a healthy dose of scepticism in relation to the perceived malleability of the concept of 'dignity',[61] in my view the most persuasive interpretation of *human* dignity regards it as the equal and elevated moral status of all persons above objects and non-human animals.[62] As I elaborate below, the archetypal character of the anti-torture norm may be understood to lie in torture's character as an attack on human dignity.

[57] J Waldron, 'Torture and Positive Law: Jurisprudence for the White House' (2005) 105 *Columbia Law Review* 1681, 1726.

[58] Waldron (n 4) 228.

[59] *Bouyid* (n 33) para 89.

[60] ibid para 81.

[61] This is acknowledged in C McCrudden, 'Human Dignity and Judicial Interpretation of Human Rights' (2008) 19 *European Journal of International Law* 655. But see the constructive account in S Riley, 'Human Dignity as a *Sui Generis* Principle' (2019) 32 *Ratio Juris* 439.

[62] On the idea of dignity as rank or status, see J Waldron, *Dignity, Rank and Rights* (Oxford University Press 2012), especially Lectures 1 and 2. See also J Whitman, '"Human Dignity" in Europe and the United States: The Social Foundations' in G Nolte (ed), *European and US Constitutionalism* (Cambridge University Press 2005) 110: '"Human dignity", as we find it on the Continent today, has been formed by a pattern of levelling up, by an extension of formerly high-status treatment to all sectors of the population'. On the idea of human dignity as encapsulating 'intrinsic worth' demanding acts consistent with respecting this worth, see McCrudden (n 61) 679.

3.3.2. The Torture Continuum

How might we understand the 'wrongs themselves'? As indicated above, I proceed on the understanding that grasping the central wrong of torture in paradigmatic terms can help illuminate the wrongs proscribed by Article 3 ECHR. This position is premised on an understanding of the wrongs at issue as being on a continuum, which we may refer to as the 'torture continuum'. On this basis, illuminating the wrong of torture can help provide the groundwork for the specification of Article 3 more broadly.

Torture is an all too widespread phenomenon and wrong. It evokes enduring images and acts, old and new, that form what we may call the paradigm of torture. Focusing on what he takes to be the paradigm case, David Luban has suggested that torture, through the exercise of control and the infliction of pain and suffering, isolates,[63] terrorises and humiliates the victim to the point of absolute powerlessness.[64] His communicative account of the paradigmatic case of torture may be encapsulated as follows:

> Torture of someone in the torturer's custody or physical control is the assertion of unlimited power over absolute helplessness, communicated through the infliction of severe pain or suffering on the victim that the victim is meant to understand as the display of the torturer's limitless power and the victim's absolute helplessness.[65]

For Luban, the torture paradigm captures the infliction of pain or suffering on someone in the torturer's control, with a view to communicating the total subordination of the victim to the torturer.[66] The goal of torture is, paradigmatically, for its victim to be so thoroughly subordinated as to be rendered a puppet in the hands of the torturer, to be bent to the torturer's will.[67]

Nonetheless, as Luban is quick to point out, the paradigm does not exhaust the substantive scope of the wrong of torture.[68] Luban's account of torture allows for situations in which the torturer has failed to 'attain' the total subordination, or breaking, of the victim, on account of the victim's physical and psychological reserves or any other reason. It is the wrong of deliberately inflicting suffering in order to bring about someone's absolute helplessness and subordination, rather than *achieving* it, that is central to torture. Moreover, given that Luban's is a paradigmatic account which does not exhaust the range of instantiations of torture, there may be instances of ill-treatment which we may properly consider torture where such a sharp communicative vision on the part of the perpetrator as that

[63] While feelings of isolation can be brought about in various ways, one way in which a sense of isolation can be achieved is through the infliction of pain. Elaine Scarry famously suggested, in E Scarry, *The Body in Pain: The Making and Unmaking of the World* (Oxford University Press 1985) 33, that 'in serious pain the claims of the body utterly nullify the claims of the world'.

[64] D Luban, *Torture, Power, and Law* (Cambridge University Press 2014) 48–50.

[65] ibid 128.

[66] ibid.

[67] David Sussman suggests that the tortured person becomes the 'medium in which someone else realizes or expresses his agency', see D Sussman, 'What's Wrong with Torture?' (2005) 33 *Philosophy and Public Affairs* 1, 32.

[68] Luban (n 64) 130.

conveyed by Luban is lacking. Nonetheless, Luban rightly highlights the 'directionality' of the pain and suffering, which typically form a 'fanfare' asserting the torturer's sovereignty over the victim.[69]

It is, therefore, not simply the infliction of excruciating pain – with the potential long-lasting trauma that accompanies it – that is central to the wrong of torture as paradigmatically conceived.[70] To begin with, persons may willingly experience excruciating pain in circumstances which could not properly be seen to amount to torture. Consider, for instance, persons who freely choose to give birth without pain medication, or persons who freely choose to engage in sadomasochistic practices. Indeed, a willing endurance of pain can, in some circumstances, be empowering.[71] The wrong of torture, however, involves the intentional infliction of unwanted suffering in a way that fundamentally *violates* a person in body and/or spirit. In torture, the human body, with its capacity for intense sensation and suffering, and its mortality and breakability, the human psyche with its capacity for intense emotion and devastation, and the interaction of the two,[72] all become tools to hurt and diminish us.

Jay Bernstein emphasises that paradigmatically torture is done '*for the sake of breaking the victim*, and hence a torture whose point is the asymmetry and non-reversibility of position between torturer and victim, the establishment of the absolute *authority* of the torturer'.[73] As Jean Améry observed in his account of the torture he experienced at the hands of the Nazis, the torturer becomes 'master over flesh and spirit, life and death'.[74] In this tyrannical occupation of body and soul,[75] we find what Colin Dayan calls 'spirit thievery',[76] a form of domination which 'recalls the debilitation of slavery'.[77] Building on Luban's account, this tyrannisation of a defenceless person's body and spirit[78] makes torture entirely inimical to the anti-totalitarian vision that underpins human rights.[79]

[69] ibid 129.

[70] This is not to discount the layered experience and significance of pain: see Scarry (n 63).

[71] See J Wisnewski, *Understanding Torture* (Edinburgh University Press 2010) 53–54.

[72] These dimensions speak both to our embodied vulnerability and to our personal integrity. On embodied vulnerability and human rights, see A Grear, *Redirecting Human Rights: Facing the Challenge of Corporate Legal Humanity* (Palgrave 2010); on human dignity as valuing human vulnerability, see M Neal, '"Not Gods But Animals": Human Dignity and Vulnerable Subjecthood' (2012) 33 *Liverpool Law Review* 177. On the personal integrity attacked in torture, see JM Bernstein, *Torture and Dignity: An Essay on Moral Injury* (University of Chicago Press 2015) 168: 'the mineness of my body intertwines bodily autonomy with bodily integrity'.

[73] Bernstein (n 72) 163. On the 'breaking' or 'deconstructing' impact of torture, see Wisnewski (n 71) 73.

[74] J Améry, *At the Mind's Limits: Contemplations by a Survivor on Auschwitz and Its Realities* (Indiana University Press 1980) 35.

[75] The idea that 'torture is government occupation of your soul' is borrowed from Henry Shue's talk at a panel discussion at King's College London: 'What Makes Torture Special? A Unique Moral Wrong and its Legal Prohibition', 26 February 2016.

[76] C Dayan, *The Law Is a White Dog* (Princeton University Press 2011) 21–22.

[77] ibid 22.

[78] Luban (n 64) 48; H Shue, 'Torture' (1978) 7 *Philosophy & Public Affairs* 124, 125, 129–30.

[79] Luban himself refers primarily to liberalism rather than human rights, ibid. See also Waldron's (arguably rose-tinted) account of the prohibition of torture as archetypal of the liberal rule of law, (n 4) 232. But see Susan Marks's account of the continuum between torture and global oppression in S Marks, 'Apologising for Torture' (2004) 73 *Nordic Journal of International Law* 365.

Linking the wrong of torture to the wrong of rape, Bernstein argues that these wrongs 'depend upon undoing the human standing of the victim, of removing her from the domain of beings deserving of human treatment',[80] and constitute 'relations whose terms require that the victim be shown that her *standing as human* is insupportable and unsustainable' (emphasis added).[81] Améry, seeing precisely this 'quality' in the torture he endured at the hands of the Nazis, argued that 'torture was not an accidental quality of this Third Reich, but its very essence'.[82] In torture, Améry located the 'negation'[83] of one's fellow man: a fundamental rupture in the relational humanity[84] of our social world. As Améry puts it,

> torture becomes the total inversion of the social world, in which we can live only if we grant our fellow man life, ease his suffering, bridle the desire of our ego to expand … in the world of torture man exists only by ruining the other person who stands before him.[85]

Understood in this sense, torture places the tortured person outside of the realm of basic respect and concern for and between human persons. William and Penelope Twining identified this aspect of torture as 'its most objectionable feature', highlighting that in accounts of torture, 'the intensity of the pain, and the seriousness of the after-affects are treated as secondary to the *denial of humanity*' (emphasis added).[86] Elaine Webster reflects that torture embodies, and indeed is an archetype of, 'symbolic exclusion from the human community'.[87] Michelle Farrell comments that torture is 'the reduction of the human … to the status of less than human'.[88] Central to the wrong of torture, then, is that it sets the human person it targets *apart* from humanity.

Torture is thus a form of radical othering.[89] In torture, the (embodied) human person is treated as profoundly – even limitlessly[90] – violable, to be manipulated and bent to the torturer's purposes. Yet there is, in torture, not just a violation of the human person themselves, but also a profound rupture in relational

[80] Bernstein (n 72) 171.

[81] ibid.

[82] Améry (n 74) 24.

[83] ibid 35.

[84] See A Maier, 'Torture' in P Kaufmann, H Kuch, C Neuhaeuser and E Webster (eds), *Humiliation, Degradation, Dehumanization: Human Dignity Violated* (Springer 2010) 111–13. On our relational humanity, see Grear (n 72); on our 'relational life', see R Harding, *Duties to Care: Dementia, Relationality and Law* (Cambridge University Press 2017).

[85] Améry (n 74) 35.

[86] WL and PE Twining, 'Bentham on Torture' (1973) 24 *Northern Ireland Legal Quarterly* 305, 354.

[87] Webster (n 20) 130. On the related idea of dehumanisation as 'moral exclusion', see S Oliver, 'Dehumanization: Perceiving the Body as (In)Human' in Kaufmann et al (eds) (n 84) 85–96.

[88] M Farrell, *The Prohibition of Torture in Exceptional Circumstances* (Cambridge University Press 2013) 246. As Andreas Maier argues, this status or standing is fundamentally moral: Maier (n 84) 113.

[89] The idea of dehumanisation as rendering someone 'radically other' is highlighted by Sophie Oliver (n 87) at 85.

[90] See Y Ginbar, 'Making Human Rights Sense of the Torture Definition' in M Başoğlu (ed), *Torture and Its Definition In International Law: An Interdisciplinary Approach* (Oxford University Press 2017) 277.

humanity and a renunciation of the equal and elevated status ascribed within the human rights edifice to all human persons,[91] and the basic respect and concern that it demands.[92] For this reason, Améry saw torture as the 'apotheosis'[93] of Nazism, which 'hated the word "humanity" like the pious man hates sin, and [thus] spoke of "sentimental humanitarianism"'.[94] The character of torture, then, illuminates human dignity by being fundamentally antithetical to it.[95] Torture radically denies the deontic, relational claim to (mutual) respect and concern that human dignity makes. Torture therefore fundamentally wrongs the person subjected to it, but also strikes more broadly at this egalitarian premise of human rights.

As a phenomenon, torture tends also to be a product and marker of othering. As Patrick Lenta has highlighted in the context of US torture practices after 9/11, 'once the identity of those that the United States designates as its enemies has been constructed as a wholly negative, uncivilized other, torture will appear to the US soldiers who inflict it on Iraqis as morally unobjectionable and even heroic'.[96] Michael Rosen, too, has underlined that atrocities like torture are often facilitated by the expressive denial of the humanity of their victims.[97] These dynamics are not new. In ancient Greece, as Page DuBois highlights, torture served as a physical 'marker' of lesser status, which delineated the boundary 'between the untouchable bodies of free citizens and the torturable bodies of slaves'.[98] Darius Rejali traces, in more recent practices, the operation of torture as a 'civic marker' demarcating those deemed worthy of being treated as fully human from those deemed less worthy, reminding those deemed 'lesser' of 'who they are and where they belong'.[99] As the UN Torture Rapporteur's mandate has repeatedly observed, torture has

[91] See Art 1 of the Universal Declaration of Human Rights. Pablo Gilabert links human dignity to 'universalist humanism' and ties this also to Art 2 of the Universal Declaration: 'Human dignity raises people above their class, ethnicity, nationality, and other conventional or narrower statuses, making them basic units of moral concern and respect for everyone everywhere', P Gilabert, *Human Dignity and Human Rights* (Oxford University Press 2018) 119.

[92] See Gilabert (n 91) 119. On human dignity as a status commanding respect, see Waldron (n 62) 33, 60; M Düwell, 'Human Dignity: Concepts, Discussions, Philosophical Perspectives' in M Düwell, J Braarvig, R Brownsword and D Mieth (eds), *The Cambridge Handbook of Human Dignity: Interdisciplinary Perspectives* (Cambridge University Press 2014) 27. On human dignity 'in the sense of being treated with respect for one's humanity', see M Rosen, *Dignity: Its History and Meaning* (Harvard University Press 2012) 157. On intrinsic worth and respect, see McCrudden (n 61) 679. See, too, N Mavronicola, 'Heeding Human Dignity's Call' (Review Essay: *The Age of Dignity* by Catherine Dupré) (2016) 36 *Legal Studies* 725, 730–31. For a distinctive account of torture as the denial of one's status as a human person, the requirement of respect and its links to torture and degradation, see J Bronsther, 'Torture and Respect' (2019) 109 *Journal of Criminal Law and Criminology* 423.

[93] Améry (n 74) 30.

[94] ibid 31.

[95] On this 'negative' method of making sense of human dignity, see R Stoecker, 'Three Crucial Turns on the Road to an Adequate Understanding of Human Dignity' in Kaufmann et al (eds) (n 84) 11.

[96] P Lenta, 'Waiting for the Barbarians after September 11' (2006) 42 *Journal of Postcolonial Writing* 71, 73. See also the extensive study of dehumanisation in D Livingstone Smith, *Less than Human: Why We Demean, Enslave, and Exterminate Others* (St Martin's Press 2011).

[97] Rosen (n 92) 158.

[98] P DuBois, *Torture and Truth* (Routledge 1991) 63.

[99] Rejali (n 34) 56–58.

been widely inflicted on persons on the margins of society's regard.[100] This cyclical relationship between torture and othering discloses the importance of paying close attention to dynamics of stigmatisation, marginalisation, inequality and discrimination in the way the 'mechanics' of torture and ill-treatment operate and proliferate.

The above reflections may be seen as guiding ideas that can help inform the legitimate specification of the wrong of torture by the ECtHR, without claiming to constitute a comprehensive account of how the wrong may be reasoned and delineated as a matter of law.[101] In contemplating the specification of torture by the ECtHR, it is important to consider, or revisit, a number of nuances. One is that 'failed' torture – torture which does not attain the perpetrator's desired consequences – should still be seen as torture. Another is that the amalgamation of intended suffering and actual suffering may vary significantly from one instantiation of torture to another, for an array of reasons, including pure contingency. Moreover, the ways in which human suffering can be created and/or sought are endlessly varied and may well operate in a way which harnesses individual or situational vulnerabilities and particular socially constructed sensibilities. Diverse personal characteristics – a testament to our humanity – may be targeted to attain the aims that torture pursues. Forcing a profoundly religious person to burn a sacred text is likely to elicit a significantly greater degree of mental anguish than forcing an atheist to do the same. The point at which the intentional infliction of mental and physical violence on someone becomes torture may be a matter of contention,[102] but torture fundamentally involves a relationship of control or substantial power asymmetry between perpetrator and victim, and physical, mental or emotional violence intended to cause suffering with a purpose or motivation which encompasses the breaking, or dehumanisation, of the victim.

To illustrate some of this, consider the following scenario. A man, A, is in the control of another person, B. A has been made to feel disorientated and intimidated through acts and statements that assert A's inability to escape from potential violence. B has repeatedly spat at him and called him 'vermin'. At some point,

[100] See, for example, Report of Special Rapporteur on Torture and Other Cruel, Inhuman or Degrading Treatment or Punishment, UN Doc A/73/207, 20 July 2018, paras 63, 74; Report of the Special Rapporteur on Torture and Other Cruel, Inhuman or Degrading Treatment or Punishment, UN Doc A/HRC/40/59, 16 January 2019, para 73.

[101] I do not mean carelessly to neglect international law's formulations of the wrong of torture. In particular, the definition provided in Art 1 of the Convention Against Torture and Other Cruel, Inhuman or Degrading Treatment or Punishment (1984) UNTS 1465 (UNCAT) forms a legal bridge between our abstract understanding of the essence of the wrong of torture and the practice of torture and can be a useful tool in specification efforts. Nonetheless, it is a definition of a *crime* of torture. The definition explicitly indicates that it does not purport to be the sole and exclusive definition of the wrong of torture at international law. Indeed, see N Rodley, 'The Definition(s) of Torture in International Law' (2002) 55 *Current Legal Problems* 467. See, further, Report A/72/178 (n 2) paras 20–33. See, too, the discussion of torture in Ch 4 of this book.

[102] See the overview and discussion of torture definitions in Rodley (n 101).

B convincingly tells A that he knows A's mother's whereabouts and intends to bring her in and rape her in front of A if A does not disclose the identities of his co-conspirators.[103] Identifying the threat against A's mother as torture might raise controversy given that no abuse is actually perpetrated on the victim's mother;[104] and the suffering inflicted on the victim through the interrogator's lies is 'mere' anguish, which some may not see as severe suffering. However, on the understanding of torture advanced in this chapter, the facts squarely make out the wrong of torture. Within a situation of relative power and powerlessness between perpetrator and victim, the victim is being intentionally subjected to significant suffering through the manipulation of his love of his mother, and the threats are (known and calculated to be) all the more believable and painfully felt in the context of A's powerlessness; A is made to believe that the suffering that may be inflicted on him is limitless, that he and those he cares about are fundamentally violable; and the purpose of what is said is to break A through inflicting and threatening inexorable anguish. Importantly, long-standing feminist insights demonstrate that the dismissal of anguish as suffering is both profoundly gendered and disingenuous, and have driven progressive change to 'feminize' the legal understanding of torture.[105]

As is the case with torture, our understanding of inhumanity and degradation cannot be exhaustively captured either by means of a comprehensive list of instantiations of such ill-treatment,[106] or by purely abstract reasoning. Therefore what is outlined here is only a brief reflection on the wrongs at issue. I would suggest that the wrongs of inhuman as well as degrading treatment and punishment remain conceptually located on a continuum with torture in the following sense: they represent wrongs that encompass something of the 'qualities' of torture and that accordingly strike at the equal and elevated moral status of the human person – human dignity – even if they might not involve the fanfare or systematicity of the paradigm case of torture.[107] Building on Waldron's observation, the wrongs at issue can encompass 'agent-oriented' and 'victim-oriented'[108] dimensions, one of which might be more prominent in one instantiation of the wrong than another. In some instances it might be the cruelty of the perpetrator that may be key to

[103] The scenario is loosely based on the threats issued to Abd al-Rahim al-Nashiri, see Senate Select Committee on Intelligence, *Committee Study of the Central Intelligence Agency's Detention and Interrogation Program: Executive Summary* (2014) 70. But see the ECtHR's finding that threats of 'physical' torture amounted to 'inhuman treatment' and not torture in the kidnap case of *Gäfgen v Germany* (2011) 52 EHRR 1, para 108.

[104] Antonin Scalia (in)famously considered this to vitiate wrongfulness: 'Scalia and Torture', *The Atlantic*, 19 June 2007.

[105] A Edwards, 'The "Feminizing" of Torture under International Human Rights Law' (2006) 19 *Leiden Journal of International Law* 349, 362–63.

[106] See, relatedly, Waldron (n 4) 284–90.

[107] A somewhat parallel approach is proposed by Yuval Ginbar in approaching cruel, inhuman or degrading treatment or punishment in international law as 'torture minus': Ginbar (n 90).

[108] J Waldron, 'Inhuman and Degrading Treatment: The Words Themselves' (2010) 23 *Canadian Journal of Law & Jurisprudence* 269, 280.

rendering a treatment inhuman or degrading, in others it might be the debilitating experience the victim has been made to endure.

The term 'inhuman' is not orientated at capturing what humans do not do to each other as a matter of fact,[109] but is fundamentally normative, a matter of 'ought', capturing treatment that falls foul of our relational, deontic humanity.[110] It might not in all instances involve the assertion of absolute power over absolute powerlessness, or the deliberate instrumentalisation of suffering to break someone, but it might nonetheless encompass shades of such tyrannisation and can be taken to involve treatment which violates rather than fundamentally respects one's body or psyche, or which is otherwise dehumanising in character, intent or effect.[111] Waldron also ties inhumanity to the denial of respect and concern for one's basic needs, suggesting that '[t]reatment may be described as inhuman if it fails in sensitivity to the most basic needs and rhythms of a human life', and gives the examples of the 'need to sleep, to defecate or urinate, the need for daylight and exercise, and perhaps even the need for human company',[112] to which many more could arguably be added.

The label 'degrading' appears to denote a reduction in rank,[113] suggestive of an intent or experience of *de*-gradation to something 'less than'.[114] It might include, for instance, forms of 'inferiorising social cruelty'[115] that treats someone as less than human, or that is capable of cutting to the core of their self-respect or tarnishing their basic sense of self-worth.[116] Insofar as degradation relationally inferiorises or treats someone as less than human, a person may be degraded in constant fashion: that is, someone may subject a person to a continuous degradation which need not necessarily involve (awareness of) any palpable diminution from a treatment previously meted out to them. Thus, degradation need not be located in a conscious 'moment' of diminution.[117] Ultimately, inhumanity and degradation may not involve the *radical* denial of human dignity that torture encompasses, but may nonetheless stand fundamentally at odds with human dignity by 'expressing' the idea 'that this creature does not matter, at least not like a person does'.[118]

[109] This is noted in Waldron (n 4) 306. Indeed, the position is similar in relation to 'crimes against humanity': see, for instance, C Macleod, 'Towards a Philosophical Account of Crimes Against Humanity' (2010) 21 *European Journal of International Law* 281; B Kuschnik, 'Humaneness, Humankind and Crimes Against Humanity' (2010) 2 *Goettingen Journal of International Law* 501.

[110] See Waldron (n 4) 306–08.

[111] For an insightful account of inhuman wrongs that dismisses the relevance and/or 'baggage' of human dignity, see A Sangiovanni, *Humanity Without Dignity* (Harvard University Press 2017) ch 2.

[112] Waldron (n 4) 308.

[113] See ibid 308.

[114] On the lowering of status involved in degradation, see Webster (n 20).

[115] Sangiovanni (n 111) 95.

[116] For a set of examples of practices that may amount to 'degradation' (though some may also be inhuman), see Waldron (n 108) 282–83; Waldron (n 4) 310–11, with reference to A Margalit, *The Decent Society* (Harvard University Press 1996).

[117] See, on such a manifestation of degradation, the account offered by Antony Duff, in RA Duff, 'Punishment, Dignity and Degradation' (2005) 25 *Oxford Journal of Legal Studies* 141, 150–51; see, further, his interesting analysis of the degradation of those subject to criminal punishment, ibid 152–55.

[118] Bronsther (n 92) 429.

Fact and value,[119] description and evaluation,[120] can become enmeshed in the process of specification of the wrongs at issue. Consider, for example, the intended purpose and likely effect of someone being subjected to the song 'I Love You' by Barney the Purple Dinosaur on repeat. The constellation of intent and effect is distinct between a familial context involving one's two-year-old daughter, who happens to be a particularly avid fan of Barney the Purple Dinosaur, and the subjection of a detained person to the song on repeat over a course of several hours in a cold prison cell in the context of the (threatened) employment of a range of other 'enhanced interrogation techniques'.[121] Such contextual factors shape the character of the act or situation at issue. Accordingly, a sensitive evaluative judgement is required to identify the wrongs within a set of facts. All relevant circumstances must be assessed in order to determine whether the relevant treatment amounts to torture or inhuman or degrading treatment or punishment.

3.3.3. Context and Contingent Circumstance

The significance of context and contingent fact(s) in the specification of torture and inhuman and degrading treatment and punishment warrants further reflection. In particular, it is important to respond to perspectives that view sensitivity to relevant context and contingent circumstance in the specification of these wrongs as posing a challenge to the absoluteness starting point. Michael Addo and Nicholas Grief, for example, contrast the position that Article 3 is an absolute right with the fact that its application in specific circumstances involves '[taking] into account … factual and personal distinctions',[122] and find that Article 3's absolute character is conceptually 'nebulous'.[123] Similarly, when David Feldman indicates that while State obligations under Article 3 are considered absolute, 'a degree of relativism cannot, in practice, be entirely excluded from the application of the notions of inhuman or degrading treatment', he appears to be referring at least partly to the manifold ways in which a variation in circumstances may impact on the character of the treatment at issue.[124] However, relevant context and contingent fact(s) can inform Article 3's specification without undermining its absolute character.

[119] On the distinction and hybridity between fact and value in jurisprudence see M Del Mar, 'Relational Jurisprudence: Vulnerability Between Fact and Value' (2012) 2 *Law and Method* 63.

[120] See Waldron (n 4) 296.

[121] That such a practice was part of the US 'Enhanced Interrogation Techniques' was revealed in J Sharrock, 'The Torture Playlist', *Mother Jones*, 22 February 2008; see the discussion in SG Cusick and BW Joseph, 'Across an Invisible Line: A Conversation about Music and Torture' (2011) 42 *Grey Room* 6.

[122] MK Addo and N Grief, 'Does Article 3 of the European Convention on Human Rights Enshrine Absolute Rights?' (1998) 9 *European Journal of International Law* 510, 515.

[123] ibid 523.

[124] D Feldman, *Civil Liberties and Human Rights in England and Wales* (2nd edn, Oxford University Press 2002) 242.

Although we might say, in general terms, that physical or psychological abuse or cruel humiliation fall within the torture continuum, relevant contextual factors play a central role in crystallising what amounts to such wrongs. *Relevant* contextual factors – say, in the above example, the familial as opposed to the interrogational setting in which Barney the Purple Dinosaur's tune is played – can and indeed ought to inform the interpretation and application of the right not to be subjected to torture or to inhuman or degrading treatment or punishment. The relevance of contextual factors entails that particular contingent facts may shape the character of certain practices. The relevant contingent contextual factors, including social norms, need not be benign or desirable. Consider, for instance, the treatment of a Guantánamo inmate:

> He was told that his mother and sister were whores. He was forced to wear a bra, and a woman's thong was put on his head. He was dressed as a woman and compelled to dance with a male interrogator. He was told that he had homosexual tendencies and that other prisoners knew this.[125]

To appreciate the full extent of the demeaning[126] and (cumulatively) coercive force of this treatment, a grasp of the matrix of gendered social norms and particular contingent moral sensibilities emerging from these is needed, as well as how being coerced into certain activities fundamentally differs from freely choosing to pursue them. An exploitation of relevant contextual and contingent factors can often drive 'interrogation techniques' and shape their wrongfulness. The specification of the torture continuum should be responsive to these factors, whose consideration can help determine whether a practice is inhuman or degrading in the here and now. If the norm interpreter is to capture the wrong being perpetrated in the relevant act, they should be aware of the social conditions in which the perpetrator inflicts or seeks to inflict 'moral injury'.[127]

The specification of the torture continuum, which demands sensitivity to relevant context, discloses the flaw in assuming that the concretisation of absolute entitlements in human rights law is meant to be somehow *a*contextual. Accepting that context may be relevant in determining whether something amounts to torture, inhumanity or degradation does not undermine the absolute character of Article 3 ECHR. There is no fundamental contradiction between the idea that Article 3 is an absolute right and the fact that its application in specific circumstances involves '[taking] into account any [relevant] factual and personal distinctions'.[128] At the same time, sensitivity to

[125] SH Miles, 'Medical Ethics and the Interrogation of Guantanamo 063' (2007) 7(4) *The American Journal of Bioethics* 1, 3.

[126] John Vorhaus highlights the significance of symbolic dimensions of degradation: 'it is important not to lose sight of the many ways in which dignity is impinged upon by the symbolic nature of much ill-treatment', J Vorhaus, 'On Degradation Part Two: Degrading Treatment and Punishment' (2003) 31 *Common Law World Review* 65, 79.

[127] See Bernstein (n 72).

[128] Addo and Grief (n 122) 515.

relevant context need not entail equanimity towards *problematic* contexts: rather, we should expect the specification of the torture continuum to take place with a readiness to identify such absolute wrongs not only in light of, but also as occurring within or because of, historically contingent 'givens'. That is, Article 3 should be specified with a preparedness to locate torture, inhumanity or degradation even in common – 'given' – practices and structures, such as, for example, the practice of solitary confinement, or the prison itself.[129]

3.3.4. Revisiting the Capacity to Guide

Much of the discussion above has been orientated at grounding the substance of Article 3's specification, broadly mapping onto the requirements of relevant reasoning and non-displacement. An issue which warrants addressing is what the discussion in this and previous sections of this chapter entails for one aspect of legitimate specification: the capacity to guide. It is apparent from Chapter 2 that the criterion of capacity to guide is a matter of degree. It can be fulfilled through specification occupying the terrain in the spectrum between an overly abstract standard (what Gewirth referred to as 'Principle Absolutism'), which offers little specific guidance regarding the contours of the right's demands, and an overly concretised standard (what Gewirth referred to as 'Individual Absolutism'), which offers little generalisable guidance beyond the finding that the particular circumstances amount to a violation of the right.[130] In its specification of Article 3, the ECtHR must therefore carefully tread the line between over-generality and over-specificity to ensure a sufficient degree of both generality and clarity.

Treading the line between over-generality (which broadly maps onto Article 3's abstract terms) and over-specificity (which we may tie to the Court's ultimate conclusions that, on the facts, the applicant has been subjected to treatment in violation of Article 3[131]) means that the Court should carefully attend to the substantive reasoning through which it determines whether the impugned activity or situation violates Article 3 ECHR. To fulfil the criterion of capacity to guide, the Court should aim for coherent and transparent reasoning that is capable of being effectively transposed, where appropriate, to sets of facts other than those in the case at hand; as the Court itself put it in *Ireland v UK*, its judgments should 'serve not only

[129] The complex approach taken by the ECtHR in the area of punishment is discussed in Ch 5. On being prepared to identify Art 3 wrongs in 'common' practices, see also Mavronicola (n 33).

[130] See the analysis in Ch 2, with reference to A Gewirth, 'Are There Any Absolute Rights?' (1981) 31 *The Philosophical Quarterly* 1.

[131] See also N Mavronicola, 'What Is an "Absolute Right"? Deciphering Absoluteness in the Context of Article 3 of the European Convention on Human Rights' (2012) 12 *Human Rights Law Review* 723, 750.

to decide those cases brought before the Court but, more generally, to elucidate, safeguard and develop the rules instituted by the Convention', in this way 'contributing to the observance by the States of the engagements undertaken by them as Contracting Parties'.[132] This means that the ECtHR should transparently set out any generalisable standards that mediate between the norm itself – that 'no one shall be subjected to torture or to inhuman or degrading treatment or punishment' – and the concrete finding in a given case, and acknowledge and explain how relevant nuances and contextual factors have shaped its particular finding. Reasoning in this fashion is vital towards meeting the legitimate specification requirement of capacity to guide, but also in providing the transparency to allow for meaningful critical engagement, not least towards the progressive (re-)interpretation of the wrongs at issue.

3.4. Article 3's Negative and Positive Obligations

3.4.1. Rights and Wrongs

On the flip side of rights are wrongs. The human rights contained in the ECHR constitute entitlements not to be wronged by the State. The right not to be subjected to torture or to inhuman or degrading treatment or punishment enshrined in Article 3 ECHR renders particular types of State wrongs unlawful. The State may be held to have wronged a person through its actions, and this maps onto the State's negative obligations, which require that the State refrain from certain action. But the State may also be held to have wronged someone by failing to take positive measures to protect them, and this is embodied in States' positive obligations to take certain action. Delimiting Article 3 involves a delineation of the wrongs it proscribes. The nexus between rights and wrongs – with obligations carved out accordingly – may be illustrated as follows:

Wrong	Obligation	Right
It is wrong of X to do A to Y.	X has a duty not to do A to Y. (negative obligation)	Y has a right against X that X not do A.
It is wrong of X not to do B for Y.	X has a duty to do B for Y. (positive obligation)	Y has a right against X that X do B.

[132] *Ireland v UK* (n 32) para 154. On the *res interpretata* implications of the ECtHR's doctrine, see OM Arnardóttir, 'Res Interpretata, Erga Omnes Effect and the Role of the Margin of Appreciation in Giving Domestic Effect to the Judgments of the European Court of Human Rights' (2017) 28 *European Journal of International Law* 819.

Article 3 can be seen as proscribing relational wrongs: ways of wronging someone.[133] These often amount to wrongful conduct which significantly harms the victim. Consider the all-too-frequently occurring scenario of the beating by a police officer of a suspect in their custody. The perpetrator acts with an intent to cause suffering, potentially for a purpose such as intimidating and/or eliciting information. The victim experiences the beating as painful, intimidating and degrading. The treatment of the victim by the perpetrator is relationally wrongful; the perpetrator has wronged the victim. The wrong committed has two dimensions: the character of the perpetrator's conduct and the way it is experienced.

Nonetheless, it is possible to contemplate that Article 3 also captures 'free-standing' wrongs, without identifying a substantial concrete harm inflicted on the victim. Consider the scenario of 'failed' torture through the deliberate beating of the soles of a victim's feet in circumstances where the victim, unbeknownst to the torturer, cannot feel pain.[134] There is, fundamentally, a relational quality to this invasion of bodily integrity with the aim of inflicting intolerable suffering, and to its wrongful character. At the same time, the central wrongdoing can be identified independently of the way it is experienced by the individual subjected to it. The wrong lies chiefly in the infliction of such treatment on another person with the aim of producing unbearable pain and a potential physical and psychological breakdown. These elements make the torturer's conduct an affront to human dignity.

That the obligations envisaged in the provision 'No one shall be subjected to torture or to inhuman or degrading treatment or punishment' can in certain circumstances have the quality of 'monadic deonticity'[135] is reflected in the fact that torture and other forms of ill-treatment can also amount to crimes. Torture is specified as a criminal act in the United Nations Convention Against Torture.[136] Moreover, as highlighted in Chapter 6, the ECtHR has indicated that 'wilful' ill-treatment must be criminally punished.[137]

At the same time, we can contemplate instances where persons are subjected to inhumanity or degradation, in violation of the negative obligation under Article 3 ECHR, without any malice or criminal(-like) level of culpability involved on the part of relevant perpetrator(s). Consider the scenario where a mentally impaired person who is not fully capable of comprehending the character of their action sexually assaults another person. The experience of inhumanity or degradation by the victim is not vitiated by the diminished culpability of the perpetrator. In the

[133] See, in this regard, J Goldberg and B Zipursky, 'Tort Law and Responsibility' in J Oberdiek (ed), *Philosophical Foundations of the Law of Torts* (Oxford University Press 2014) 27; see further M Thompson, 'What Is It to Wrong Someone? A Puzzle about Justice' in RJ Wallace, P Pettit, S Scheffler and M Smith (eds), *Reason and Value: Themes from the Moral Philosophy of Joseph Raz* (Oxford University Press 2004).

[134] I am grateful to David Feldman for challenging me with a similar scenario.

[135] Thompson (n 133) 344.

[136] Art 4 UNCAT.

[137] *Gäfgen v Germany* (2011) 52 EHRR 1, para 119.

human rights law context,[138] such a victim-centred perspective can be important in identifying circumstances where the State has wronged someone even as the inhumanity or degradation inflicted may lack a specific intent, arise out of genuine error, or be diffuse or systemic.[139] Moreover, the State may wrong us by failing to take sufficient measures to protect us from torture, inhumanity or degradation, and this is captured by the recognition of positive obligations.

3.4.2. The Specification of Positive Obligations

Negative obligations constitute obligations to refrain from certain acts. Article 3 ECHR establishes negative obligations on the State to refrain from subjecting anyone to torture or inhuman or degrading treatment or punishment. Delimiting the negative obligations imposed by Article 3 on the State involves specifying what amounts to subjecting persons to torture or inhuman or degrading treatment or punishment, which is conclusively unlawful when engaged in by the State. The complexity raised by this specification, in light of the absoluteness starting point, is evident in the preceding analysis, and further concretised in the Court's doctrine as examined in Chapters 4, 5 and 7.

Positive obligations, on the other hand, constitute duties to take positive action to secure – or, in other words, protect and fulfil[140] – a right. Positive obligations under the right enshrined in Article 3 ECHR delineate what amounts to wrongful omission on the part of the State in the protection and fulfilment of the right not to be subjected to torture or inhuman or degrading treatment or punishment.[141] Additional complexity arises in determining how the delimitation of

[138] Which I take to be distinct from the criminal law – see, in this regard, *Denis Vasilyev v Russia* App no 32704/04 (ECtHR, 17 December 2009) para 114; see, further, some of the discussion in Ch 6. On the 'objective social meaning' of a wrongful action, see Sangiovanni (n 111) 76.

[139] Cathryn Costello suggests that while the wrong of torture is 'agent-centred', inhumanity and degradation should be determined in a more victim-centred manner (C Costello, *The Human Rights of Migrants and Refugees in European Law* (Oxford University Press 2015) 191), while Jeremy Waldron identifies both agent-oriented and victim-oriented aspects of the wrongs at issue (Waldron (n 108) 280).

[140] See DJ Harris, M O'Boyle, E Bates and C Buckley, *Harris, O'Boyle and Warbrick: Law of the European Convention on Human Rights* (4th edn, Oxford University Press 2018) 24. It may also be argued that the duty to *respect* entails duties to take positive measures to avert breaches of the negative obligation by State agents. See also D Shelton and A Gould, 'Positive and Negative Obligations' in D Shelton (ed), *The Oxford Handbook of International Human Rights Law* (Oxford University Press 2013) 570.

[141] Of course, it should be acknowledged that understanding positive obligations as duties to take action raises questions. Where does direct infliction end and failure to secure begin? An institutional system can, arguably, in the combination of what it does and does not do, *subject* persons to inhumanity or degradation. It is conceivable that the law *treats* and the law *punishes*; and the law is the creation – the doing – of the State. We could therefore speak of a legal framework of property, employment, welfare and other laws as treating or punishing individuals in a way that is inhuman or degrading. See, for example, L Oette, 'Austerity and the Limits of Policy-induced Suffering: What Role for the Prohibition of Torture and Other Ill-treatment?' (2015) 15 *Human Rights Law Review* 669; M Adler, *Cruel, Inhuman or Degrading Treatment?: Benefit Sanctions in the UK* (Palgrave 2018).

duties to take positive action might interact with the absoluteness starting point. A crucial starting point in unpacking this complexity is that positive obligations cannot be boundless. To reiterate a point made in Chapter 2, the absolute character of Article 3 does not entail practical inviolability: it is not a guarantee, nor can the State practically guarantee, that no one will ever in fact endure torture or inhuman or degrading treatment or punishment. At the same time, in view of the significance of the imperative of protecting persons from torture and related ill-treatment in upholding human dignity, the State ought to be held to a demanding standard regarding the action it takes to minimise and offer protection from such ill-treatment and to provide redress where it materialises, and held to account where it fails to take sufficient measures towards this.[142] I use the term 'sufficient' to reflect the point made just above: namely, that protection will never be total, but must nonetheless be substantial.

The absolute character of Article 3 should mean that the State's overarching duty to take positive action to secure the right cannot be simply displaced by extraneous concerns, such as the 'bad' behaviour of the person in peril. Additionally, positive obligations to secure the right enshrined in Article 3 should be more onerous than those obligations corresponding to rights that are displaceable, since the latter's infringement can in principle be withstood. Yet the specification of positive obligations under Article 3 (of what the State is compelled to do) must inevitably admit of a wider set of relevant considerations than the specification of negative obligations (of what the State is compelled to refrain from doing), not least given the infinite variety of potential action as well as relevant constraints on the State's action. As Matthias Klatt highlights, 'not any [or every] action that amounts to or causes protection … is obligated'.[143] The specification of what *is* obligated can incorporate a range of relevant factors that shape what may appropriately be required of the State in the circumstances at issue. These factors include relevant constraints on State action, such as practical possibility,[144] intra-Convention (il)legality, and competing claims to limited resources.[145] An additional concern in the specification of positive obligations is institutional competence: arguably, the evaluative judgement of a

[142] On the related concept of 'due diligence', Dinah Shelton and Ariel Gould comment that 'a state's diligence is not legally deficient because of the act that causes the injury, but rather because of what was lacking in the authorities' prevention of or response to said act': Shelton and Gould (n 140) 578. See also the distinction drawn between positive obligations and attribution of conduct in H Keller and R Walther, 'Evasion of the International Law of State Responsibility? The ECtHR's Jurisprudence on Positive and Preventive Obligations under Article 3' (2019) *International Journal of Human Rights* (advance online access).

[143] M Klatt, 'Positive Obligations under the European Convention on Human Rights' (2011) 71 *Heidelberg Journal of International Law* 691, 694.

[144] See L Lavrysen, *Human Rights in a Positive State: Rethinking the Relationship between Positive and Negative Obligations under the European Convention on Human Rights* (Intersentia 2016) 157. Note the more wide-ranging and interesting discussion of the 'practicability constraint' in delineating moral human rights in E Ashford, 'The Nature of Violations of the Human Right to Subsistence' in A Etinson (ed), *Human Rights: Moral or Political?* (Oxford University Press 2018).

[145] For a distinct thematic analysis of relevant considerations, see Lavrysen, ibid ch 3.

supranational court such as the ECtHR may appropriately be shaped by according due consideration, though not complete or undue deference or latitude, to the institutional competence of State actors making such assessments.[146]

Consequently, while the Court ought to demand substantial good faith efforts capable of securing the right, it should also acknowledge key limiting factors and specify positive obligations accordingly. The Court should not require action that is impossible to undertake (ought implies can), and should not identify a duty to take action that is itself unlawful under the Convention. The Court should exercise a final judgement on the objective adequacy of the action taken to secure the right, while duly taking into account relevant institutional and resource constraints and the relative institutional competence of the authorities determining the options available and action(s) to be taken. Such an approach represents both a standard of stringency and scrutiny to be applied by the Court, and a recognition of the substantive and institutional limitations that may be relevant to delineating States' positive obligations and assessing whether they have been discharged.

Lawfulness under the Convention is a key limiting factor identified above and previously highlighted in Chapter 2. While the imperative to protect individuals from torture, inhumanity and degradation may be very strong indeed, it cannot displace non-displaceable negative obligations. As argued in relation to the kidnap scenario discussed in Chapter 2, there is no positive duty to torture or ill-treat a kidnapper in order to discover the kidnapped person's whereabouts – to put it differently, the kidnapped person and their next of kin are not wronged on account of the State refraining from subjecting the suspected kidnapper to interrogational torture.[147] As to *displaceable* negative obligations, with respect to rights which may be lawfully infringed, these may be displaced insofar as necessary and proportionate – a principle applicable generally in relation to interference with these rights.

How does this account square with the requirements of legitimate specification? As the above makes clear, positive obligations under Article 3 cannot extend to the point of guaranteeing freedom from torture, inhumanity and degradation in the sense of securing their total eradication. Positive obligations' limits may be drawn on the basis of rigid and fluid constraints, such as intra-Convention (il)legality, and the reasonable distribution of limited resources. It might thus appear as though, in blunt terms, positive obligations under Article 3 are not absolute. Yet this would be to misread what the absolute character of a right

[146] This is noted in I Leijten, 'Defining the Scope of Economic and Social Guarantees in the Case Law of the ECtHR' in E Brems and J Gerards (eds), *Shaping Rights in the ECHR: The Role of the European Court of Human Rights in Determining the Scope of Human Rights* (Cambridge University Press 2013) 113, citing E Palmer, 'Protecting Socio-economic Rights through the European Convention on Human Rights: Trends and Developments in the European Court of Human Rights' (2009) 2 *Erasmus Law Review* 397, 398. For an interesting account of the competence dynamics at play shaping the standard of scrutiny in relation to the discharge of positive obligations, see M Klatt, 'Positive Rights: Who Decides? Judicial Review in Balance' (2015) 13 *International Journal of Constitutional Law* 354; Klatt notes that the significance of the right can augment the judicial scrutiny called for: ibid 371.

[147] See Mavronicola (n 55) 484.

such as that enshrined in Article 3 entails. Absoluteness means that the right, and its correlative obligations, are not displaceable; they may not be *extinguished* in respect of a person deemed undeserving, for example. Absoluteness does not entail that positive obligations under that right require limitless action;[148] no right can demand that. To uphold the absolute character of Article 3, the ECtHR must nonetheless rigorously police the distinction between delimitation and displacement. While the delimitation of the substantive scope of positive obligations to protect from or redress ill-treatment can allow for a variation in approaches to safeguarding these obligations, it must remain subject to a rigorous scrutiny of the appropriateness, sufficiency and good faith character of the State's efforts. It is, in this regard, not appropriate to take States' word for their assessment of what positive action was sufficient in the circumstances, and the ECtHR must demand, and establish through careful scrutiny, that States go substantially further than offering nominal 'nods' to their positive duties. Such vigilance is key to ensuring that Article 3's positive obligations offer meaningful protection and are not hollowed out or displaced.

As to the criterion of relevant reasoning in the specification of positive obligations, this requires us to appreciate the nexus between State inaction and State blameworthiness. What amounts to a wrongful omission and, on the flip side, what is to be expected of the State, is shaped both by the significant imperative of pursuing effective measures capable of protecting people from ill-treatment, and by attention to constraints such as those outlined above. The application of relevant limiting criteria amounts to relevant reasoning: it delimits the *wrong* of failing to take the measures that may appropriately be expected to secure the right.[149]

According a degree of latitude to the State machinery's good faith efforts to protect persons from ill-treatment raises the risk that such leeway may be abused by State authorities to offer inadequate protection to individuals. This is why a robust assessment, which does not necessarily assume the good faith or sufficiency of State efforts, is required. Beyond this, however, latitude combined with a context-sensitive specification of positive obligations in light of relevant constraints can also deepen the challenges raised in respect of the requirement of capacity to guide. Yet, as underlined above, this requirement is inevitably a matter of degree. No specification of legal standards can lay claim to perfect certainty, in the sense of total *ex ante* elaboration of the entire substantive scope of application of the standard, and the ECtHR cannot and ought not to seek such 'total' certainty in its specification of Article 3. Nonetheless, the ECtHR can – and should – pursue principled coherence in the specification of positive

[148] Klatt (n 143) 694.

[149] Shelton and Gould highlight that identifying violations of the State's positive obligations 'is not the same as saying the state is complicit in the wrongful act … it is the state's own behaviour that is judged wrongful' – Shelton and Gould (n 140) 579.

obligations under Article 3 ECHR, ensuring that its pronouncements on positive obligations and the measures by which they are fulfilled in particular contexts are as clear, transparent and coherently generalisable as possible.

3.5. Conclusion

Specifying the absolute right enshrined in Article 3 ECHR involves the delimitation of particular wrongs. This chapter outlined and addressed some of the scepticism, challenges and pitfalls surrounding this morally loaded evaluative endeavour. A key argument advanced in this chapter is that the uncertainty and contestation surrounding Article 3's terms should not entail an abdication by the ECtHR of its evaluative interpretive task. The prohibition on inflicting torture or inhuman or degrading treatment signifies a 'red line' and requires the ECtHR to specify that line, without abandoning the norm's interpretation to undue minimalism, pragmatism, majoritarianism or variation across States.

Substantively, this chapter advanced an understanding of the 'torture continuum' that conceives of torture as a form of radical renunciation of the equal and elevated status ascribed to the human person in the human rights edifice: human dignity. Inhumanity and degradation lie on this continuum and may be understood as wrongs which attack human dignity in particular ways, though not necessarily in the deliberate and structured 'fanfare' of abuse paradigmatically found in torture. From this premise we can begin to understand the way that a court such as the ECtHR may distinguish between relevant and extraneous reasoning in the specification of the wrongs proscribed by Article 3 ECHR. In undertaking this specification, the Court should be alert to the way in which contextual factors may shape the character of the act or situation under consideration. Moreover, a nuanced approach is required in delimiting positive obligations to protect from, and provide redress for, torture or inhuman or degrading treatment or punishment. The overarching duty to take appropriate and sufficient protective action is non-displaceable. At the same time, a number of relevant factors and constraints may justifiably limit the range of particular positive measures States should be expected to pursue. These are important starting points in thinking through the way in which the ECtHR can navigate the legitimate specification requirements of relevant reasoning and non-displacement outlined in Chapter 2.

While the ECtHR should boldly seek to specify the 'wrongs themselves', it should not be complacent in doing so. The morally loaded character of what is at stake calls for wide-ranging critical engagement, which it is incumbent on the ECtHR – and any other interpreter of the right enshrined in Article 3 ECHR – to heed. There should be scope, therefore, for a progressive (re-)interpretation of the right and its corresponding wrongs. Ultimately, the dynamic and context-sensitive approach necessitated in the specification of the right enshrined in

Article 3 ECHR entails that the ECtHR must navigate the line between the undue abstraction of what Gewirth referred to as 'principle absolutism' and the all-things-considered, ex post facto specificity of 'individual absolutism' by seeking principled coherence, transparency and a degree of generalisability in its pronouncements. This means that overarching principles as well as relevant nuances, where appropriate, should be acknowledged and reasoned through. By doing this, the ECtHR can provide not only guidance to norm-appliers, right-holders and duty-bearers, but also a basis for meaningful critique and for potentially rethinking or reimagining prevailing understandings of the wrongs at issue.

4

The Specification of Torture under Article 3 ECHR

4.1. Introduction

While Article 3 ECHR absolutely proscribes torture as well as inhuman or degrading treatment or punishment, torture is often seen as being at the apex of wrongfulness of what Article 3 proscribes. This chapter explores the way in which torture has been specified by the ECtHR in light of the legitimate specification requirements. Recalling the legitimate specification requirements of capacity to guide, non-distortion and non-displacement, the account offered here aims to sharpen the way aggravation and 'severity' are understood in distinguishing torture from other forms of inhuman or degrading treatment or punishment. The examination of the contours of torture provided in this chapter is complemented significantly by the discussion of the Court's specification of inhuman and degrading treatment and punishment offered in Chapter 5, and these two chapters should be read together.

4.2. Torture as an Aggravated Wrong within Article 3

The ECtHR has, at least since *Ireland v UK*, viewed a finding of torture as carrying a particular stigma.[1] Previously, the European Commission of Human Rights in *The Greek Case* had referred to torture as 'an *aggravated* form of inhuman treatment' (emphasis added).[2] Yet the distinction between torture and other ill-treatment proscribed by Article 3 ECHR is occasionally glossed over.[3] This may, in part, be attributed to the fact that Article 3 ECHR absolutely proscribes torture *as well as* inhuman or degrading treatment or punishment. While the ECtHR in *Ireland v UK* referred to the 'special stigma' attached to torture among the ill-treatment

[1] *Ireland v UK* (1979–80) 2 EHRR 25, para 167.

[2] *The Greek Case (Denmark, Norway, Sweden and the Netherlands v Greece)* (1969) 12 *Yearbook of the European Convention on Human Rights* 1, 186.

[3] See, for example, P Gaeta, 'When Is the Involvement of State Officials a Requirement for the Crime of Torture?' (2008) 6 *Journal of International Criminal Justice* 183, 185.

proscribed by Article 3,[4] it also underlined that both ill-treatment falling within the category of torture and ill-treatment amounting to inhuman or degrading treatment or punishment (generally shortened, for the purposes of this chapter to 'IDTP', unless otherwise specified) are absolutely prohibited by Article 3.[5] Indeed, it bears underlining that the ECtHR has affirmed that Article 3 proscribes the expulsion of persons to places where they face a real risk of torture *or* of inhuman or degrading treatment or punishment.[6]

Nonetheless, torture is seen as a particularly aggravated form of ill-treatment within the range of ill-treatment absolutely proscribed by Article 3 ECHR. It is often pointed out that a finding of *torture*, as distinct from inhuman or degrading treatment or punishment, would particularly damage the human rights record of a State – it is considered significant, for example, that the UK has never been found by the ECtHR to have 'committed' torture under Article 3;[7] in 1999, a finding of torture in *Selmouni v France*[8] sparked significant media interest, with media commentators suggesting that '[t]he European Court of Human Rights … made France the first European state to be convicted of torture'.[9] The distinction between torture and other ill-treatment proscribed by Article 3 ECHR also carries legal ramifications. John Cooper indicates that 'criminal sanctions should be applied to torture but may not always be an appropriate step for treatment found to be inhuman or degrading'.[10] Moreover, in *Gäfgen v Germany*[11] the Grand Chamber of the ECtHR established – not without attracting well-reasoned criticism[12] – that the distinction can carry important implications in

[4] *Ireland v UK* (n 1) para 167.

[5] ibid para 163.

[6] See Ch 7.

[7] S Foster, *Human Rights & Civil Liberties* (2nd edn, Pearson Education 2008) 203. It should be noted that many regard the UK practices at issue in *Ireland v UK* (n 1) to have amounted to torture. A response to, and analysis of, the case can be found in RJ Spjut, 'Torture under the European Convention on Human Rights' (1979) 73 *American Journal of International Law* 267. See, more recently, B Dickson, *The European Convention on Human Rights and the Conflict in Northern Ireland* (Oxford University Press 2010) 146–53. See also the account of the UK's wider involvement in torture in I Cobain, *Cruel Britannia: A Secret History of Torture* (Portobello Books 2012).

[8] *Selmouni v France* (2000) 29 EHRR 403.

[9] G Reilhac, 'Court finds France guilty of torture', *The Guardian*, 29 July 1999. See also BBC News, 'France guilty of torture', 28 July 1999, available at: http://news.bbc.co.uk/1/hi/world/europe/406036.stm (accessed 3 January 2020): 'France is the only member of the European Union to have been convicted of torture by the human rights court, although Turkey, a member of the Council of Europe, has been convicted on these grounds'. Turkey had been found to have inflicted torture in *Aksoy v Turkey* (1997) 23 EHRR 553.

[10] J Cooper, *Cruelty – An Analysis of Article 3* (Sweet & Maxwell 2003) 17. Another argument highlights the difference that a finding of torture can potentially make to the measure of damages awarded by the Strasbourg Court – see MK Addo and N Grief, 'Does Article 3 of the European Convention on Human Rights Enshrine Absolute Rights?' (1998) 9 *European Journal of International Law* 510, 511–12; on damages before the ECtHR, see V Fikfak, 'Changing State Behaviour: Damages before the European Court of Human Rights' (2019) 29 *European Journal of International Law* 1091.

[11] *Gäfgen v Germany* (2011) 52 EHRR 1.

[12] See, for example, M Spurrier, 'Gafgen v Germany: Fruit of the Poisonous Tree' (2010) 5 *European Human Rights Law Review* 513.

terms of the relationship between Article 3 and Article 6 ECHR, the right to a fair trial.[13] The Grand Chamber indicated that the use of real evidence obtained by torture to incriminate someone in criminal proceedings always violates Article 6 ECHR, while the use of real evidence obtained by other Article 3 ill-treatment *may* (but will not in all cases) entail violation of Article 6 ECHR.[14]

In examining the ECtHR's specification of torture in light of the legitimate specification requirements, I take torture to be an aggravated *wrong* within the wrongs proscribed by Article 3 ECHR. This is distinct from aggravated harm (including physical or mental suffering) or injury; the aggravated wrongfulness and associated 'stigma' attached to torture pertains to the character of the act, rather than its repercussions.

4.3. Distinguishing Torture: From Intensity of Suffering to Severity of Treatment

4.3.1. The Intensity Criterion

The first institution to make a finding of torture under the ECHR was the European Commission of Human Rights in *The Greek Case*. An oft-quoted passage of the Commission's Report, addressing the range of ill-treatment proscribed by Article 3, runs as follows:

> It is plain that there may be treatment to which all these descriptions apply, for all torture must be inhuman and degrading treatment, and inhuman treatment also degrading. The notion of inhuman treatment covers at least such treatment as deliberately causes severe suffering, mental or physical, which, in the particular situation, is unjustifiable. The word 'torture' is often used to describe inhuman treatment which has a purpose, such as the obtaining of information or confessions, or the infliction of punishment, and it is generally an aggravated form of inhuman treatment. Treatment or punishment of an individual may be said to be degrading if it grossly humiliates him before others or drives him to act against his will or conscience.[15]

The Commission thus portrayed torture as an aggravated form of inhuman treatment and also placed emphasis on the purposive dimension of torture, reflecting the notion that torture involves the employment of ill-treatment as a means towards attaining a particular purpose.[16]

[13] For a critical take on the distinction, see *Gäfgen* (n 11), Joint Partly Dissenting Opinion of Judges Rozakis, Tulkens, Jebens, Ziemele Bianku and Power.

[14] *Gäfgen*(n 11) para 167. This issue, despite being of great significance, relates primarily to Art 6, and will not be a focal point in this study.

[15] *The Greek Case* (n 2) 186.

[16] On this idea, see also the Report of the Special Rapporteur on torture and other cruel, inhuman or degrading treatment or punishment, UN Doc A/72/178, 20 July 2017, para 31.

It is worth noting that the reference to justifiability in the Commission's report became a matter of controversy given that the defining characteristic of an absolute right is that it leaves no room for a justifiable infringement.[17] The Commission clarified its approach in *Ireland v UK*, underlining that 'it did not have in mind the possibility that there could be a justification for any treatment in breach of Art. 3'.[18]

The starting point in the *Court's* specification of torture is the judgment in *Ireland v UK*, where the ECtHR pointed to an 'intention that the Convention with its distinction between torture and inhuman treatment should by the first of these terms attach a special stigma to *deliberate inhuman treatment causing very serious and cruel suffering*' (emphasis added).[19] The Court preceded this remark by stating that 'In the Court's view, this distinction derives principally from a difference in the intensity of the suffering inflicted'.[20] The Court considered its approach to be consistent with UN General Assembly Resolution 3452, which declares: 'Torture constitutes an aggravated and deliberate form of cruel, inhuman or degrading treatment or punishment'.[21]

The ECtHR thereby appeared to draw a quantitative distinction, in terms of the 'intensity of suffering' inflicted,[22] between torture and other ill-treatment proscribed by Article 3, with the additional proviso that torture is *deliberate* inhuman treatment. Yet the Court's method for measuring intensity of suffering has been opaque at best. For instance, in *Ireland v UK*, the Court simply reasoned that the five techniques, consisting of wall standing, hooding, subjection to noise, deprivation of sleep and deprivation of food and drink, 'did not occasion suffering of the particular intensity and cruelty implied by the word torture as so understood'.[23] The majority did not provide particulars of the 'particular intensity' required for

[17] Note, however, the complexity arising in relation to the justified use of force and justified punishment, discussed in Ch 5.

[18] *Ireland v UK* App no 5310/71 (Report of the Commission, 25 January 1976), 378; see also, among others, *Ireland v UK* (n 1) para 163; *Tomasi v France* (1993) 15 EHRR 1, para 115; *Chahal v UK* (1997) 23 EHRR 413, para 79; *Saadi v Italy* (2009) 49 EHRR 30, para 127.

[19] *Ireland v UK* (n 1) para 167.

[20] ibid.

[21] Declaration on the Protection of All Persons from Being Subjected to Torture and Other Cruel, Inhuman or Degrading Treatment or Punishment (UN General Assembly Resolution 3452, 9 December 1975) A/RES/3452, referred to in para 167 of the *Ireland v UK* (n 1) judgment. But see C De Vos, 'Mind the Gap: Purpose, Pain, and the Difference between Torture and Inhuman Treatment' (2006) 14(2) *Human Rights Brief* 4, 4: 'Although the Commission's decision heavily influenced the 1975 United Nations Declaration against Torture, which similarly adopted the notion of torture as an aggravated form of inhuman treatment … the case of *Ireland v. United Kingdom* challenged the Commission's purpose-driven test with the approach of the European Court of Human Rights'. See also N Rodley, 'The Definition(s) of Torture in International Law' (2002) 55(1) *Current Legal Problems* 467, 472.

[22] Note, however, the Separate Opinions of Judge Evrigenis and of Judge Matscher in *Ireland v UK* (n 1).

[23] *Ireland v UK* (n 1) para 167. See the critique in Spjut (n 7); see also L Doswald-Beck, 'What Does the Prohibition of "Torture or Inhuman or Degrading Treatment or Punishment" Mean? The Interpretation of the European Commission and Court of Human Rights' (1978) 25 *Netherlands International Law Review* 24, 40–41.

a finding of torture, even as some such particulars were given regarding inhuman and degrading treatment.[24]

In its first finding of torture in *Aksoy v Turkey* in 1996,[25] the ECtHR established that the subjection of the applicant to 'Palestinian hanging' was clearly deliberate ill-treatment which, in addition to the 'severe pain which it must have caused at the time', had been medically shown to have led to a paralysis of both arms 'which lasted for some time'.[26] It held that 'this treatment was of such a serious and cruel nature that it can only be described as torture'.[27] In the subsequent case of *Aydin v Turkey*,[28] concerning the rape and other forms of ill-treatment inflicted on a 17-year-old girl in detention, the ECtHR observed that not only had the applicant 'experienced the acute physical pain of forced penetration, which must have left her feeling debased and violated both physically and emotionally', but also that 'rape leaves deep psychological scars on the victim which do not respond to the passage of time as quickly as other forms of physical and mental violence'.[29] The ECtHR noted the other 'terrifying and humiliating experiences' to which the applicant had been subjected, including being kept blindfolded, being beaten, being paraded naked and being pummelled with high-pressure water while being spun around in a tyre (a sheer litany of inhumanity),[30] and that the purpose of eliciting information or related purposes must have underpinned this ill-treatment.[31] It held that 'the accumulation of acts of physical and mental violence inflicted on the applicant and the especially cruel act of rape to which she was subjected amounted to torture in breach of Article 3 of the Convention', clarifying too that it 'would have reached this conclusion on either of these grounds taken separately'.[32]

The Grand Chamber's 1999 judgment in *Selmouni v France*[33] (21 years after the judgment in *Ireland v UK*) is notable for affirming the dynamic character of the Court's interpretive endeavour. The ECtHR maintained the premise that torture amounts to 'deliberate inhuman treatment causing very serious and cruel suffering'.[34] For the Court, determining whether torture had occurred in *Selmouni* rested on whether the particular 'severity' of pain or suffering was made out, which the Court also linked to the definition of torture in Article 1 of the United Nations Convention Against Torture (UNCAT).[35] In respect of its assessment of 'severity' of pain or suffering, the Court stated:

[24] *Ireland v UK* (n 1) paras 162 and 167. See also the analysis in Ch 5.

[25] *Aksoy* (n 9). A detailed account of 'the tortures of Aksoy' in wider context is offered in M Goldhaber, *A People's History of the European Court of Human Rights* (Rutgers University Press 2007) ch 12.

[26] ibid para 64.

[27] ibid.

[28] *Aydin v Turkey* (1998) 25 EHRR 251.

[29] ibid para 83.

[30] ibid para 84.

[31] ibid para 85.

[32] ibid para 86.

[33] *Selmouni* (n 8).

[34] ibid para 96, citing *Ireland v UK* (n 1) para 167. See, too, *Aksoy* (n 9) para 63; *Aydin* (n 28) para 82.

[35] *Selmouni* (n 8) para 100, citing Art 1 of the United Nations Convention Against Torture and Other Cruel, Inhuman or Degrading Treatment or Punishment (1984) 1465 UNTS 85.

> [H]aving regard to the fact that the Convention is a 'living instrument which must be interpreted in the light of present-day conditions' … certain acts which were classified in the past as 'inhuman and degrading treatment' as opposed to 'torture' could be classified differently in future.[36]

With this statement, and the indication that 'an increasingly high standard' and 'greater firmness' are required in this area,[37] the Court established that it was taking a progressively developing approach to its assessment, such that it would potentially be recognising a wider range of ill-treatment as torture over time.

The Court in *Selmouni* elaborated on its 'severity' assessment for the purpose of distinguishing torture from IDTP as follows:

> [T]his 'severity' is, like the 'minimum severity' required for the application of Article 3, in the nature of things, relative; it depends on all the circumstances of the case, such as the duration of the treatment, its physical or mental effects and, in some cases, the sex, age and state of health of the victim, etc.[38]

It then proceeded to highlight the 'large number of blows'[39] inflicted on the victim, whose intensity was shown by marks all over his body, commenting: 'Whatever a person's state of health, it can be presumed that such intensity of blows will cause substantial pain'.[40] The Court then outlined other elements of the treatment, such as the fact that the victim was dragged along by his hair, made to run along a corridor with police officers positioned on either side to trip him up, urinated on by a police officer, and threatened with a blowlamp and then with a syringe over prolonged periods.[41] It concluded that 'the physical and mental violence, considered as a whole, committed against the applicant's person caused "severe" pain and suffering and was particularly serious and cruel', thus amounting to torture.[42] It is worth registering that finding such facts to substantiate torture does not necessarily point to a significant 'lowering' of the intensity or aggravation 'threshold', given the substantial extent of humiliation and suffering this ill-treatment deliberately and systematically inflicted.

While what distinguishes the 'intensity' or 'severity' of pain or suffering warranting the label of 'torture' has been opaque in the jurisprudence of the Court, certain key determinants do emerge in its assessment. In particular, the Court has often highlighted the injuries and/or long-term consequences resulting from the treatment at issue. In *Aksoy* the Court considered it important to note, regarding the applicant's subjection to 'Palestinian hanging', that this had brought about 'a paralysis of both arms which lasted for some time'.[43] The particular long-term

[36] *Selmouni* (n 8) para 101.
[37] ibid.
[38] ibid para 100. On the 'minimum level of severity' and the Art 3 'threshold', see Ch 5.
[39] *Selmouni* (n 8) para 102.
[40] ibid.
[41] ibid paras 102–04.
[42] ibid para 105.
[43] *Aksoy* (n 9) para 64.

trauma associated with rape was highlighted in *Aydin*.[44] In *Selmouni*, the applicant's injuries – 'the marks of the violence Mr Selmouni had endured covered almost all of his body' – were highlighted in concluding that the ill-treatment at issue amounted to torture.[45] In *Denizci v Cyprus*, just before concluding that a heavy police beating, to the point where one of the applicants was urinating blood,[46] did *not* amount to torture, the Court considered it relevant to point out that 'despite the serious injuries sustained by some of the applicants, no evidence was adduced to show that the ill-treatment in question had any long-term consequences for them'.[47] The point was also made in *Egmez v Cyprus* in the same fashion and with the same proximity to the conclusion that the ill-treatment did not amount to torture.[48] In *Cestaro v Italy*, which led to a finding that the severe beating of an unarmed anti-globalisation protester taking shelter in a school amounted to torture, the ECtHR made reference to the fractures and hospitalisation endured by the applicant, among an array of other factors leading the Court to a finding of torture.[49] Indeed, the Court in *Cestaro* cited *Egmez* as attesting to 'the absence of long-term after-effects' precluding a finding of torture.[50] Long-term effects and/or injuries appear to have been key determinants in several of the ECtHR's findings of torture.[51]

As formulated and applied in some of the cases outlined above, the criterion of 'intensity' or 'severity' of pain or suffering raises concerns in relation to the legitimate specification requirements. The opacity of the threshold of 'severe' or particularly intense pain or suffering, and the uncertainty involved in its application, which transforms into the *ex post facto* question of 'has this body suffered enough?',[52] undermine the guidance requirement. At the same time, the emphasis on tangible injuries and/or long-term consequences tends towards irrelevant reasoning capable of distorting the specification of torture. Even assuming that the extent of suffering caused should be a key criterion distinguishing torture from

[44] *Aydin* (n 28) para 83. See also *Zontul v Greece* App no 12294/07 (ECtHR, 17 January 2012), para 88.

[45] *Selmouni* (n 8) para 102.

[46] *Denizci and others v Cyprus* App nos 25316–25321/94 and 27207/95 (ECtHR, 23 May 2001), para 329.

[47] ibid para 385.

[48] *Egmez v Cyprus* (2002) 34 EHRR 29, para 78. Note also that this approach can be linked to the Bush administration's lawyers' adoption of a narrow definition of torture under US and international law – see the critical commentary in RK Goldman, 'Trivializing Torture: The Office of Legal Counsel's 2002 Opinion Letter and International Law Against Torture' (2004) 12(1) *Human Rights Brief* 1; and see D Cole (ed), *The Torture Memos: Rationalising the Unthinkable* (The New Press 2009).

[49] *Cestaro v Italy* App no 6884/11 (ECtHR, 7 April 2015), paras 177–90.

[50] ibid para 175, citing *Egmez* (n 48) paras 76, 78–79.

[51] See, for example, *Bartesaghi Gallo and others v Italy* App nos 12131/13 and 43390/13 (ECtHR, 22 June 2017), para 118; *Zakharin and others v Russia* App no 22458/04 (ECtHR, 12 November 2015), para 82; *Ilhan v Turkey* (2002) 34 EHRR 36, paras 86–88; *Akkoç v Turkey* (2002) 34 EHRR 51, paras 116–17.

[52] This is taken from Michelle Farrell's presentation titled 'The Tortured Body' at *The Body and Human Rights Symposium*, Brunel University, 12 February 2018; see further M Farrell, 'Just How Ill-treated Were You? An Investigation of Cross-fertilisation in the Interpretative Approaches to Torture at the European Court of Human Rights and in International Criminal Law' (2015) 84 *Nordic Journal of International Law* 482.

other ill-treatment (a matter that is interrogated further below), it should be questioned how far long-term consequences or tangible injuries are appropriately to be used as a proxy for the intensity of suffering experienced. Insofar as injuries or long-term consequences are, separately or in combination, treated as a *sine qua non* of the 'intensity' element for a finding of torture, this is problematic. A focus on these makes central the tangible or long-term impact of the treatment suffered rather than the intensity of pain or suffering inflicted in the moment of torture.[53]

Accordingly, an emphasis on such tangible consequences risks unduly transforming what is at most an evidentiary shortcut for proving intense suffering into a central element in the specification of torture. Yet even treating it as an evidentiary shortcut is problematic, given that a focus on locating tangible proof of injury or lasting damage risks eliding much of modern torture.[54] Several judges and commentators disagreed forcefully with the ECtHR majority's rejection of the Commission's finding of torture in *Ireland v UK* on precisely this ground[55] – as Judge Evrigenis put it:

> The interpretation adopted by the Court in this case also seems to point towards a conception of torture which is attached to devices for inflicting suffering which are now outdistanced by the ingenuity of modern methods of oppression. Torture does not necessarily involve violence, a notion to which the judgment refers expressly and generically. It can be – and indeed is – carried out by subtle techniques, perfected in multidisciplinary laboratories which call them-selves scientific. It aims, through new forms of suffering which have little in common with the bodily pain caused by the conventional torments, at inducing even temporarily the disintegration of the human personality, the destruction of man's mental and psychological balance and the annihilation of his will. I should be extremely sorry if the definition of torture which comes out of the Judgment could not cover these different forms of technologically-refined torture. Such an interpretation would lose sight of the context and the historical perspectives in which the European Convention on Human Rights should be situated.[56]

Judge Evrigenis's concerns are particularly relevant today, as torture methods leaving (virtually) no 'traces' continue to be 'refined'.[57] Insofar as the Court might place

[53] The difficulties in the evaluation of suffering in the context of defining torture are addressed in M-H McDonnell, L Nordgren and G Loewenstein, 'Torture in the Eyes of the Beholder: The Psychological Difficulty of Defining Torture in Law and Policy' (2011) 44 *Vanderbilt Journal of Transnational Law* 87.

[54] This is noted in *Jalloh v Germany* (2007) 44 EHRR 32, Concurring Opinion of Judge Zupančič (footnote), citing Judge Posner in *Cooper v Casey*, 97 F3d 914, 917 (Seventh Circuit 1996).

[55] See the Separate Opinions of Judge Evrigenis, Judge Matscher and Judge O'Donoghue in *Ireland v UK* (n 1); see also the commentary in Spjut (n 7); N Rodley and M Pollard, *The Treatment of Prisoners under International Law* (3rd edn, Oxford University Press 2009) 90–95; De Vos (n 21) 4–5.

[56] *Ireland v UK* (n 1), Separate Opinion of Judge Evrigenis.

[57] The Court has expressed its concerns on this: 'due regard must be had to the special difficulties in proving allegations of torture. Torture is uniquely evil both for its barbarity and its corrupting effect on the criminal process. It is practised in secret, often by experienced interrogators who are skilled at ensuring that it leaves no visible signs on the victim. All too frequently, those who are charged with ensuring that torture does not occur – courts, prosecutors and medical personnel – are complicit in its concealment.' *Othman (Abu Qatada) v UK* (2012) 55 EHRR 1, para 276. On the enduring need to sharpen relevant legal standards in respect of psychological torture, see E Cakal, 'Debility, Dependency and Dread: On the Conceptual and Evidentiary Dimensions of Psychological Torture' (2018) 28(2) *Torture* 15.

injury – and not just violence – at the centre of its inquiry, even if it does this in respect of instances of physical ill-treatment, it bears underlining that this can serve to sideline the reality of mental or psychological (or indeed some forms of physical) torture methods focused on creating, exacerbating and exploiting disorientation, humiliation, anguish and fear.[58] Consider, for example, mock executions, threats against one's family, attacks on personal, religious and cultural sensibilities, or even the practice of waterboarding.[59] Indeed, the Court has observed, in assessing Bulgaria's legislative framework in *Myumyun v Bulgaria*, that 'one of the distinguishing characteristics of torture is that it not only – *and not always* – seriously damages the physical health of the person subjected to it but also affects in a very serious way that person's dignity and psychological well-being' (emphasis added).[60]

Yet making the distinction between torture and IDTP hinge on a difference in the degree of pain or suffering successfully inflicted can also be challenged on a wholesale basis. Torture is an aggravated wrong because of its particular wrongfulness, not just the additional pain or suffering it inflicts in comparison to IDTP. The specification of torture can and should be reconfigured to capture the essence of the wrong, which is relational and qualitative.[61] A reassessment of the function of the concept of 'severity' holds the key to this reconfiguration.

4.3.2. From Enhanced Intensity to Aggravated Severity

The Court does not always focus on injuries and long-term health consequences to make a finding of torture. In *Polonskiy v Russia*, for instance, it reasoned as follows:

> The applicant was hit at least several times in his face, shoulders, back and legs and was subjected to electric shocks, which is a particularly painful form of ill-treatment. Such treatment must have caused him severe mental and physical suffering, even though it did not apparently result in any long-term damage to his health. Moreover, it appears that the use of force was aimed at debasing the applicant, driving him into submission and making him confess to criminal offences. Therefore, the Court finds that the

[58] But on the emphasis on *trauma* in the context of (psychological) torture, see T Kelly, *This Side of Silence: Human Rights, Torture, and the Recognition of Cruelty* (University of Pennsylvania Press 2013) 38, 44–45.

[59] See S Sayeed, 'Guantanamo Bay – Five Years On' (2007) 21 *Journal of Immigration Asylum and Nationality Law* 109, 114–15. See generally D Luban and H Shue, 'Mental Torture: A Critique of Erasures in U.S. Law' (2011) 100 *Georgetown Law Journal* 823; Rodley and Pollard (n 55) 103. See also JT Parry, 'The Shape of Modern Torture: Extraordinary Rendition and Ghost Detainees' (2005) 6 *Melbourne Journal of International Law* 516, 525; Goldman (n 48); E Peters, *Torture* (University of Pennsylvania Press 1996) 169–71. See generally D Rejali, *Torture and Democracy* (Princeton University Press 2009).

[60] *Myumyun v Bulgaria* App no 67258/13 (ECtHR, 3 November 2005), para 74.

[61] On the relational wrongness of torture, see A Maier, 'Torture' in P Kaufmann, H Kuch, C Neuhaeuser and E Webster (eds), *Humiliation, Degradation, Dehumanization: Human Dignity Violated* (Springer 2010) 111–13.

> treatment to which the applicant was subjected was serious enough to be considered as torture.[62]

The Court's reasoning in *Polonskiy* escapes the conflation of suffering with evidentiary shortcuts for proving suffering. Moreover, instead of focusing on the intensity of the suffering inflicted in determining whether the ill-treatment amounts to torture, it opts for treating the severity of the *treatment* as determinative: the treatment was clearly capable of – 'must have' – and oriented at causing substantial suffering, and was 'serious' enough to be considered to amount to torture. This is the better approach to the torture 'threshold': a focus on the severity of the treatment can and should supersede the criterion of augmented intensity of suffering, or of evidentiary shortcuts for proving it masquerading as substantive elements of torture.

Moving from the intensity of pain or suffering to the *severity of the treatment* transforms a seemingly quantitative criterion – has the victim suffered 'enough', and demonstrably so? – into a qualitative standard, whereby severity and aggravation attach to the *conduct* rather than its repercussions. Despite the problematic tendencies critiqued above,[63] the ECtHR's determination of the torture 'threshold' can be reframed as hinging on the severity of the conduct itself. A number of elements in the Court's reasoning can be adduced in support of this.

One key element is that the ECtHR has expressly attached the 'severity' label to the treatment at issue, rather than solely to the pain or suffering it caused. It has, for example, referred to 'the severity of the ill-treatment',[64] to 'ill-treatment serious enough to be considered as torture',[65] and to the severity of 'acts of violence'.[66] Moreover, the Court's Article 3 'threshold' mantra is that 'ill-treatment must attain a minimum of severity if it is to fall within the scope of Article 3'.[67]

Another important element in the Court's reasoning is the ECtHR's allusion to cruelty. The Court's conclusion in *Ireland v UK* that 'the five techniques … did not occasion suffering of the particular intensity and *cruelty* implied by the word torture as so understood'[68] illustrates that cruelty is a notion distinct from intensity of suffering. In its judgment in *Gäfgen*, the ECtHR referred to treatment reaching the 'level of cruelty required to attain the threshold of torture'.[69] Cruelty

[62] *Polonskiy v Russia* App no 30033/05 (ECtHR, 19 March 2009) para 124.

[63] See also A Cullen, 'Defining Torture in International Law: A Critique of the Concept Employed by the European Court of Human Rights' (2003) 34 *California Western International Law Journal* 29.

[64] See, for example, *Cestaro* (n 49) para 185; *Akkoç* (n 51) para 117; see also *Olisov and others v Russia* App nos 10825/09, 12412/14 and 35192/14 (ECtHR, 2 May 2017), paras 86–87.

[65] See, for example, *Zhyzitskyy v Ukraine* App no 57980/11 (ECtHR, 19 February 2015), para 44; *Grigoryev v Ukraine* App no 51671/07 (ECtHR, 15 May 2012), para 65; for variations of this, see *Polonskiy* (n 62) para 124; *Pomilyayko v Ukraine* App no 60426/11 (ECtHR, 11 February 2016), para 51.

[66] See, for example, *Sergey Ivanov v Russia* App no 14416/06 (ECtHR, 15 May 2018), para 79; *Abdulkadyrov and Dakhtayev v Russia* App no 35061/04 (ECtHR, 10 July 2018), para 70.

[67] *Keenan v UK* (2001) 33 EHRR 38, para 108.

[68] *Ireland v UK* (n 1) para 167.

[69] *Gäfgen* (n 11) para 108; see also *Cestaro* (n 49) para 176.

is primarily a perpetrator-focused concept, as Waldron posits, relating particularly to one's (callous or malevolent) attitude to another's suffering.[70] It is a concept that can go some way towards capturing the dehumanising totalitarianism of torture, which ruptures the deontic mutual bond that human dignity encapsulates.

An additional factor which suggests that the ECtHR attaches torture's particular severity to the character of the conduct is that, in distinguishing torture from other ill-treatment, the Court has on occasion ascribed significance to whether the ill-treatment was inflicted within 'a short period of heightened tension and emotions',[71] the latter situation tending more to be seen as a still likely unacceptable (over-)reaction to events but as not necessarily involving the deliberate and/or systematic infliction of suffering (for a purpose). For instance, the ECtHR reasoned as follows in *Selmouni*:

> The Court notes, lastly, that the above events were not confined to any one period of police custody during which – without this in any way justifying them – heightened tension and emotions might have led to such excesses. It has been clearly established that Mr Selmouni endured repeated and sustained assaults over a number of days of questioning.[72]

This point is deemed worthy of its own paragraph and just precedes the finding of torture. It thus appears quite significant in determining the gravity of the conduct at issue. While over-emphasising systematicity and duration may be substantively questionable,[73] it is indicative of an (arguably flawed) attempt by the Court to delineate the severity of the treatment – notably its deliberate and purposeful character – rather than purely the gravity of its consequences, *particularly* for the purpose of distinguishing between the aggravated wrong of torture and the (still absolutely proscribed) wrongs of inhuman and/or degrading treatment or punishment.

Finally, and crucially, conduct- and perpetrator-focused criteria have, in many instances, taken centre stage over intensity and consequences in the Court's delineation of torture. The following excerpt from *Krastanov v Bulgaria* identifies, by highlighting their absence in the circumstances, key elements of the ECtHR's understanding of the aggravated wrong of torture:

> However, it does not appear that the pain and suffering were inflicted on the applicant intentionally for the purpose of, for instance, making him confess to a crime or breaking his physical and moral resistance. Also, the injuries were caused during a short

[70] J Waldron, *Torture, Terror and Trade-offs: Philosophy for the White House* (Oxford University Press 2012) 299–302. But note that the Court sometimes refers to 'cruel suffering': see, for example, *Ireland v UK* (n 1) para 167; text to n 85, below.

[71] *Selmouni* (n 8) para 104; *Krastanov v Bulgaria* (2005) 41 EHRR 50, para 53; *Egmez* (n 48) para 78.

[72] *Selmouni* (n 8) para 104.

[73] Note, however, the Court's nuanced dismissal of the argument of 'heightened tensions' in *Cestaro* (n 49) paras 171–90. On systematicity and duration, see also *Cirino and Renne v Italy* App nos 2539/13 and 4705/13 (ECtHR, 26 October 2017), para 83.

> period of time, in the course of a police operation for the arrest of suspected offenders, which was apparently accompanied by heightened tension ... In these circumstances, the Court concludes that the ill-treatment complained of was sufficiently serious to be considered as inhuman, but that it cannot be qualified as torture.[74]

The passage above highlights that the lack of intentionality, purposefulness, or full control of the situation played a role in differentiating treatment that is sufficiently severe to be considered *inhuman* from treatment sufficiently severe to be qualified as *torture*. A similar emphasis on intentionality and purposefulness transpires in *Egmez*, alongside the ill-conceived emphasis on long-term consequences.[75] In other case law in which it has made a finding of torture, the ECtHR has underlined that the ill-treatment took place in circumstances where 'the applicant had no means of resisting', and was bound to cause not only physical pain or injury but also 'feelings of helplessness, acute stress and anxiety'.[76] In several findings of torture, the Court has also repeatedly emphasised, as in *Polonskiy*,[77] that the perpetrators acted 'intentionally' and 'with the aim of ... driving [the victim] into submission'.[78]

There is much to tie these considerations to the way that the wrong of torture was conceptualised in Chapter 3. If torture paradigmatically constitutes the tyrannisation of a defenceless person's body and/or spirit, then focus should lie on the authoritarian cruelty that it involves. When the Court alludes to the special stigma pertaining to torture, the word stigma is not independent of object. Torture is an aggravated *wrong*, and the stigma pertains to the character of the treatment inflicted on the person. It makes sense therefore to speak of the severity of the *treatment* at issue, as the Court often does.[79]

Returning to something akin to the hypothetical scenario set out in Chapter 3, of an individual unable to feel anything even while the perpetrators are acting in a way that is deliberately aimed at inflicting maximum suffering, the wrong committed arguably amounts to torture because it intentionally and purposefully seeks to break someone through the infliction of suffering, regardless of its success in bringing about suffering. Many would also point out, of course, that a perpetrator seeking to break someone – or drive them 'into submission' – would not stop at a 'failed' attempt to cause pain, but would proceed to other body parts, or use other methods to attain their aim. Those bent on breaking someone through suffering

[74] *Krastanov* (n 71) para 53.

[75] *Egmez* (n 48) para 78.

[76] See, for example, *Skomorokhov v Ukraine* App no 58662/11 (ECtHR, 26 September 2019), paras 69–70; *Pankiv v Ukraine* App no 37882/08 (ECtHR, 28 February 2019), paras 65–66. See also the reference to the overpowering of the applicant and her feelings of helplessness in the finding of torture in *Pomilyayko* (n 65) para 51.

[77] See text to n 62 above.

[78] See, for example, *Shestopalov v Russia* App no 46248/07 (ECtHR, 28 March 2017), para 46; *Zhyzitskyy* (n 65) para 43; *Grigoryev* (n 65) para 64; *Polonskiy* (n 62) para 124.

[79] See text to n 64 above; see, further, *Ilhan* (n 51) para 85; *Salman v Turkey* (2002) 34 EHRR 17, para 114; *El-Masri v Former Yugoslav Republic of Macedonia* (2013) 57 EHRR 25, para 197, among others.

will be doing their best to bring about substantial suffering, and indeed to create circumstances in which the potential suffering the victim comes to expect is limitless.[80] As Waldron points out, a perpetrator of torture 'knows that he is inflicting considerable pain; that is his intention'.[81] Given the Court's tendency to infer,[82] it is accordingly strange that it sometimes takes a lot to persuade it that a particular intensity of suffering was reached in cases where there is a clear and enacted intent to cause serious suffering (with a view to breaking the person). The Court's approach in *Ireland v UK* is particularly problematic on this account: the 'five techniques' were clearly performed with a view to creating the kind of overwhelming suffering that would subvert the will of the victims, which also makes the refusal to view them as reaching the enhanced 'intensity of suffering' threshold at best misguided.[83]

The Court itself appears in other cases to be more open to drawing the inference that treatment intended to inflict and capable of inflicting substantial suffering has inflicted it. The Court's finding in *Diri v Turkey* that the use of *falaka* – foot whipping – amounted to torture is instructive:

> In this connection, the Court considers that the treatment complained of was inflicted on the applicant intentionally by the prison guards with the purpose of punishing him and of breaking his physical and moral resistance to the prison administration. In these circumstances, the Court finds that this act was particularly serious and cruel and capable of causing severe pain and suffering. It is [*sic*] therefore concludes that this sort of ill-treatment amounted to torture within the meaning of art.3 of the Convention.[84]

There is in this passage, more generally, a promising redirection from the emphasis on the *actual* suffering caused to the severity of the treatment itself and whether and to what extent it is *intended to* cause, and capable of causing, grave suffering. Similarly, the Court's approach to the infliction of electric shocks in judgments such as *Grigoryev v Ukraine* is instructive in looking beyond the extent of tangible injuries or long-term harm brought about by ill-treatment:

> As to the Government's submission about the supposedly minor nature of the applicant's injuries, the Court has already held in its case-law that subjecting a person to electric shocks is a particularly serious form of ill-treatment capable of provoking

[80] The idea that torture knows no boundaries is put forward in Y Ginbar, *Why Not Torture Terrorists? Moral, Practical and Legal Aspects of the 'Ticking Bomb' Justification for Torture* (Oxford University Press 2010) 66.

[81] J Waldron, 'Torture and Positive Law: Jurisprudence for the White House' (2005) 105 *Columbia Law Review* 1681, 1700.

[82] See, for example, *Güler and Öngel v Turkey* App nos 29612/05 and 30668/05 (ECtHR, 4 October 2011), para 26: 'Furthermore, in assessing evidence, the standard of proof "beyond reasonable doubt" is generally applied. However, such proof may follow from the coexistence of sufficiently strong, clear and concordant inferences or of similar unrebutted presumptions of fact. Further, where allegations are made under Articles 2 and 3 of the Convention, the Court must apply a particularly thorough scrutiny'.

[83] See critique by Cullen (n 63) 38–40.

[84] *Diri v Turkey* (2010) 50 EHRR 1, para 45. See also *Othman (Abu Qatada)* (n 57) para 270.

severe pain and cruel suffering, and therefore falling to be treated as torture, even if it does not result in any long-term damage to health.[85]

Torture's particular 'severity' can and should therefore be seen as being tied to the relational and qualitative wrongfulness of torture rather than to whether it has 'successfully' brought about an enhanced intensity of suffering or proxies thereof. This reconceptualisation of the 'aggravation' involved in torture calls for a shift of focus from associating aggravation with torture's *outcomes*, namely an increased intensity of suffering, to associating aggravation with the character of the ill-treatment. It is therefore a departure from how Nigel Rodley understood 'aggravation' in a landmark article on the definition(s) of torture, where he treated 'aggravation' as pertaining to a higher scale of suffering (and argued for suppressing its significance).[86] On the other hand, it coheres with the premise of an argument advanced by Malcolm Evans in another key article on torture – in 'Getting to Grips with Torture', Evans argued that the purposive element, rather than an augmented level of suffering, should be seen as the key 'aggravating factor' constituting torture. Evans's argument rightly tied aggravation to the character of the act, rather than its consequences. In the remainder of the chapter, I consider the key elements that make up torture's aggravated severity, focusing on the element of control and the dual dimension of intent and purpose.[87]

4.3.3. The Element of Control

Until recently, the ECtHR's findings of torture had pertained solely to ill-treatment of individuals deprived of their liberty.[88] In *Cestaro v Italy*,[89] and, two years later, in *Bartesaghi Gallo v Italy*,[90] the ECtHR found that the violent beating, including with the use of rubber truncheons, of anti-globalisation protesters taking shelter within a school amounted to torture. None of the victims had acted violently or had been in any position effectively to resist the violence. The police subjected them to violent beatings, intentionally inflicting substantial physical and psychological

[85] *Grigoryev* (n 65) para 64. See also *Polonskiy* (n 62) para 124; *Zhyzitskyy* (n 65) para 43.

[86] Rodley (n 21) 491.

[87] See, in this regard, the Report of the Special Rapporteur on Torture and Other Cruel, Inhuman or Degrading Treatment or Punishment, UN Doc A/HRC/13/39, 9 February 2010, para 60. See the relevant commentary in Rodley and Pollard (n 55) ch 3; but note their distinct treatment of 'aggravation' (also present in Rodley (n 21)).

[88] Even in cases which did not involve formal State custody, the Court only came close to a finding of torture in circumstances where it appeared that the victim was in the control of the perpetrator(s): for instance, in *Kaya v Turkey*, which concerned a case of enforced disappearance, the Court considered the possibility that a kidnapped individual had been subjected to torture (though ultimately making a finding of inhuman treatment) – *Kaya v Turkey* App no 22535/93 (ECtHR, 28 March 2000), paras 110–19.

[89] *Cestaro* (n 49), decided in 2015.

[90] *Bartesaghi Gallo* (n 51).

suffering.[91] The Court noted that the domestic courts had interpreted these acts as having the purposes of punishing and humiliating the protesters.[92] It concluded that the ill-treatment amounted to torture.

While (State) custody is often associated with torture, notably in the scope of operation envisaged for key torture prevention bodies such as the European Committee for the Prevention of Torture and the United Nations Subcommittee on Prevention of Torture,[93] the circumstances in *Cestaro* and *Bartesaghi Gallo* were not typically custodial. They nonetheless involved what can be seen as an integral element of torture: control over the victim. Although control is most obviously present in situations where the victim is in custody, custody does not exhaust the circumstances in which the victim may be in the control of the perpetrator(s).[94] Rather, control primarily has to do with relative power and powerlessness.[95] The tyrannisation at the centre of torture occurs in circumstances where one person (or more) possesses and asserts power over another, and paradigmatically where they act as 'master over flesh and spirit', as Jean Améry put it.[96] The person subjected to torture is, or is rendered, effectively powerless.[97] As Manfred Nowak explains, it is typically 'one of the principal aims of the perpetrator of torture to show the victims that they exercise total control over them and that they are able to do with them whatever they wanted to do'.[98] Thus, control underlines the limitlessness of the victim's potential suffering and aggravates the cruelty of its infliction. In this respect, the ECtHR in *Cestaro* and *Bartesaghi Gallo* stressed that the victims in the cases at hand were neither attacking the police nor in a position meaningfully to resist them,[99] while at the same time the anti-riot police were 'well-armed',

[91] *Cestaro* (n 49) paras 170–90; *Bartesaghi Gallo* (n 51) paras 114–20.

[92] *Cestaro* (n 49) para 177; *Bartesaghi Gallo* (n 51) para 114.

[93] European Convention for the Prevention of Torture and Inhuman or Degrading Treatment or Punishment (1987) ETS 126, Arts 1 and 2; Optional Protocol to the United Nations Convention Against Torture, A/RES/57/199, Arts 1 and 19.

[94] The International Criminal Court (ICC) Statute's definition of torture is interesting on this point. According to the ICC Statute, '"Torture" means the intentional infliction of severe pain or suffering, whether physical or mental, upon a person in the custody or under the control of the accused'. Rome Statute of the International Criminal Court (adopted 17 July 1998, entered into force 1 July 2002) 2187 UNTS 90, Art 7(2)(e). Note, too, the Committee Against Torture's finding in *V.L. v Switzerland*, CAT/C/37/D/262/2005, 22 January 2007, para 8.10.

[95] In *Pomilyayko v Ukraine*, for example, the ECtHR emphasised the perpetrators' 'overwhelming power' over the victim – see *Pomilyayko* (n 65) para 51.

[96] J Améry, *At the Mind's Limits: Contemplations by a Survivor on Auschwitz and Its Realities* (Indiana University Press 1980) 35.

[97] The element of 'powerlessness' is highlighted by Manfred Nowak and Elizabeth McArthur in relation to UNCAT, see M Nowak and E McArthur, *United Nations Convention against Torture: A Commentary* (Oxford University Press 2008) 76–77; see also the Report of the Special Rapporteur on Torture and Other Cruel, Inhuman or Degrading Treatment or Punishment, UN Doc A/HRC/13/39, 9 February 2010, para 60.

[98] M Nowak, 'Powerlessness as a Defining Characteristic of Torture' in M Başoğlu (ed), *Torture and Its Definition in International Law: An Interdisciplinary Approach* (Oxford University Press 2017) 437.

[99] *Cestaro* (n 49) para 180; *Bartesaghi Gallo* (n 51) paras 116–17.

being equipped with both weapons and defensive equipment.[100] The ECtHR also dismissed the Italian government's allusions to the tension pervading the policing operations at issue in *Cestaro* and *Bartesaghi Gallo* as irrelevant in what was clearly a controlled situation in which the State's agents systematically but also indiscriminately inflicted violence on persons whose behaviour did not necessitate the use of force in defence of anyone's bodily integrity.[101]

That the element of control, or the assertion of power over powerlessness, is not exhausted by custodial contexts is affirmed in a recent report by the United Nations Special Rapporteur on Torture.[102] As the Rapporteur explains, powerlessness is a matter of whether someone, at the time of the relevant act or omission, is within the control of the perpetrator and is not in a position effectively to resist or escape the infliction of pain or suffering.[103]

It is important that this aggravating element is not understood too rigidly or in a purely spatial or physical sense. Control can operate in a multitude of ways and be shaped by varied forms of coercion and power asymmetry beyond the physical exercise of power or deprivation of liberty.[104] Moreover, while control may in certain circumstances be built up systematically and over a prolonged duration, circumstances of control need not be of a particular duration, and in this respect any myopia towards circumstances of control or profound power asymmetry in the Court's allusion to 'a short period of heightened tension and emotions'[105] should be rethought.

4.3.4. Intent and Purpose

The ECtHR refers to '*deliberate* inhuman treatment' in its definition of torture.[106] This does not merely denote acts which are intended, as distinct from acts which are unintended.[107] Instead, the element of intentionality is attached to the *character* of the action and, in particular, its (likely) consequences. The idea of 'deliberate inhuman treatment' implies an intention *to cause suffering*.[108] Indeed,

[100] *Cestaro* (n 49) para 189; *Bartesaghi Gallo* (n 51) para 115.

[101] *Cestaro* (n 49) paras 185–90; *Bartesaghi Gallo* (n 51) paras 116–17. On Art 3's application to the use of force in defence of self or others, see Ch 5; see also N Mavronicola, '*Güler and Öngel v Turkey*: Article 3 of the European Convention on Human Rights and Strasbourg's Discourse on the Justified Use of Force' (2013) 76 *Modern Law Review* 370.

[102] Report of the Special Rapporteur on Torture and Other Cruel, Inhuman or Degrading Treatment or Punishment, UN Doc A/72/178, 20 July 2017, para 47.

[103] ibid para 31; see also Report of the Special Rapporteur on Torture and Other Cruel, Inhuman or Degrading Treatment or Punishment, UN Doc A/74/148, 12 July 2019, para 8.

[104] Report A/74/148 (n 103) paras 8–9, 62.

[105] *Selmouni* (n 8) para 104; *Krastanov* (n 71) para 53; *Egmez* (n 48) para 78.

[106] See, for instance, *Gäfgen* (n 11) para 90.

[107] But see *Aksoy* (n 9) para 64.

[108] Gail Miller makes the point regarding the UNCAT definition, GH Miller, *Defining Torture* (Benjamin N Cardozo School of Law 2005) 14. John Vorhaus also suggests that 'The concept of torture implies

in delineating its own understanding of torture, the Court has frequently alluded to Article 1 of the UNCAT, which establishes that torture involves the 'intentional infliction'[109] of pain or suffering. The Court's (arguably flawed) finding that the forceful administration of emetics to a drug trafficking suspect in *Jalloh v Germany* did not involve deliberate cruelty is instructive on this point: '*Although this was not the intention*, the measure was implemented in a way which caused the applicant both physical pain and mental suffering. He has therefore been subjected to *inhuman and degrading treatment* contrary to Article 3' (emphasis added).[110] *Jalloh* highlights that, as distinct from torture, IDTP can be made out without this element of intent.[111]

Moreover, the intent to cause suffering that is central to torture distinguishes it from most situations of medical necessity or self-defence, where suffering may be an 'unintended side-effect'.[112] In his account of the definition of torture in the UNCAT, Manfred Nowak explains:

> Intent must intend that the conduct inflict severe pain or suffering and intend that the purpose be achieved by such conduct … If severe pain or suffering is inflicted, for instance, in the course of a fully justified medical treatment, such conduct cannot constitute torture because it lacks both the purpose and intent [of torture] …[113]

Nowak alludes both to an intent to cause suffering and to a purpose. Found in the UNCAT definition of torture,[114] the dual elements of intention and purpose have appeared in many ECtHR judgments, notably *Selmouni*,[115] and were set out in the following terms in the Grand Chamber judgment in *Salman*:

> In addition to the severity of the treatment, there is a purposive element as recognised in the United Nations Convention against Torture and Other Cruel, Inhuman or Degrading Treatment or Punishment, which came into force on 26 June 1987, which defines torture in terms of the intentional infliction of severe pain or suffering with the aim, *inter alia*, of obtaining information, inflicting punishment or intimidating.[116]

agency, and the victim's agony is neither an accident nor the unintended consequence of the torturer's deeds. Torture implies purposeful ill-treatment': J Vorhaus, 'On Degradation. Part One: Article 3 of the European Convention on Human Rights' (2002) 31 *Common Law World Review* 374, 386.

[109] See, for example, *El-Masri* (n 79) para 197.

[110] *Jalloh* (n 54) para 82.

[111] See also *MSS v Belgium and Greece* (2011) 53 EHRR 2, para 220; *RR v Poland* (2011) 53 EHRR 31, para 151; *V v UK* (2000) 30 EHRR 121, para 71.

[112] JH Burgers and H Danelius, *The United Nations Convention against Torture: A Handbook on the Convention against Torture and Other Cruel, Inhuman or Degrading Treatment or Punishment* (Martinus Nijhoff 1988) 119.

[113] M Nowak, 'What Practices Constitute Torture? US and UN Standards' (2006) 28 *Human Rights Quarterly* 809, 830, also citing Burgers and Danelius (n 112) 119.

[114] See Art 1 UNCAT (n 35).

[115] *Selmouni* is considered key in establishing the relevance of the UNCAT and the element of purpose; see *Selmouni* (n 8) paras 96–98. Note *Jalloh* (n 54), Concurring Opinion of Judge Zupančič: 'In *Selmouni v France* we integrated Article 1 of the United Nations Convention against Torture … into our own case law'.

[116] *Salman* (n 79) para 114.

In judgments such as *Gäfgen*[117] and *El-Masri v FYROM*,[118] the Grand Chamber has reiterated the above passage from *Salman*. It was similarly noted by the Grand Chamber in *Othman (Abu Qatada) v UK* in relation to *falaka*, that '*when its purpose has been to punish or to obtain a confession*, the Court has had no hesitation in characterising it as torture'.[119] The two layers of intent and purpose are evident: '*intentional* infliction of severe pain or suffering with the *aim* … of …' (emphasis added).[120]

The ECtHR takes the purposive element to lie within its own understanding of torture under Article 3 ECHR *as well as* within Article 1 UNCAT: 'there is a purposive element to torture, as recognised *also* in the United Nations Convention against Torture' (emphasis added).[121] The treatment's purpose is now frequently alluded to by the Court in making a finding of torture, sometimes even apart from references to the UNCAT.[122] The 'purposive element',[123] which Judge Zupančič refers to as '*dolus specialis*',[124] is therefore, as Clare McGlynn has put it, 'an important element to any torture inquiry'.[125] In much of the case law, the element of purpose is presented as a *sine qua non*. For instance, the Court in *Denizci*, justifying its finding of inhuman treatment but not torture, stated: 'at the time of the applicants' detention, the police officers had intentionally subjected them to ill-treatment of varying degrees of severity … *However, it is not established that the police officers' aim was to extract a confession*' (emphasis added).[126]

Judgments such as this prompted Malcolm Evans, in 2002, to suggest that

> the Chambers of the Court have concluded that ill-treatment which would seem to qualify as torture on the *Selmouni* approach to the threshold is to be categorized as inhuman and degrading treatment because of [*sic*] the nature of the purpose underlying its infliction was not sufficiently closely linked to extracting a confession.[127]

Writing in 2009, McGlynn also remarked that, within ECtHR analysis, 'the discussion of purpose has been solely linked to the extraction of confessions and

[117] *Gäfgen* (n 11) para 90.

[118] *El-Masri* (n 79) para 197.

[119] *Othman (Abu Qatada)* (n 57) para 270. See also *Diri* (n 84) para 45.

[120] Text to n 116.

[121] *Kaçiu and Kotorri v Albania* App nos 33192/07 and 33194/07 (ECtHR, 25 June 2013), para 90.

[122] See, for example, *Menesheva v Russia* (2007) 44 EHRR 56, paras 57–59; *Pankiv* (n 76) paras 65–66; *Skomorokhov* (n 76) paras 69–70.

[123] The Court regularly refers to 'a purposive element as recognised in the United Nations Convention against Torture': see, for example, *Salman* (n 79) para 114; *Ilhan* (n 51) para 85; *Akkoç* (n 51) para 115; *Aktaş v Turkey* (2004) 38 EHRR 18, para 313; *El-Masri* (n 79) para 197.

[124] *Jalloh* (n 54), Concurring Opinion of Judge Zupančič. See also *Korobov v Ukraine* App no 39598/03 (ECtHR, 21 July 2011), Joint Concurring Opinion of Judges Zupančič, Berro-Lefèvre and Yudkivska, para 9.

[125] C McGlynn, 'Rape, Torture and the European Convention on Human Rights' (2009) 58 *International & Comparative Law Quarterly* 565, 580.

[126] *Denizci* (n 46) para 384.

[127] M Evans, 'Getting to Grips with Torture' (2002) 51 *International & Comparative Law Quarterly* 365, 377. See also *Aydin* (n 28) para 85.

information'.[128] This no longer holds. Punishment, for example, has been central to several findings of torture, such as the finding that the applicant's force-feeding amounted to torture in *Nevmerzhitsky v Ukraine*,[129] and the ruling that the retaliatory beating of a prisoner with rubber truncheons amounted to torture in *Vladimir Romanov v Russia*.[130] In *El-Masri*, the ECtHR indicated that the aim of the applicant's ill-treatment had been 'to cause severe pain or suffering in order to obtain information, inflict punishment or intimidate the applicant'[131] before making a finding of torture. In *Cestaro* and *Bartesaghi Gallo* the Court viewed the ill-treatment inflicted on protesters taking shelter in a school as being orientated towards punishment and intimidation rather than pursuing the objectives typically associated with 'interrogational torture',[132] before making a finding of torture.[133]

As indicated above, the ECtHR frequently cites the element of purpose alongside reference to Article 1 UNCAT. Article 1 UNCAT encompasses

> such purposes as obtaining from [the victim] or a third person information or a confession, punishing him for an act he or a third person has committed or is suspected of having committed, or intimidating or coercing him or a third person, or for any reason based on discrimination of any kind.[134]

The words 'such purposes as' suggest that the list is not exhaustive,[135] but also that for a purpose besides those enumerated to fall within the definition, it should have something in common with the purposes listed.[136] The latter point should not be overstated, however: the instrumentalisation of intentionally inflicted pain or suffering, which aims to contort a person's body or psyche so it serves towards a certain purpose, is what aggravates the ill-treatment and substantiates the severity of torture. The specifics of the purpose need not, therefore, take centre stage, and to that extent the ECtHR's willingness to look beyond interrogational torture should be welcomed.

At the same time, it is important to highlight that 'discrimination' features in Article 1 UNCAT, chiefly as underlying reason or motivation rather than purpose. Feminist scholars have sought to highlight the discrimination element in the

[128] McGlynn (n 125) 582.

[129] *Nevmerzhitsky v Ukraine* (2006) 43 EHRR 32, paras 93–99.

[130] *Vladimir Romanov v Russia* App no 41461/02 (ECtHR, 24 July 2008), paras 68–70.

[131] *El-Masri* (n 79) para 211.

[132] On the particular challenge posed by interrogational torture to liberal ideals, see D Luban, 'Liberalism, Torture, and the Ticking Bomb' (2005) 91 *Virginia Law Review* 1425.

[133] *Cestaro* (n 49) para 177; *Bartesaghi Gallo* (n 51) para 114. See also *Cirino and Renne* (n 73) para 85, where the purposive element was identified as being 'to punish the detainees, to enforce discipline and to deter future disorderly behaviour'.

[134] Art 1 UNCAT (n 35).

[135] See, also, Burgers and Danelius (n 112) 118. But see *Delalić et al* (IT-96-21-T), Trial Chamber Judgment, 16 November 1998, para 470.

[136] Miller (n 108) 16.

definition of torture with regard to gender-based violence.[137] Writing on rape as torture, for example, McGlynn furnishes a forceful argument that all rape, as 'an act of power and therefore with purposes beyond sexual gratification',[138] is a gendered and discriminatory act irrespective of whom it is inflicted upon.[139] Although the ECtHR recognises rape as amounting to proscribed ill-treatment under Article 3 ECHR,[140] and in many instances as amounting to torture, the ECtHR has not shown clear signs of explicitly applying discrimination in this way in its case law on rape as torture. The applicant's rape in *Aydin* was linked explicitly to the purpose of eliciting information before the Court made a finding of torture.[141] In a more recent judgment in *Zontul v Greece*,[142] concerning the anal penetration of a man with a truncheon, the argument that the victim's sexuality motivated the attack was mentioned in a relevant report and in the applicant's allegations, but did not feature in the ECtHR's findings. The ECtHR found the forcible penetration of the applicant to constitute torture, on account of its brutality and intentionality.[143] It did so referring approvingly[144] to judgments of the International Criminal Tribunal for the former Yugoslavia (ICTY),[145] the International Criminal Tribunal for Rwanda (ICTR)[146] and the Inter-American Court of Human Rights (IACtHR).[147] It quoted, in particular, the following passage from *Akayesu* at the ICTR:

[137] See L Davis, 'The Gendered Dimensions of Torture: Rape and Other Forms of Gender-Based Violence as Torture Under International Law' in Başoğlu (ed) (n 98). See also the insightful account in FD Gaer, 'Rape as a Form of Torture: The Experience of the Committee Against Torture' (2012) 15 *CUNY Law Review* 293. For an important general overview of the application of the anti-torture norm to violence against women in particular, see A Edwards, *Violence against Women under International Human Rights Law* (Cambridge University Press 2011) ch 5. On gender perspectives on the prohibition of torture, see Report of the Special Rapporteur on Torture and Other Cruel, Inhuman or Degrading Treatment or Punishment, UN Doc A/HRC/31/57, 5 January 2016.

[138] McGlynn (n 125) 582. See C MacKinnon, *Are Women Human? And Other International Dialogues* (Harvard University Press 2006) 240–41; R Copelon, 'Surfacing Gender: Re-Engraving Crimes Against Women in Humanitarian Law' (1994) 5 *Hastings Women's Law Journal* 243, 246.

[139] The former UN Special Rapporteur on Torture, Manfred Nowak, has also indicated that 'the purpose element is always fulfilled, if the acts can be shown to be gender-specific', in the sense of being 'aimed at "correcting" behaviour perceived as non-consonant with gender roles and stereotypes or at asserting or perpetuating male domination over women', see Report of the Special Rapporteur on Torture and Other Cruel, Inhuman or Degrading Treatment or Punishment, UN Doc A/HRC/7/3, 15 January 2008, para 30 and footnote. See also P Pérez-Sales and M Zraly, 'From Sexualized Torture and Gender-based Torture to Genderized Torture: The Urgent Need for a Conceptual Evolution' (2018) 28(3) *Torture* 1.

[140] As Edwards highlights, 'rape per se satisfies the threshold level of severity for Article 3 of the ECHR, regardless of the type of rape at issue', Edwards (n 137) 236. See, further, *MC v Bulgaria* (2005) 40 EHRR 20 and *Aydin* (n 28).

[141] *Aydin* (n 28) para 85.

[142] *Zontul* (n 44).

[143] ibid paras 92–93.

[144] ibid para 91.

[145] *Kunarac* (IT-96-23 & IT-96-23/1-A), Appeal Chamber Judgment, 12 June 2002, para 150; *Furundžija* (IT-95-17/1), Trial Chamber Judgment, 10 December 1998, para 181.

[146] *Musema* (ICTR-96-13), Trial Chamber Judgment, 27 January 2000, paras 221–22; *Akayesu* (ICTR-96-4), Trial Chamber Judgment, 2 September 1998, para 597.

[147] *Caso del Penal Miguel Castro Castro v Perú* Serie C No 160 (IACtHR, 25 November 2006), para 312.

> Like torture, rape is used for such purposes as intimidation, degradation, humiliation, discrimination, punishment, control or destruction of a person. Like torture, rape is a violation of personal dignity, and rape in fact constitutes torture when inflicted by or at the instigation of or with the consent or acquiescence of a public official or other person acting in an official capacity.[148]

While the potential discriminatory 'purpose' or motivation behind torture and rape is acknowledged in this eloquent passage, and was thus implicitly a feature of the finding in *Zontul*, the ECtHR in *Zontul* also relied on domestic findings indicating that the perpetrator had been aiming to punish the applicant for what he deemed to be troublesome behaviour, and concluded that the ill-treatment inflicted amounted to torture on account of its brutality and intentionality.[149]

More generally, the ECtHR does not systematically focus on discrimination in its specification of torture. In *Denizci*, for example, the Turkish-Cypriot applicants ill-treated by Greek-Cypriot police officers had also complained of an Article 14 violation – not addressed by the Court 'in the light of its findings [of violation of Articles 3 and 5(1)]'[150] – and there was a strong possibility that their ill-treatment was tied to a discrimination of *some* kind, to paraphrase the UNCAT. Yet, in finding the ill-treatment not to constitute torture, the Court noted that it had not been shown that the police officers' purpose was to extract a confession, without considering this other significant possibility. Similarly, in cases concerning the ill-treatment of persons of Roma background in Greece, the ECtHR has not systematically considered discrimination allegations as part of its assessment of the characterisation of the ill-treatment itself,[151] as distinct from the application of Article 14 ECHR. In *Antayev and others v Russia*, the ECtHR found police officers to have ill-treated several persons in an apparently racially motivated attack 'with the aim to intimidate, humiliate and debase them'.[152] Nonetheless, it characterised the ill-treatment as inhuman and degrading,[153] except in respect of one of the applicants, who had had a rope tightened around his neck until he lost consciousness: his heightened suffering, according to the Court, meant that the way he was treated could be characterised as 'torture'.[154] The Court noted that it was 'especially disturbing that this treatment seems to have had a racial element to it',[155] and, observing that 'Racial violence is a particular affront to human dignity',[156] it ultimately found a violation of Article 14 ECHR taken together with the substantive limb of Article 3 ECHR.[157]

[148] *Akayesu* (n 146) para 597, cited in *Zontul* (n 44) para 64.

[149] *Zontul* (n 44) para 31 and para 92.

[150] *Denizci* (n 46) para 414.

[151] See, for example, *Zelilof v Greece* App no 17060/03 (ECtHR, 24 May 2007); *Petropoulou-Tsakiris v Greece* (2009) 48 EHRR 47.

[152] *Antayev and others v Russia* App no 37966/07 (ECtHR, 3 July 2014), para 97.

[153] ibid.

[154] ibid.

[155] ibid.

[156] ibid para 120.

[157] ibid para 129.

There is cause for systematically treating discrimination as a central element in the specification of torture. On a general level, discrimination is evidently an aggravating factor in respect of any instance of physical or psychological violence or other ill-treatment.[158] More importantly, while discrimination may appear 'both conceptually and grammatically distinct from the other purposes' set out in the UNCAT definition,[159] as discrimination does not disclose a goal but an underlying reason, it is certainly not conceptually alien to the wrong of torture. The Court itself acknowledges racist violence as being a particular affront to human dignity.[160] As argued in Chapter 3, torture operates as a form of radical othering, with the dehumanisation of the person at its core.[161] In his sharp and devastating account of torture at the hands of the Nazi regime, Jean Améry underlined this denial of mutual humanity in torture and concluded that 'torture was not an accidental quality of this Third Reich, but its very essence'.[162] As many who have grappled with the phenomenon of torture have highlighted, torture is often underpinned by a stark othering of the person(s) targeted.[163] Discrimination is therefore closely connected to torture: torture others and is premised on othering.

4.3.5. State Involvement

As the account above elaborates, the aggravated wrong of torture encompasses intentional and purposeful infliction of pain or suffering in circumstances of control over the victim. A question that endures in respect of what fundamentally constitutes the aggravated wrong of torture as a matter of human rights law concerns the element of State involvement: is State involvement an essential element of torture? To elucidate the relevance of State involvement in the ECtHR's

[158] Indeed, the Court appears to recognise the aggravated severity of 'cases of violence motivated by racial discrimination' and requires a proper investigation of such incidents, including their discriminatory motivation – see, for example, *Škorjanec v Croatia* (2018) 66 EHRR 14. On discrimination as an 'aggravating factor', see also *Moldovan and others v Romania* (2007) 44 EHRR 16, para 111.

[159] Miller (n 108) 16.

[160] See, for example, *Antayev* (n 152) para 120; *Petropoulou-Tsakiris* (n 151) para 61; *Zelilof* (n 151) para 72. See also, on discrimination and Article 3 more broadly, *Cyprus v Turkey* (2002) 35 EHRR 30, paras 302–11.

[161] See the analysis in Ch 3; see also N Mavronicola, 'Torture and Othering' in B Goold and L Lazarus (eds), *Security and Human Rights* (2nd edn, Hart Publishing 2019).

[162] Améry (n 96) 24.

[163] See, for example, P Lenta, 'Waiting for the Barbarians after September 11' (2006) 42 *Journal of Postcolonial Writing* 71, 73: 'once the identity of those that the United States designates as its enemies has been constructed as a wholly negative, uncivilized other, torture will appear to the US soldiers who inflict it on Iraqis as morally unobjectionable and even heroic'. Nigel Rodley put this as follows: 'when [torture] is part of an institutional practice … the victim is – must be – dehumanised, seen as an object. This is the traditional and inevitable means of considering "the enemy", be it a class enemy, a race enemy, a religious enemy, or a foreign enemy. Whatever the group, its members must be stripped of their inherent dignity as human beings in order to mobilise the rest against them'. N Rodley, *The Treatment of Prisoners under International Law* (Oxford University Press 1999) 14–15. See further discussion in Ch 3.

specification of torture, it is important to avoid conflating two distinct questions: the question of the specification of torture itself and the question of the State's responsibility in respect of incidents of torture or IDTP. My focus is the former, and not the latter – that is, the substance of the wrong of torture rather than the attribution of responsibility.[164]

The element of State involvement is incorporated into the definition of torture in the UNCAT: pain or suffering must, for the purposes of fitting within the UNCAT definition of torture, be 'inflicted by or at the instigation of or with the consent or acquiescence of a public official or other person acting in an official capacity'.[165] In 2008, McGlynn observed that 'in every case in which there has been a positive finding of torture by the ECtHR, the conduct in question has been *meted out* by a state official' (emphasis added).[166] In other words, the ECtHR had only made findings of torture in cases of infliction – and not of instigation, consent or acquiescence – by State officials. At the same time, the ECtHR had regularly quoted the UNCAT definition in its case law, notably in *Selmouni*,[167] a case which is sometimes taken to mark the importation or integration of the UNCAT definition on torture into ECtHR jurisprudence.[168]

Hints remained of the possibility of recognising torture absent State involvement. For example, in *Kaya v Turkey*,[169] considering Hasan Kaya's suffering before being killed at the hands of unidentified persons, the ECtHR explicitly stated that the acts in question were not shown to be acts of State agents[170] but proceeded to note:

> The obligation imposed on High Contracting Parties under Article 1 of the Convention to secure to everyone within their jurisdiction the rights and freedoms defined in the Convention, taken together with Article 3, requires States to take measures designed to ensure that individuals within their jurisdiction are not subjected to *torture* or inhuman or degrading treatment, including such ill-treatment administered by private individuals (emphasis added).[171]

[164] See also Report A/74/148 (n 103) para 5. For an important discussion focusing on the attribution of responsibility (through the lens of 'due diligence'), see L McGregor, 'Applying the Definition of Torture to the Acts of Non-State Actors: The Case of Trafficking in Human Beings' (2014) 36 *Human Rights Quarterly* 210.

[165] Art 1(1) UNCAT.

[166] McGlynn (n 125) 588.

[167] *Selmouni* (n 8) para 97. See also *Othman (Abu Qatada)* (n 57) para 266.

[168] See, for instance, *Jalloh* (n 54), Concurring Opinion of Judge Zupančič: 'In *Selmouni v. France* we integrated Article 1 of the United Nations Convention against Torture (hereinafter "the UNCAT") into our own case law'. For Rodley and Pollard, writing in 2009, the UNCAT approach represents the position in international human rights law on the State actor element: Rodley and Pollard (n 55) 88.

[169] *Kaya* (n 88).

[170] ibid para 114.

[171] ibid para 115.

Ultimately, however, the ECtHR considered that the evidence did not disclose torture but 'inhuman and degrading treatment'.[172]

Relevant academic commentators have suggested there may be closer linkages between Article 3 ECHR and understandings of torture in international criminal law, where State involvement is not an essential component of the definition of torture.[173] Judgments such as *Kunarac* (at the ICTY),[174] as well as the ICC Statute, provided definitions of torture that are independent of the State involvement parameter, with the ICC Statute specifying torture as 'the intentional infliction of severe pain or suffering, whether physical or mental, upon a person in the custody or under the control of the accused'.[175] Nonetheless, although the ECtHR has cited some of the case law of international criminal tribunals approvingly in cases such as *Zontul*, it has also continued to place emphasis on State involvement; in *Zontul*, for example, it underlined the fact that the sexual violence had been inflicted by a State agent.[176]

While State involvement appears to remain a feature of the ECtHR's specification of torture, the nature and degree of State involvement that the ECtHR tends to look for may have evolved. In *El-Masri*,[177] the Court considered the applicant's subjection to torture and his expulsion to face further torture in a set of facts amounting to extraordinary rendition. The applicant was detained on entry into the Former Yugoslav Republic of Macedonia (FYROM) in 2003 by Macedonian agents for several days, during which he was threatened and ill-treated, and then was handed to CIA agents, who performed on him the so-called 'capture shock' treatment, involving various forms of ill-treatment. He was, for example, sodomised with an object and drugged. After being forcefully placed in a CIA aircraft, he was flown out of FYROM to Afghanistan, where he was subjected for four months to torture and repeated interrogation about his alleged involvement in terrorism. The ECtHR in *El-Masri* held a Contracting State (FYROM) responsible for torture, even where such torture had been inflicted by a non-Contracting State's agents (CIA agents).[178] Considering the ill-treatment the applicant had endured at Skopje airport at the hands of CIA rendition agents, the Court found that

[172] ibid para 118. It appears from the Court's analysis that the lack of evidence concerning perpetrators, intention and purpose played a key role in the finding.

[173] See Gaeta (n 3); O de Frouville, 'The Influence of the European Court of Human Rights' Case Law on International Criminal Law of Torture and Inhuman or Degrading Treatment' (2011) 9 *Journal of International Criminal Justice* 633.

[174] *Kunarac* (IT-96-23 & IT-96-23/1-T), Trial Chamber Judgment, 22 February 2001, para 496: 'the Trial Chamber is of the view that the presence of a state official or of any other authority-wielding person in the torture process is not necessary for the offence to be regarded as torture under international humanitarian law'.

[175] See n 94 above.

[176] *Zontul* (n 44) para 88.

[177] *El-Masri* (n 79).

[178] ibid paras 205–11.

it amounted to torture,[179] emphasising 'that the acts complained of were carried out in the presence of officials of the respondent State and within its jurisdiction' and involved 'the acquiescence or connivance of its authorities'.[180] On one reading, the Court may be taken to be adopting the full spectrum of State involvement – including acquiescence – that can fulfil the State involvement parameter of the *definition* of torture under the UNCAT for identifying, as well as for attributing responsibility for, the wrong of torture.[181]

Acquiescence, which reflects the minimum of State involvement under the UNCAT definition, is a far-reaching concept, which arguably extends to circumstances where State officials are culpably failing to provide effective protection from ill-treatment, including ill-treatment by non-State actors.[182] An alternative interpretation of this position from a human rights perspective would be that State involvement need not be present for an act of torture, as a matter of *definition*, to be made out. On this account, the State's failure to take adequate measures – in effect, to discharge positive obligations[183] – to provide effective protection from torture would entail State responsibility for failing to take such measures[184] in respect of acts of torture which need not, in their infliction, have involved (even in an attenuated way) the State. As a matter of *human rights law*, in other words, the State may be responsible for failing to provide protection from torture, while the person responsible – and criminally liable – for the commission of torture may be a non-State actor.[185]

In contemplating this possibility, it is worth considering what the requirement of relevant reasoning entails in relation to State involvement, notably whether State involvement is necessarily a mark of aggravated severity and an integral element of torture. Feminist authors in particular have challenged the State-centric approach to defining torture for eliding the grave violence, not least gender-based violence, experienced by a significant number of persons across the world at the hands of 'private' individuals (that is, non-State actors).[186] McGlynn has expressed the hope

[179] ibid para 211.

[180] ibid para 206.

[181] See, however, the distinction drawn between attribution and failure to discharge positive obligations in H Keller and R Walther, 'Evasion of the International Law of State Responsibility? The ECtHR's Jurisprudence on Positive and Preventive Obligations under Article 3' (2019) *International Journal of Human Rights* (advance online access). See also *Al Nashiri v Poland* (2015) 60 EHRR 16.

[182] Office of the UN High Commissioner for Human Rights, *Human Rights Fact Sheet: No 4 Combating Torture* (May 2002) 34, available at: www.ohchr.org/Documents/Publications/FactSheet4rev.1en.pdf (accessed 3 January 2020).

[183] See Keller and Walther (n 181). See also the discussion of positive obligations in Ch 6.

[184] As Dinah Shelton and Ariel Gould put it, 'a state's diligence is not legally deficient because of the act that causes the injury, but rather because of what was lacking in the authorities' prevention of or response to said act': D Shelton and A Gould, 'Positive and Negative Obligations' in D Shelton (ed), *The Oxford Handbook of International Human Rights Law* (Oxford University Press 2013) 578.

[185] See R McCorquodale and R La Forgia, 'Taking Off the Blindfolds: Torture by Non-State Actors' (2001) 1 *Human Rights Law Review* 189, 217.

[186] See, among others, C MacKinnon, 'On Torture: A Feminist Perspective on Human Rights' in KE Mahoney and P Mahoney (eds), *Human Rights in the Twenty-First Century: A Global Challenge*

that the ECtHR, through 'recognizing torture beyond the paradigmatic … will begin to address the varied ways in which women are tortured and the fact that their torturers are so often private individuals'.[187]

On the other hand, McGlynn has also acknowledged that the involvement of a State official may be an aggravating or at least relevant differentiating factor, indicating that 'It may be that we should recognise that while all rapes are serious crimes, the circumstances and context of some rapes may make them different',[188] including on account of the status of the perpetrator – even if the act is no less harmful to the victim.[189] McGlynn has put the point as follows:

> All rapes are serious crimes and must be treated as such, though almost every legal system fails to do so. Nonetheless, the circumstances of some rapes may mean that the offences committed vary. In the case of Sukran Aydin, her rape was rape, but it was also torture by virtue of her perpetrator being a state official. It was rape and torture. In the case of mass rapes of Bosnian women, there were rapes of individual women and arguably also genocide: rape and genocide.[190]

Nonetheless, the State involvement parameter may distort, or simply unduly narrow, the specification of torture as a matter of human rights law. After all, within Article 3 ECHR, findings of torture are chiefly about fair labelling, about attaching 'special stigma' to what warrants such stigma. Accordingly, it is important to interrogate whether incorporating State involvement into the specification of torture appropriately encapsulates the essence of the wrong of torture and the element of aggravation it involves. We should interrogate this in light of the imperative of showing a readiness to recognise the 'egregious in the everyday'[191] infliction of long-overlooked or under-recognised gendered wrongs.

Arguably, it is the State's power over persons within its reach that makes the deliberate and purposeful infliction of pain or suffering on persons by State agents particularly severe, as an abuse of said power. If so, then the element of control captures this element of aggravation in a more principled manner: the abuse of power over relative powerlessness. Seeing control as the more salient element of

(Martinus Nijhoff 1993) 21–31; H Charlesworth, 'Worlds Apart: Public/Private Distinctions in International Law' in Margaret Thornton (ed), *Public and Private: Feminist Legal Debates* (Oxford University Press 1995) 248–51; C Romany, 'State Responsibility Goes Private: A Feminist Critique of the Public/Private Distinction in International Human Rights Law' in R Cook (ed), *Human Rights of Women: National and International Perspectives* (University of Pennsylvania Press 1994) 85–87; R Copelon, 'Recognizing the Egregious in the Everyday: Domestic Violence As Torture' (1994) 25 *Columbia Human Rights Law Review* 291; H Charlesworth, 'The Mid-life Crisis of the Universal Declaration of Human Rights' (1998) 55 *Washington & Lee Law Review* 781; C Chinkin, 'A Critique of the Public/Private Dimension' (1999) 10 *European Journal of International Law* 387.

[187] McGlynn (n 125) 594–95.

[188] C McGlynn, 'Rape as "Torture"? Catharine MacKinnon and Questions of Feminist Strategy' (2008) 16 *Feminist Legal Studies* 71, 78.

[189] ibid 80.

[190] ibid 80, referring to *Aydin* (n 28).

[191] Copelon (n 186).

aggravation would not so much enable the recognition of torture 'beyond the paradigmatic',[192] to borrow from McGlynn, as better illuminate how the 'paradigm' ought to be understood.[193] It would allow the ECtHR to label abuses of power involving the deliberate and purposeful infliction of suffering appropriately, across all settings in which they occur, both public and private (as public and private are traditionally, though not uncontestedly, understood).[194] This would be in line with the growing recognition, at international law, of gender-based violence as falling within the purview of the anti-torture norm,[195] and would better capture the way in which microcosms of tyranny arise and proliferate in homes, bedrooms, workplaces, delivery rooms and other settings beyond those in which persons come face to face with the coercive force of the State.

4.3.6. Anchoring the Above Assessment

The above appraisal of the ECtHR's specification of torture is pursued in the spirit of integrity and is premised on the idea that the Court's specification of torture should capture the aggravated wrong of torture. As I argue, an assessment focused on the severity of the treatment, rather than focusing unduly on its tangible consequences, best maps onto the aggravated wrongfulness of torture. The elements of control as well as intentionality and purposefulness, including discriminatory motivation, make up the augmented severity of torture. It is worth anchoring this appraisal with reference to two relatively recent judgments.

The first set of facts emerges from the case of *Al Nashiri v Poland*,[196] concerning the rendition and torture of two 'High Value Detainees' (HVD) in the United States' extraordinary rendition programme after the attacks of 9/11. The facts of this case are a testament to human cruelty. The applicants in *Al Nashiri*, Mr Al Nashiri and Mr Abu Zubaydah, were subjected to a range of ill-treatment euphemistically referred to by the CIA as 'standard measures', including shaving, stripping, diapering, hooding, isolation, white noise or loud music, continuous light or darkness, uncomfortably cool environment, restricted diet, shackling, water dousing and sleep deprivation. In addition, they were subjected to the so-called 'Enhanced Interrogation Techniques', including the attention grasp (whereby they would be grabbed and pulled into close proximity with the interrogator, usually face to face), the walling technique, facial hold, facial or insult slap, cramped confinement, the use of insects, wall standing, stress positions, sleep deprivation and waterboarding. Other 'techniques' included subjection to prolonged nudity, beatings, confinement

[192] McGlynn (n 125) 594–95.
[193] Edwards (n 137) chs 2 and 5.
[194] For a call for such recognition within the ECtHR, see *Volodina v Russia* App no 41261/17 (ECtHR, 9 July 2019), Separate Opinion of Judge Pinto de Albuquerque, joined by Judge Dedov, paras 6–10; see also the Separate Opinion of Judge Serghides in the same case.
[195] Edwards (n 137) ch 5.
[196] *Al Nashiri* (n 181).

in a box, exposure to cold temperatures, threats of ill-treatment of family members, threats of rape, forced shaving and deprivation of solid food.

Consider one 'technique' employed in the case as an isolated example: walling. Walling consists of pulling a person forward and then firmly pushing them into a 'false wall' so that their shoulder blades hit the wall while their head and neck may be 'supported' with a rolled towel to reduce the risk of whiplash. According to the CIA, it is

> one of the most effective interrogation techniques because it wears down the HVD physically, heightens uncertainty in the detainee about what the interrogator may do to him, and creates a sense of dread when the [detainee] knows he is about to be walled again.[197]

Consider, too, another 'technique': threats of ill-treatment against oneself or a loved one.[198] In Chapter 3 I contemplated such a scenario and argued that within a situation of control, such a threat issued to an effectively powerless person is all the more believable and painfully felt; crucially, the torturer is intentionally inflicting what, in the circumstances, he calculates will be experienced as inexorable anguish, with a view to subordinating the will of that person. Each scenario discloses torture. The purpose is 'spirit thievery',[199] and the conduct involves the tyrannisation of the victim's body and spirit through the infliction of considerable intended suffering.

Let us reflect on a distinct case, *Volodina v Russia*, in which Russia was held responsible for failing to fulfil its positive obligations under Article 3 ECHR.[200] For the purposes of the analysis here, I will focus on the label given to the ill-treatment at issue. The applicant in *Volodina* was subjected to repeated acts of domestic violence, including coercive control,[201] at the hands of a man, S. She was physically attacked on several occasions, including when she was pregnant, leading to the premature termination of her pregnancy. Moreover, she experienced significant psychological violence, including harassment, stalking, death threats, the theft of her identity documents, and the destruction of her property.[202] Her abuser's behaviour was a systematic and comprehensive assault on her body and spirit, in circumstances of power asymmetry and control, and for the purpose of maintaining and indeed strengthening the abuser's coercive grip on her. It also took place against a backdrop of systemic gender-based abuse, discrimination and subordination.[203] The Court underlined the 'feelings of fear, anxiety and powerlessness that the applicant must have experienced in connection with [her abuser's]

[197] ibid para 67.
[198] ibid para 99.
[199] C Dayan, *The Law Is a White Dog* (Princeton University Press 2011) 21–22.
[200] *Volodina* (n 194).
[201] E Stark, *Coercive Control: How Men Entrap Women in Personal Life* (Oxford University Press 2009).
[202] *Volodina* (n 194) paras 74–75.
[203] This is outlined in the Court's finding of an Art 14 violation in Russia's discharge of its positive obligations under Art 3 ECHR, see ibid paras 103–33.

controlling and coercive behaviour'[204] and which the abuser surely sought to create through this behaviour. While the majority of the ECtHR considered this abuse to amount to 'inhuman treatment', the tyrannisation of body and spirit that she had been subjected to should properly be seen as torture. In a Separate Opinion, Judge Pinto de Albuquerque, joined by Judge Dedov, also argued that the ill-treatment experienced by the applicant amounted to torture, rightly highlighting the wider structural circumstances of patriarchal power in which grave suffering was inflicted on, and continued to be experienced by, the applicant.[205]

The arguments made above in relation to capturing torture's particular severity are orientated at the legitimate specification requirements, and premised on the idea that the ECtHR's specification of torture should correspond to the (aggravated) wrong of torture. With regard to the ECtHR doctrine's capacity to guide, three key points may be distilled from the analysis and argument in this chapter. The first is that, while the Court has taken steps to elaborate its specification of torture in case law such as *Cestaro*,[206] there is scope for further *ex ante* guidance to be offered by the Court with respect to the elements that make up torture as distinct from IDTP. The second is that a focus on aggravated *severity* as the overarching criterion, made up of the component elements of control as well as intentionality and purposefulness, including discriminatory motivation, offers more clarity and coherence than a distinction premised on enhanced intensity of suffering, which benefits from neither precise measurement nor a clear benchmark. Finally, the dynamic approach affirmed in *Selmouni*[207] appropriately allows scope for improving the Court's exercise of evaluative judgement in establishing the contours of torture and identifying instances of torture. By combining a dynamic approach with an effort to provide generalisable pronouncements, the Court can suitably navigate the line between undue uncertainty and undue rigidity or complacency.

4.4. Conclusion

Article 3 prohibits torture as well as inhuman and/or degrading treatment or punishment irrespective of extraneous countervailing considerations. Although one could say that there is still a spectrum of 'wrongfulness' within Article 3, the absolute prohibition substantively operates across the whole scope of ill-treatment captured by Article 3 ECHR. Nonetheless, the specification of torture, and getting it right, matters. Besides the specification's legal significance, it is more broadly important that the ECtHR should appropriately label the deliberate, purposeful

[204] ibid para 75.
[205] ibid, Separate Opinion of Judge Pinto de Albuquerque, joined by Judge Dedov, paras 6–10.
[206] See *Cestaro* (n 49) paras 171–176.
[207] *Selmouni* (n 8).

tyrannisation of one's body and spirit. The specification of torture under Article 3 ECHR should reflect the premise that torture is an aggravated *wrong* within a sphere of absolutely proscribed wrongs. What makes torture stand out from IDTP pertains to the character of the conduct: the particular *severity* of the treatment, rather than an augmented intensity of suffering or gravity of injuries inflicted, is key to the aggravated wrong of torture. Torture's aggravated severity, in the account offered in this chapter, is the gateway through which the elements of control and intentionality and purposefulness, including any discriminatory motive, take centre stage in delineating what is appropriately to be understood as torture. On this understanding, we may see torture more clearly, and appreciate that it is as egregious as it may be pervasive.

5

The Article 3 'Threshold': The Specification of Inhuman or Degrading Treatment or Punishment

5.1. Introduction

Ill-treatment which crosses the Article 3 'threshold' is conclusively unlawful. Accordingly, more so than the 'line' separating torture and other Article 3 ill-treatment, the threshold of severity at which treatment or punishment is found to be inhuman and/or degrading is crucial to the lawfulness of State (in)action. This chapter considers the ECtHR's specification of the Article 3 threshold in light of the legitimate specification parameters, addressing a number of conceptual challenges as they relate to the absoluteness starting point. Through a reframing of 'severity', elements of the Court's jurisprudence are clarified, reassessed or critiqued. The chapter tackles a number of issues of contention, including: the meaning of 'relative' in the assessment of potential Article 3 ill-treatment; the variables applied in the specification of the terms 'inhuman' and 'degrading'; the idea of the justified use of force, as well as justificatory reasoning in respect of other practices impinging upon bodily integrity; and the particularities of 'punishment' and treatment associated with punishment. As indicated in Chapter 4, Chapters 4 and 5 should be read together.

5.2. Starting Points in Identifying Inhumanity and Degradation

5.2.1. The Court's 'Tests'

Central to the 'tests' by which the ECtHR specifies the Article 3 'threshold' is the position, repeated in much of the ECtHR's Article 3 jurisprudence since *Ireland v UK*, that 'ill-treatment must attain a *minimum level of severity* if it is to fall within the scope of Article 3' (emphasis added).[1] The Court has indicated that

[1] *Ireland v UK* (1979–80) 2 EHRR 25, para 162.

'[t]he assessment of this minimum is, in the nature of things, relative; it depends on *all the circumstances of the case*, such as the duration of the treatment, its physical or mental effects and, in some cases, the sex, age and state of health of the victim, etc' (emphasis added).[2] Within the 'all the circumstances' formula, the Court has alluded broadly to 'the nature and context of the treatment or punishment, the manner and method of its execution',[3] as well as to 'whether the victim [was] in a vulnerable situation'.[4]

The Court has often reiterated that treatment 'has been held by the Court to be "inhuman" because, inter alia, it was premeditated, was applied for hours at a stretch and caused either actual bodily injury or intense physical and mental suffering'.[5] Degrading treatment has been described as treatment that 'humiliates or debases an individual showing a lack of respect for, or diminishing, his or her human dignity or arouses feelings of fear, anguish or inferiority capable of breaking an individual's moral and physical resistance'.[6] The Court has also suggested that a 'measure which does not involve physical ill-treatment but lowers a person in rank, position, reputation or character may … constitute degrading treatment'[7] and indicated that '[t]he public nature of the treatment may be a relevant or aggravating factor in assessing whether it is "degrading" within the meaning of Article 3'.[8] Endorsing a Commission decision,[9] the Court has underlined that 'publicly to single out a group of persons for differential treatment on the basis of [ethnic origin, race or religion] might, in certain circumstances, constitute a special affront to human dignity'[10] and amount to degrading treatment.[11]

Some academic commentary supports the view that 'degrading' treatment (or punishment) represents the 'lowest' level of ill-treatment caught by Article 3.[12]

[2] ibid; see also, for example, *Svinarenko and Slyadnev v Russia* App nos 32541/08 and 43441/08 (ECtHR, 17 July 2014), para 114.

[3] See, for example, *Garabayev v Russia* (2009) 49 EHRR 12, para 75.

[4] See, for example, *Khlaifia and others v Italy* App no 16483/12 (ECtHR, 15 December 2016), para 160.

[5] See, for example, *Stanev v Bulgaria* (2012) 55 EHRR 22, para 203; *Jalloh v Germany* (2007) 44 EHRR 32, para 68.

[6] *Pretty v UK* (2002) 35 EHRR 1, para 52.

[7] *Raninen v Finland* (1998) 26 EHRR 563, para 50. On the idea of 'lowering' in status, see E Webster, *Dignity, Degrading Treatment and Torture in Human Rights Law: The Ends of Article 3 of the European Convention on Human Rights* (Routledge 2017).

[8] *Svinarenko* (n 2) para 115.

[9] *East African Asians v UK* (1981) 3 EHRR 76 (CD), para 207.

[10] *Cyprus v Turkey* (2002) 35 EHRR 30, para 306.

[11] See ibid para 310. In making its finding, at paras 307–11, the Court cited the applicants' ethnic origin, race and religion as being the basis for their differential (and debasing) treatment (para 309).

[12] Vorhaus suggests that degrading treatment (and punishment) 'has the lowest threshold for entry' into the Art 3 prohibition: see J Vorhaus, 'On Degradation. Part One: Article 3 of the European Convention on Human Rights' (2002) 31 *Common Law World Review* 374, 375. Yutaka Arai-Yokoi also argues that the prohibition on degrading treatment is the '"lowest" form of an absolute right on the graded scale of ill-treatment under Article 3 of the ECHR': see Y Arai-Yokoi, 'Grading Scale of Degradation: Identifying the Threshold of Degrading Treatment or Punishment under Article 3 ECHR' (2003) 21 *Netherlands Quarterly of Human Rights* 385, 420–21.

This is largely premised on indications by the Court that degrading treatment involves the least amount of suffering within the spectrum of proscribed ill-treatment, which emerge from the Court's dicta in cases like *Tyrer v UK*.[13] In *Tyrer*, upon the Court's finding that the level of suffering associated with 'inhuman' punishment was not attained, the Court indicated that 'the only question for decision [was] whether he was subjected to a "degrading punishment" contrary to that Article'.[14]

Nonetheless, looking more generally at the Court's doctrine, the idea that degrading treatment or punishment is of lesser *severity* is not necessarily representative of the approach adopted in the case law of the Court. Indeed, 'minimum level of severity' also delineates degrading treatment: the 'threshold' identified is one of 'humiliation or debasement attaining a minimum level of severity'.[15] The Court has also added this proviso in its assessment of measures lowering the person in rank, position or reputation, indicating such a measure 'may constitute' degrading treatment 'provided it attains a minimum level of severity, thereby interfering with human dignity'.[16]

Consequently, while it makes sense to view Article 3 as proscribing a spectrum of wrongful conduct, this does not necessarily imply that degrading treatment or punishment is to be found at the *least wrongful* end of the spectrum. Rather, the distinction between inhuman and degrading treatment (and punishment) is primarily qualitative. The two terms – 'inhuman' and 'degrading' – can encompass distinct qualities, with potentially distinct effects on the victim, captured in the differing terms used in the tests just outlined. In broad terms, while the Court ascribes the label 'inhuman' to ill-treatment inflicting pain or suffering, the label 'degrading' primarily captures subjection to fear, anguish, humiliation or debasement.[17] At the same time, there is no denying that suffering is closely – perhaps inextricably – tied to fear, anguish, humiliation and debasement, or that certain instances of ill-treatment will involve all or most of these elements. For example, the subjection of Mark Keenan to solitary confinement, in the context of his mental ill-health and coupled with the inadequate provision of medical care, inflicted on him suffering and feelings of anguish that were capable of breaking his moral and physical resistance.[18] He was accordingly found, in *Keenan v UK*, to have been subjected to inhuman *and* degrading treatment and punishment.[19]

[13] *Tyrer v UK* (1979–80) 2 EHRR 1.

[14] ibid para 29. See also the Commission's analysis in *The Greek Case*: 'It is plain that there may be treatment to which all these descriptions apply, for all torture must be inhuman and degrading treatment, and inhuman treatment also degrading'. *The Greek Case (Denmark, Norway, Sweden and the Netherlands v Greece)* (1969) 12 *Yearbook of the European Convention on Human Rights* 1, 186.

[15] *Campbell and Cosans v UK* (1982) 4 EHRR 293, para 28; see also *Costello-Roberts v UK* (1995) 19 EHRR 112, paras 30–32.

[16] *Raninen* (n 7) para 50.

[17] See Vorhaus (n 12) 395.

[18] *Keenan v UK* (2001) 33 EHRR 38, para 115.

[19] ibid. See also *Ketreb v France* App no 38447/09 (ECtHR, 19 July 2012) para 115.

5.2.2. 'Severity' as Qualitative

The 'minimum level of severity' appears to delineate the Article 3 threshold by means of a requirement that a certain quantum of suffering or humiliation be made out.[20] Yet this warrants reconsideration. Building on the reconceptualisation of severity offered in relation to torture in Chapter 4, the 'minimum level of severity' can also be reframed on the basis that the Court is grappling with a qualitative, morally loaded concept of 'severity' through which inhumanity and degradation are understood. Severity, on this account, goes beyond the degree of pain, suffering, humiliation or anguish inflicted, although it is clear that the Article 3 threshold is only crossed when these are more than negligible. Severity, rather, is tied to the *wrong* in inhuman and in degrading treatment or punishment. The case of *Bouyid v Belgium*[21] is illuminating in making sense of this account of severity.

The case concerned two young men, one of whom was 17 at the time the events took place, who alleged that they had been slapped once in the face by local police officers while being detained at a police station. They claimed to have been victims of degrading treatment. In its judgment, the Fifth Section Chamber of the ECtHR had referred to the principle that in order for ill-treatment to fall within the scope of Article 3 it had to attain a 'minimum level of severity' and had suggested that some forms of violence, although morally condemnable and likely domestically unlawful, would not fall within Article 3.[22] It concluded that the slaps, 'though unacceptable, cannot be regarded as generating a sufficient degree of humiliation or debasement for a breach of Article 3 of the Convention to be established'; that, '[i]n other words', the 'threshold of severity has not been reached in the present case'.[23] The majority (14 judges) at the Grand Chamber disagreed with the Fifth Section of the ECtHR on this issue.

The Grand Chamber stressed that Article 3 ECHR is 'closely bound up with respect for human dignity'.[24] It indicated that

> in respect of a person who is deprived of his liberty, or, more generally, is confronted with law-enforcement officers, any recourse to physical force which has not been made strictly necessary by his own conduct diminishes human dignity and is, in principle, an infringement of the right set forth in Article 3.[25]

The facts suggested that the slaps were impulsive responses to what was perceived to be the applicants' disrespectful attitude, which, the Grand Chamber observed,

[20] See, on this, Michelle Farrell's critical examination of ECtHR doctrine on torture and ill-treatment: M Farrell, 'Just How Ill-treated Were You? An Investigation of Cross-fertilization in the Interpretive Approaches to Torture at the European Court of Human Rights and in International Criminal Law' (2015) 84 *Nordic Journal of International Law* 482.

[21] *Bouyid v Belgium* (2016) 62 EHRR 32 [Grand Chamber].

[22] *Bouyid v Belgium* App no 23380/09 (ECtHR, 21 November 2013) [Fifth Section], paras 43–48.

[23] ibid para 51.

[24] *Bouyid* [Grand Chamber] (n 21) para 81.

[25] ibid para 88, citations omitted.

was 'certainly insufficient to establish such necessity'.[26] The Court therefore found that the applicants' human dignity had been undermined and there had been a breach of Article 3 ECHR.[27]

In their general remarks, the majority of the Grand Chamber underlined that a slap by a law enforcement agent of an individual under their control is a 'serious attack on the individual's dignity'.[28] The majority indicated that 'even one unpremeditated slap devoid of any serious or long-term effect on the person receiving it may be perceived as humiliating by that person'.[29] This, in the majority's account, is particularly the case when the slap is inflicted by law enforcement officials on persons under the officials' control 'because it highlights the superiority and inferiority which by definition characterise the relationship between the former and the latter in such circumstances' and may arouse in the person(s) on whom it is inflicted 'a feeling of arbitrary treatment, injustice and powerlessness'.[30] The majority highlighted that persons in police custody or in the control of the police 'or a similar authority' are 'in a situation of vulnerability'.[31] Accordingly, the State's authorities are under a duty to protect them; and slapping them amounted to the antithesis, or 'flouting', of this duty.[32]

Bouyid potently illustrates that 'severity' does not stem straightforwardly from the degree of harm or suffering inflicted, but relates rather to the character of the treatment at issue. The violation inflicted on the applicants in *Bouyid* was an abuse of power that we may view as a microcosm of the totalitarianism found in torture.[33] The treatment's severity pertained to its character and not merely to its consequence. The assessment of 'minimum level of severity' therefore ultimately involves grappling with *the wrongs themselves*, and takes place in a context-sensitive way, where power asymmetry and the vulnerability it creates may play an important role in shaping the character of the treatment. Treatment is found to reach or not to reach the 'minimum' level of severity on an assessment of all the *relevant* facts of the particular situation, on a case-by-case basis, but with the guidance of a growing body of case law,[34] which includes positions of principle such as those outlined in *Bouyid*.[35]

[26] ibid para 102.
[27] ibid.
[28] ibid para 103.
[29] ibid para 105.
[30] ibid para 106, citing *Petyo Petkov v Bulgaria* App no 32130/03 (ECtHR, 7 January 2010), paras 42 and 47.
[31] *Bouyid* [Grand Chamber] (n 21) para 107.
[32] ibid.
[33] See Ch 3; see also N Mavronicola, '*Bouyid v Belgium*: The "Minimum Level of Severity" and Human Dignity's Role in Article 3 ECHR' (2020) 1(1) *ECHR Law Review* 105. For an account of the connections between torture, degradation and (dis)respect, see J Bronsther, 'Torture and Respect' (2019) 109 *Journal of Criminal Law and Criminology* 423.
[34] See, for example, *Bouyid* [Grand Chamber] (n 21) paras 81–90. The Court generally alludes to its past case law and repeats or builds on quotations from past cases in interpreting and applying Art 3.
[35] See ibid paras 81–113.

5.2.3. The Perspective Taken

The doctrine discloses that the minimum level of severity test operates as an objective standard set and applied by the Court, which ultimately does not defer to the government's or the alleged victim's viewpoint on severity. Although the Court reiterates the 'relative' approach it takes, which is sensitive to matters ranging from the age and gender of the victim to the wider context of the treatment,[36] and although it considers the victim's account of the experience of the treatment as outlined in the application before the Court,[37] the Court's 'relative' assessment is a means of ascertaining objectively the severity of the conduct. The Court does not tend to engage in determining as accurately as possible the victim's subjective experience of suffering,[38] although it has often relied on well-supported findings regarding the impact of certain practices on individuals.[39] The way the Court's approach is connected to the 'relative' assessment involved and the requirements of legitimate specification is addressed below.

5.3. The Court's 'Relative' Assessment in Light of the Legitimate Specification Criteria

5.3.1. Is the 'Relative' Assessment Relativist?

The Court has described its assessment of whether the Article 3 threshold has been crossed as being 'in the nature of things, relative'.[40] This raises the question of whether this 'relative' assessment signifies a form of 'relativism' which undermines or defeats the absoluteness starting point. As alluded to in Chapter 2, David Feldman has remarked that 'a degree of relativism cannot, in practice, be entirely

[36] See, for example, *Selmouni v France* (2000) 29 EHRR 403; *A v UK* (1999) 27 EHRR 611.

[37] The importance of a subjective test is emphasised by Judge Zekia in *Ireland v UK* (n 1), Separate Opinion of Judge Zekia. See also Cordula Droege's take on the matter in relation to Common Article 3 in C Droege, '"In Truth the Leitmotiv": The Prohibition of Torture and Other Forms of Ill-treatment in International Humanitarian Law' (2007) 89 *International Review of the Red Cross* 515.

[38] Note Anthony Cullen's point that in *Ireland v UK* (n 1) 'a subjective test, assessing the ill-treatment from the point of view of the victim, was not applied by the Court, which chose not to call witnesses', in A Cullen, 'Defining Torture in International Law: A Critique of the Concept Employed by the European Court of Human Rights' (2003) 34 *California Western International Law Journal* 29, 39.

[39] See, for example, its reliance on expert findings on solitary confinement in, among other cases, *Gorbulya v Russia* App no 31535/09 (ECtHR, 6 March 2014), para 78; *Razvyazkin v Russia* App no 13579/09 (ECtHR, 3 July 2012), paras 89, 104, 106 – in both judgments, the ECtHR relied on the *21st General Report of the European Committee for the Prevention of Torture and Inhuman or Degrading Treatment or Punishment* (CPT/Inf (2011) 28). The Court also acknowledges that mentally ill persons may not be in a position to describe their suffering 'coherently', see, for example, *Keenan* (n 18) para 110.

[40] See text to n 2 above.

excluded from the application of the notions of inhuman or degrading treatment'.[41] Michael Addo and Nicholas Grief, too, refer to the severity 'threshold' *itself* as 'relative'[42] and the requisite assessment as inevitably 'subjective'.[43]

Relativism may be understood in several ways, and perhaps those most likely to be understood as undermining the absoluteness starting point would be: (a) 'relativism' as the opposite of objectivity; (b) 'relativism' as the opposite of universalism; and (c) 'relativism' as the opposite of absoluteness, that is, of non-displaceability. In spite of suggestions that the Court's 'relative' assessment entails relativism, the Court's 'relative' assessment does not necessarily connote 'relativism' in any of these three senses. What the Court's doctrine conveys is that the assessment of whether a particular treatment experienced by a particular individual constitutes inhuman or degrading treatment is relative in a fourth sense, simply reflecting the context-sensitive nature of the assessment: that it *relates to* a number of contextual variables, such as potentially intersecting factors shaping the individual's particular vulnerability or the perpetrator's knowledge, attitude and/or intent.[44] As argued in Chapter 3, the key issue is whether reference to, or reliance by the Court on, these factors amounts to relevant reasoning and whether *relating* the assessment to such factors is therefore legitimate or illegitimate specification.

5.3.2. Key Variables in the Court's 'Relative' Assessment

The factors to which the Court has frequently made reference in its assessment of severity have included 'the duration of the treatment, its physical and/or mental effects and, in some cases, the sex, age and state of health of the victim …'[45] as well as the 'nature and context'[46] of the treatment. In this regard, the Court has increasingly considered 'whether the victim [was] in a vulnerable situation'.[47] In broad terms, the Court suggests that it considers 'all the circumstances of the case'.[48]

[41] D Feldman, *Civil Liberties and Human Rights in England and Wales* (2nd edn, Oxford University Press 2002) 242. Omer Ze'ev Bekerman makes this point regarding torture: see O Ze'ev Bekerman, 'Torture – The Absolute Prohibition of a Relative Term: Does Everyone Know What Is in Room 101?' (2005) 53 *American Journal of Comparative Law* 743.

[42] MK Addo and N Grief, 'Does Article 3 of the European Convention on Human Rights Enshrine Absolute Rights?' (1998) 9 *European Journal of International Law* 510, 511.

[43] ibid 517.

[44] Cathryn Costello makes the argument that '[w]hile torture may be understood principally (although not exclusively) in agent-centred terms, focusing on the perpetrator's actions and intentions, inhuman and degrading treatment demands a victim-centred approach, and so is necessarily relative in this sense', and that this 'relativity, and the contextual assessment it demands, in no way undermines the absolute nature of the right, indeed it supports it': C Costello, *The Human Rights of Migrants and Refugees in European Law* (Oxford University Press 2015) 191.

[45] See text to n 2 above.

[46] See text to n 3 above.

[47] See text to n 4 above.

[48] *Ireland v UK* (n 1) para 162; *A v UK* (1999) (n 36) para 20.

Approaching these variables in light of the legitimate specification requirements, it is possible to (re)conceptualise the Court's 'all the circumstances' approach as one which distinguishes between circumstances that may be considered relevant and those that may be seen as irrelevant to determining whether the treatment at issue is inhuman or degrading.

5.3.2.1. *Physical or Mental Effects*

The physical or mental effects of the treatment tend to be ascribed significance by the ECtHR and may be taken to refer to the pain, suffering, anguish or humiliation to which the person was subjected. The Court does not regularly engage in its own technical evaluation of the physical or mental pain or suffering actually experienced by the particular individual in the instant of the particular treatment,[49] although it accepts medical evidence and expert input that it treats as indicative of the suffering or anguish that can be shown or assumed to have been experienced as a result of the treatment at issue. In *Keenan v UK* the ECtHR indicated that 'there are circumstances where proof of the actual effect on the person may not be a major factor'.[50] It found that the imposition on a mentally ill person of a disciplinary punishment involving an extension of imprisonment and solitary confinement 'may well have threatened his physical and moral resistance' and was 'not compatible with the standard of treatment required in respect of a mentally-ill person', holding it to be 'inhuman and degrading treatment and punishment'.[51] This is illustrative of the Court's readiness to consider likely or anticipated effects rather than effects as shown to have been subjectively endured.

The Court's context-sensitive but nonetheless objective stance in assessing physical or mental effects entails a complex assessment, which encompasses sensitivity to the individual's particular circumstances and resultant experience, as well as a more generalised account of the implications of a particular type of treatment. For instance, in *Erdoğan Yağız v Turkey*, the ECtHR rather interestingly considered both the general humiliation involved in being paraded around one's home town in handcuffs and the particular humiliation experienced by the applicant, who was a doctor, in encountering his patients while in handcuffs;[52] finding that Turkey had offered no basis for the necessity of the prolonged public handcuffing, it held that Erdoğan Yağız had been subjected to degrading treatment.[53]

At the same time, the emphasis on 'physical or mental effects' sometimes pushes the Court towards a focus on the tangible injuries – indeed, the Court

[49] Indeed, Cullen points out that the Court did not call witnesses in *Ireland v UK*: see Cullen (n 38) 39.

[50] *Keenan* (n 18) para 112.

[51] ibid para 115.

[52] *Erdoğan Yağız v Turkey* (2014) 59 EHRR 4, paras 34–47. Of course, the implication that the prestige of the applicant's profession entailed deeper humiliation in his public handcuffing is not unproblematic.

[53] ibid para 47.

has frequently alluded to 'actual bodily injury' in its account of inhuman treatment[54] – or long-term trauma resulting from the particular treatment. The Court's conclusions in *Muradova v Azerbaijan* are indicative of the reasoning at play:

> [T]he Court finds that the injuries sustained by the applicant establish the existence of serious physical pain and suffering. These injuries had lasting consequences for her health, as she became permanently blind in her right eye. The ill-treatment and its consequences must have also caused the applicant considerable mental suffering diminishing her human dignity. In these circumstances, the Court considers that the ill-treatment complained of was sufficiently serious to attain a minimum level of severity falling within the scope of Article 3 and to be considered as inhuman and degrading treatment.[55]

Conveying the link the Court sometimes draws between injuries and the wrongs of inhumanity and degradation more starkly, the conclusion in *Ribitsch v Austria* was that 'the injuries suffered by Mr Ribitsch show that he underwent ill-treatment which amounted to both inhuman and degrading treatment'.[56] In *Costello-Roberts v UK* (decided in 1993), the Court observed that the applicant, who had been subjected to corporal punishment that involved being 'slippered three times on his buttocks through his shorts with a rubber-soled gym shoe' but had no visible injuries, had 'adduced no evidence of any severe or long-lasting effects as a result of the treatment complained of'[57] in finding that the treatment at issue had *not* reached the minimum level of severity.

A focus on the physical or mental effects of the treatment appears prima facie to constitute relevant reasoning in delimiting the concepts of inhuman and degrading treatment, insofar as 'effects' refer to the suffering, anguish or sense of humiliation the treatment at issue has subjected someone to; and, particularly if marked by intent, callousness or indifference, to the character of the perpetrator's conduct. However, treating tangible injury or long-term effects as a *sine qua non* for a finding that the minimum level of severity has been reached would unduly conflate the experience of suffering with injury or long-term trauma. It is notorious that some of the most egregious forms of ill-treatment, from mock executions to waterboarding, can cause considerable mental and/or physical suffering without leaving tangible injuries or marks, as the post-9/11 reckoning with 'enhanced' interrogation techniques has starkly reminded us. Moreover, a focus on long-term repercussions misconstrues the question of the particular physical or mental suffering intended or inflicted. Ultimately, the Court's frequent reliance on tangible injury or long-term effects, which appears primarily to be linked to evidentiary 'convenience', should not carry the implication of wholly transposing a practical matter – the evidentiary issue of proving suffering – into the specification of inhumanity or degradation. As such, treating injury or long-term impact as

[54] See text to n 5 above.
[55] *Muradova v Azerbaijan* (2011) 52 EHRR 41, para 134.
[56] *Ribitsch v Austria* (1996) 21 EHRR 573, para 39.
[57] *Costello-Roberts* (n 15) paras 31–32.

essential for reaching the minimum level of severity would fall foul of the legitimate specification criterion of non-distortion.[58]

5.3.2.2. *Duration*

Duration is regularly cited as a factor in the Court's 'relative' assessment, and as an element of inhuman treatment in the Court's allusions to past jurisprudence: that a treatment has been recognised as inhuman because it 'was applied for hours at a stretch'.[59] The duration of the treatment may relate to the suffering caused or intended or expected.[60] One hour in solitary confinement, for instance, can be very different from one month or an indefinite period in terms of its impact on the person. Duration may also pertain to the intentionality or systematicity of the cruelty involved. It is notable that, in the ECtHR's case law, although 'heat-of-the-moment' reactions may well cross the Article 3 threshold,[61] a longer-lasting – and thereby more obviously deliberate in its cruelty – infliction of suffering tends more readily to be found to amount to torture.[62]

The duration of the treatment may be a relevant factor in determining its severity – it may be significant in shaping the character of a treatment and how such treatment is experienced. At the same time, duration's potential relevance as a factor should not obscure or foreclose the prospect of finding a brief 'encounter' to be inhuman, degrading or indeed torturous in character on account of other relevant factors.

5.3.2.3. *Age*

The ECtHR views age as a relevant factor in assessing the particular vulnerability of individuals[63] and their experience of suffering, humiliation and/or debasement.

[58] This issue is elaborated further in Ch 4 on torture.

[59] *Kudla v Poland* (2002) 35 EHRR 11, para 92; *Jalloh* (n 5) para 68; *Gäfgen v Germany* (2011) 52 EHRR 1, para 89.

[60] See, for instance, *Soering v UK* (1989) 11 EHRR 439, para 111: 'in the Court's view, having regard to the very long period of time spent on death row in such extreme conditions, with the ever-present and mounting anguish of awaiting execution of the death penalty, and to the personal circumstances of the applicant, especially his age and mental state at the time of the offence, the applicant's extradition to the United States would expose him to a real risk of treatment going beyond the threshold set by Article 3'. See also *Kurt v Turkey* (1999) 27 EHRR 373, paras 133–34; *Timurtaş v Turkey* (2001) 33 EHRR 6, paras 97–98; *Z and others v UK* (2002) 34 EHRR 3, para 74.

[61] See, for instance, *Muradova* (n 55); *Güler and Öngel v Turkey* App nos 29612/05 and 30668/05 (ECtHR, 4 October 2011).

[62] See, for example, *Selmouni* (n 36); *Cirino and Renne v Italy* App nos 2539/13 and 4705/13 (ECtHR, 26 October 2017).

[63] See, on this, C Heri, 'Shaping Coercive Obligations through Vulnerability: The Example of the ECtHR' in L Lavrysen and N Mavronicola (eds), *Coercive Human Rights: Positive Duties to Mobilise the Criminal Law under the ECHR* (Hart Publishing 2020).

Treatment that may fall outside the scope of Article 3 if experienced by a person of a certain age may fall foul of Article 3 when imposed on someone of a different age. This issue was live in the Court's assessment in *V and T v UK*,[64] concerning the criminal trial of two 11-year-old defendants for the murder of a two-year-old boy. The issue at stake regarding the criminal trial's compatibility with Article 3 was whether attributing criminal responsibility to children of such age and putting them through a trial with significant elements of adult Crown Court trials was inhuman or degrading. The ECtHR (dubiously) found that what they had endured did not cross the Article 3 severity threshold.[65] Nonetheless, the Court appeared to acknowledge that certain treatment which may not be inhuman or degrading when experienced by adults may cross the Article 3 threshold when inflicted on and experienced by a child.[66]

Quite a distinct – and troubling – argument was embraced in *Costello-Roberts*, where the Court suggested that some disciplinary uses of force may be acceptable if administered on a school boy within a school disciplinary process, as compared with similar force being administered on a young man within the criminal justice system (the circumstances in *Tyrer v UK*).[67] Nonetheless, the Court has recognised the particular vulnerability of children in subsequent cases such as *A v UK*, concerning parental chastisement,[68] and the Court's view on disciplinary use of force by adults against children does not appear to be the same today. Indeed, the Court has stated that 'to avoid any risk of ill-treatment and degrading treatment of children, the Court considers it commendable if member States prohibit in law all forms of corporal punishment of children'[69] and has indicated that 'domestic corporal punishment' is 'invariably degrading'.[70] It would be at odds with the Court's context-sensitive assessment of abuse of power, exemplified in *Bouyid*,[71] to maintain the position that violence in such profoundly asymmetrical power relationships may be less, rather than more, egregious by reason of the victim's youth.[72]

[64] *V v UK* (2000) 30 EHRR 121.

[65] ibid paras 70–80.

[66] ibid para 79. See, too, *Bouyid* [Grand Chamber] (n 21) para 109; and the striking case of *Popov v France* (2016) 63 EHRR 8, paras 96–103.

[67] *Costello-Roberts* (n 15) para 31, referring to *Tyrer* (n 13): 'Mr Costello-Roberts was a young boy punished in accordance with the disciplinary rules in force within the school in which he was a boarder. This amounted to being slippered three times on his buttocks through his shorts with a rubber-soled gym shoe by the headmaster in private … Mr Tyrer, on the other hand, was a young man sentenced in the local juvenile court to three strokes of the birch on the bare posterior'.

[68] *A v UK* (1999) (n 36); see also the child abuse case of *DMD v Romania* App no 23022/13 (ECtHR, 3 October 2017), para 50.

[69] *Tlapak and others v Germany* App nos 11308/16 and 11344/16 (ECtHR, 22 March 2018), para 90; see the analysis in C Fenton-Glynn, 'The End of Corporal Punishment?' [2018] *Family Law* 954. See, too, C O'Mahony, 'Is Time Running Out for Corporal Punishment under the ECHR?' (2019) 1 *European Human Rights Law Review* 55.

[70] *DMD* (n 68) para 50.

[71] *Bouyid* [Grand Chamber] (n 21).

[72] See, further, S Bitensky, *Corporal Punishment of Children: A Human Rights Violation* (Brill 2006).

The majority in the Grand Chamber judgment in *Bouyid* highlighted 'as a secondary consideration' – that is, a relevant factor, but not decisive of the outcome in the particular case – that the first applicant in *Bouyid* had been a minor (17 years old) and thus liable to be even more vulnerable, especially in psychological terms, in respect of such ill-treatment.[73] The Court made a general statement that certain behaviour towards minors may be incompatible with Article 3 ECHR because they are minors, even if it might be found acceptable in the case of adults, and that law enforcement officers must therefore 'show greater vigilance and self-control when dealing with minors'.[74]

Persons of an advanced age may also find themselves in circumstances of heightened vulnerability,[75] which the Court appears to recognise. For instance, advanced age was recognised as a relevant factor in *Grigoryev v Russia*,[76] where an applicant's arrest at his home was effected with the use of considerable force, which the Court found to be 'manifestly disproportionate'[77] and to amount to inhuman and degrading treatment. The Court observed that the relevant State agents

> applied force against the applicant, a man who was sixty-three years old at the time of the arrest, who was wearing nothing but his underclothes since the events in question took place at night-time, was holding no arms, and did not show any active resistance when asked to lay face down on the floor …[78]

The Court appropriately recognises that youth or advanced age may entail particular vulnerability or frailty. This can contribute to bringing a set of facts 'over' the Article 3 severity threshold on the basis that the suffering inflicted, or the iniquity of the treatment, is amplified because of this heightened vulnerability.

5.3.2.4. *State of Health*

The state of health of the person subjected to the treatment at issue can be an important factor in the Court's assessment of severity. A particular treatment may be Article 3-compatible in respect of a person who is not experiencing any

[73] *Bouyid* [Grand Chamber] (n 21) para 109.

[74] ibid para 110. Further examples of the Court citing the relevance of the victim's youth in the application of Art 3 ECHR include *Menesheva v Russia* (2007) 44 EHRR 56, para 58; *Zherdev v Ukraine* App no 34015/07 (ECtHR, 27 April 2017) paras 84–95; *Khan v France* App no 12267/16 (ECtHR, 28 February 2019) paras 76–95. On the importance of the child's best interests in delineating Art 3-(in)compatible treatment or punishment, see *Blokhin v Russia* App no 47152/06 (ECtHR, 23 March 2016), para 138.

[75] See M O'Rourke, *Older People, Dignity and Human Rights: Towards the Development of the Rule against Torture and Ill-treatment in International Human Rights Law* (PhD thesis, University of Birmingham, 2018).

[76] *Grigoryev v Russia* App no 22663/06 (ECtHR, 23 October 2012).

[77] ibid para 84. The issue of the proportionate use of force is considered in further detail below.

[78] ibid para 83.

ill-health or disability, but may reach the Article 3 severity threshold when inflicted on someone who is unwell or is disabled. For example, in *Price v UK* the detention in a regular cell of a person whose disability impeded access to the bed or toilet and who was bound to, and did, experience considerable suffering and anguish in these circumstances, was found to constitute degrading treatment contrary to Article 3.[79]

The ECtHR's judgment in *Keenan* highlights how a person's mental ill-health may render their particular treatment or punishment inhuman or degrading.[80] The Court's view was that the way Mark Keenan was treated, notably the extension of his sentence and the imposition of solitary confinement on him, was 'not compatible with the standard of treatment required in respect of a mentally-ill person'.[81] Importantly, the Court established in its judgment in *Keenan* that 'treatment of a mentally-ill person may be incompatible with the standards imposed by Article 3 in the protection of fundamental human dignity, even though that person may not be able, or capable of, pointing to any specific ill-effects'.[82] Through this stance, the Court overcomes, to a limited extent, the problematic tendency to look for tangible injury or long-term physical or psychological trauma to establish suffering.[83] The *Keenan* principle was decisive towards a finding of degrading treatment of a seriously mentally ill person placed in custody in *MS v UK*, where the Court pointed out that 'the mentally ill are in a position of particular vulnerability, and clear issues of respect for their fundamental human dignity arise whenever such persons are detained by the authorities'.[84] It found that the detention of a seriously mentally ill person without prompt or sufficient medical attention in circumstances of escalating distress constituted degrading treatment.[85]

References to human dignity are particularly prominent in this context, as in the above statement in *Keenan*.[86] In *MS v UK*, the Court highlighted the applicant's 'dire need of appropriate psychiatric treatment' and found that his continued detention without such treatment was 'an affront to human dignity'.[87] The same perspective, in relation to physical ill-health, is evident in *Aleksanyan v Russia*, where the Court found that the way the authorities had treated a person in prison suffering from AIDS, including blocking his access to vital healthcare treatment, 'undermined his dignity and entailed particularly acute hardship, causing suffering beyond that inevitably associated with a prison sentence and the illnesses

[79] *Price v UK* (2002) 34 EHRR 53, para 30.
[80] See *Keenan* (n 18) para 115.
[81] ibid.
[82] ibid para 112.
[83] But see *Ramirez Sanchez v France* (2007) 45 EHRR 49, paras 140–42.
[84] *MS v UK* (2012) 55 EHRR 23, para 39.
[85] *MS v UK*, ibid paras 45–46.
[86] See also *Boukrourou v France* App no 30059/15 (ECtHR, 16 November 2017), para 80.
[87] *MS v UK* (n 84) paras 44–45. The interplay between human dignity, vulnerability and health is highlighted in D Bedford, 'MS v United Kingdom: Article 3 ECHR, Detention and Mental Health' (2013) 1 *European Human Rights Law Review* 72.

he suffered from', and thus 'amounted to inhuman and degrading treatment'.[88] These references are illustrative of the deontic operation of human dignity, whose demands by way of respect, concern and care are responsive to persons' particular vulnerabilities and needs, as shaped by their state of health.

5.3.2.5. Sex

The Court has regularly cited the sex of the victim in its frequently reiterated account of the relevant variables shaping the severity of the treatment at issue. The variable of 'sex' has played a role in delineating the unequal power dynamics of a particular treatment or situation – the Court has, for example, highlighted such dynamics in circumstances where a young woman was confronted by several male police officers.[89] It has also been raised as a factor contributing to the experience of humiliation in circumstances where someone has been stripped naked and/or put through an intimate search[90] or helped to the bathroom[91] by or in the presence of a person of the opposite sex. The Court has commented that the presence of persons of the opposite sex in contexts such as a strip search showed 'a clear lack of respect' for the person being stripped naked and 'diminished [their] human dignity'.[92]

Clare McGlynn has interrogated the variable of 'sex' in relation to its relevance to the finding in *Aydin v Turkey*[93] that the rape of a woman in custody by a police officer constituted torture:

> [I]t is not immediately clear what the Court has in mind in relation to 'sex' … Was the Court making a broader statement that for the victim to endure rape, and/or the other forms of torture inflicted on the victim in *Aydin v Turkey*, was worse as she was female, than had she been male? It would certainly be wrong to class female rape as 'worse' and therefore more harmful than male rape …[94]

The Court's allusion to 'sex' may have been related to the 'psychological impact of the rape on a virgin (as Aydin was) in a cultural context in which the loss of virginity, prior to marriage, even through rape, could have serious adverse consequences for a woman's future marriage prospects', as McGlynn pointed out.[95] On this understanding, it may be *gender* (rather than sex),[96] a construct based on 'social

[88] *Aleksanyan v Russia* (2011) 52 EHRR 18, para 158.
[89] *Menesheva* (n 74) para 58.
[90] See *Valašinas v Lithuania* App no 44558/98 (ECtHR, 24 July 2001), para 117; *Wiktorko v Poland* (2013) 56 EHRR 30, para 54.
[91] *Price* (n 79) para 28.
[92] *Valašinas* (n 90) para 117; *Wiktorko* (n 90) para 54.
[93] *Aydin v Turkey* (1998) 25 EHRR 251.
[94] C McGlynn, 'Rape, Torture and the European Convention on Human Rights' (2009) 58 *International & Comparative Law Quarterly* 565, 575.
[95] ibid.
[96] For an analysis of the distinction between sex and gender, see A Edwards, *Violence Against Women under International Human Rights Law* (Cambridge University Press 2011) 13–19.

relations that are culturally contingent and without foundation in biological necessity',[97] that is treated as a relevant variable in the Court's severity assessment. That the Court is prepared to recognise the gendered character of particular instances or forms of violence is evident in judgments such as *Volodina v Russia*, where the domestic violence endured by the applicant was recognised as a manifestation of gender-based violence.[98]

Looking at inhumanity and degradation through the lens of gender helps illuminate how a complex set of (contingent) contextual factors, including (patriarchal) social norms, may shape the way a treatment is experienced or intended to be experienced. A relevant example here is the abuse of a detainee through the demeaning force of gendered prejudice, outlined in Chapter 3. On the other hand, as McGlynn points out, 'Were it an argument from chivalry that to inflict pain and torture on a woman is somehow worse than on a man, due to social assumptions about the role of women, this … would be undesirable'.[99] The latter would be undesirable because it would concede undue normative force to problematic paradigms – such as toxic masculinity – and effectively dent the protection offered to men, rather than more broadly amplify awareness of and sensitivity to gendered wrongs and harms. But acknowledging how a combination of contingent and potentially deeply problematic social norms may be taken advantage of to bring about suffering, anguish or humiliation, or contribute to exacerbating the character or effects of a particular treatment, amounts to relevant reasoning.

5.3.2.6. *Vulnerability*

In its assessment of severity, the Court often considers whether (potential) victims are in a 'vulnerable situation'[100] or a 'situation of vulnerability',[101] and indeed many of the variables alluded to above have been linked to vulnerability. The Court's increasing recognition of circumstances of pronounced vulnerability in its assessment of severity[102] and in wider jurisprudence[103] helps, as Alexandra

[97] H Charlesworth and C Chinkin, *The Boundaries of International Law: A Feminist Analysis* (Manchester University Press 2000) 3.

[98] See *Volodina v Russia* App no 41261/17 (ECtHR, 9 July 2019) and the case law cited therein; see also C Heri, 'Volodina, Article 3, and Russia's systemic problem regarding domestic violence', *Strasbourg Observers*, 30 July 2019, available at: https://strasbourgobservers.com/2019/07/30/volodina-article-3-and-russias-systemic-problem-regarding-domestic-violence/ (accessed 3 January 2020).

[99] McGlynn (n 94) 575.

[100] See text to n 4 above.

[101] See text to n 31 above.

[102] See, on this, C Heri, *The Rights of the Vulnerable under Article 3 ECHR: Promoting Dignity, Equality and Autonomy by Reconceptualizing the Human Rights Subject* (PhD thesis, University of Zurich 2017). I refer to pronounced vulnerability in acknowledgement of Martha Fineman's observation that vulnerability is 'universal and constant, inherent in the human condition': M Fineman, 'The Vulnerable Subject: Anchoring Equality in the Human Condition' (2008) 20 *Yale Journal of Law and Feminism* 1, 1.

[103] See L Peroni and A Timmer, 'Vulnerable Groups: The Promise of an Emerging Concept in European Human Rights Convention Law' (2013) 11 *International Journal of Constitutional Law* 1056.

Timmer suggests, produce appropriately context-sensitive judgments.[104] As a 'relational' concept,[105] vulnerability is shaped by relationships between persons,[106] and between persons and the circumstances in which they find themselves, and is a dynamic rather than a static attribute.[107] *Bouyid*, for example, involved the combination of situational vulnerability – arising in respect of both applicants in light of the power asymmetry inherent in circumstances of custody[108] – and the particular vulnerability faced by the 17-year-old applicant in light of his age.[109] Vulnerability can both deepen the severity of the ill-treatment, *and*, in its consideration by the Court, operate as 'a magnifying glass'[110] through which the severity of a particular treatment becomes more palpable.[111] Accordingly, the variable of vulnerability exemplifies the relational, qualitative and context-sensitive character of the assessment involved in identifying circumstances of inhumanity or degradation.

5.3.3. The Significance of 'Nature and Context'

The variable of 'nature and context of the treatment' may be seen as a wide-ranging residual or overarching factor in the ECtHR's 'relative' assessment. It forms the basis for considering relevant contextual factors that may pertain particularly to the relational and qualitative severity at issue. The 'nature' of the treatment, in particular, offers a gateway for considering the intent, purpose and/or attitude of those engaging in the act or omission under consideration. As the ECtHR's Grand Chamber emphasised in *Bouyid*, relevant factors beyond the frequently restated can include the purpose, intention or motivation behind a treatment,[112] although an absence of an intent to humiliate or otherwise harm does not rule out an Article 3 breach.[113] Furthermore, as Elaine Webster suggests, ill-treatment may encompass a certain attitude. Suggesting that degrading treatment involves acts which 'undermine a minimal kind of regard towards … human beings',[114] she indicates

[104] A Timmer, 'A Quiet Revolution: Vulnerability in the European Court of Human Rights' in M Fineman and A Grear (eds), *Vulnerability: Reflections on a New Ethical Foundation for Law and Politics* (Ashgate 2013) 162–64.

[105] F Luna, 'Elucidating the Concept of Vulnerability: Layers Not Labels' (2009) 2 *International Journal of Feminist Approaches to Bioethics* 121, 129.

[106] But *cf* ibid fn 22.

[107] See generally Luna (n 105).

[108] *Bouyid* [Grand Chamber] (n 21) para 83.

[109] ibid para 109.

[110] Peroni and Timmer (n 103) 1079.

[111] See Heri (n 102).

[112] *Bouyid* [Grand Chamber] (n 21) para 86, citing inter alia *Egmez v Cyprus* (2002) 34 EHRR 29, para 78; and *Krastanov v Bulgaria* (2005) 41 EHRR 50, para 53.

[113] *Bouyid* [Grand Chamber] (n 21) para 86.

[114] This is a central claim across Webster's book: see Webster (n 7) 86.

that this can be located – though not exclusively – in a way of being 'looked at'[115] or dealt with that involves an attitude of callousness or disregard.[116]

An example of how the nature and context of the treatment can impact upon both the intensity of suffering and severity more broadly can be found in the Court's case law on the treatment of relatives of disappeared persons. The Court has outlined its assessment as follows:

> Whether a family member is [a victim of a violation of Article 3] will depend on the existence of special factors which gives the suffering of the applicant a dimension and character distinct from the emotional distress which may be regarded as inevitably caused to relatives of a victim of a serious human rights violation. Relevant elements will include the proximity of the family tie (in that context, a certain weight will attach to the parent-child bond), the particular circumstances of the relationship, the extent to which the family member witnessed the events in question, the involvement of the family member in the attempts to obtain information about the disappeared person and the way in which the authorities responded to those enquiries …[117]

The context of the treatment in this account notably includes the proximity of the family bond, while the nature of the treatment includes the authorities' response to enquiries concerning the disappearance. Certainly, the ECtHR's emphasis on the parent–child bond and an implicit suggestion that the family tie, and accordingly the suffering caused, becomes attenuated beyond this is open to challenge. But it is the authorities' handling of the case at hand and their attitude to relatives that the Court has increasingly viewed as key to the severity of the treatment inflicted.[118] As the Court has put it:

> The essence of the violation [in relation to the *relatives* of the missing person] is not that there has been a serious human rights violation concerning the missing person; it lies in the authorities' reactions and attitudes to the situation when it has been brought to their attention.[119]

The inhumanity identified in cases such as *Varnava v Turkey*[120] and *Cyprus v Turkey*[121] in respect of the relatives of disappeared persons arose from their continued subjection to 'a prolonged state of acute anxiety' through the authorities' silence and inaction in respect of their loved ones' fate.[122] The degradation found

[115] ibid 102.
[116] ibid 135.
[117] *Çakici v Turkey* (2001) 31 EHRR 5, para 98.
[118] See the (critical) discussion in R Rubio-Marín, C Sandoval and C Díaz, 'Repairing Family Members: Gross Human Rights Violations and Communities of Harm' in R Rubio-Marín (ed), *The Gender of Reparations: Unsettling Sexual Hierarchies while Redressing Human Rights Violations* (Cambridge University Press 2009) 233–37.
[119] *Varnava and Others v Turkey* App nos 16064/90, 16065/90, 16066/90, 16068/90, 16069/90, 16070/90, 16071/90, 16072/90 and 16073/90 (ECtHR, 18 September 2009), para 200; see also *Çakici* (n 117) para 98.
[120] *Varnava* (n 119) para 201.
[121] *Cyprus v Turkey* (2002) 35 EHRR 30, para 157.
[122] ibid.

in *Akkum v Turkey*,[123] in relation to a father who was ultimately presented with the mutilated body of his son, can be understood, as Webster puts it, as encompassing 'an attitude of disrespect',[124] one which cuts to the core of the deontic humanity encapsulated by human dignity. The Court locates inhumanity and degradation in authorities' 'flagrant, continuous and callous disregard of an obligation to account for the whereabouts and fate of a missing person'[125] and in their lack of concern in relation to the emotional distress their behaviour is producing or compounding.

This residual consideration of 'nature and context' is therefore a gateway through which an amalgamation of relevant factors – from the particular sensibilities of the victim(s) to the attitude of the authorities – may be found to render a treatment inhuman or degrading. The operation of this residual variable in cases such as those discussed above exemplifies the context-sensitive, relational and qualitative severity assessment at play. This wide-ranging variable also unlocks the area of the case law in which the specification of inhuman and degrading treatment can raise particular controversy: the use of force, and its justification.

5.3.4. The Justified Use of Force

The extent to which the use of force falls foul of Article 3 ECHR brings to the fore questions surrounding the absolute character of the right and the right's non-displaceability. The issue becomes especially pronounced in relation to the ECtHR's assessment of justifications for the use of physical force or incursion on bodily integrity, particularly force used to fend off immediate violence,[126] to effect a lawful arrest,[127] or in situations of medical necessity.[128] This is because the Court's reasoning may appear at first sight to amount to *displacement*, rather than specification, of the right.[129]

This issue can be illustrated by a brief examination of the ECtHR's judgment in *Güler and Öngel v Turkey*.[130] In this judgment, the Court alluded to the 'justified'

[123] *Akkum v Turkey* (2006) 43 EHRR 26, para 259.

[124] Webster (n 7) 99.

[125] *Varnava* (n 119) para 200.

[126] See, for instance, *Muradova* (n 55) paras 109, 133; *Güler* (n 61) paras 28–29.

[127] See, for instance, *Shchukin and others v Cyprus* App no 14030/03 (ECtHR, 29 July 2010), para 93; *Ivan Vasilev v Bulgaria* App no 48130/99 (ECtHR, 12 April 2007), para 63; *Rehbock v Slovenia* App no 29462/95 (ECtHR, 28 November 2000), paras 68–78; *Krastanov* (n 112) paras 52–53.

[128] See, for instance, *Nevmerzhitsky v Ukraine* (2006) 43 EHRR 32, para 94; *Naumenko v Ukraine* App no 42023/98 (ECtHR, 10 February 2004), para 112; *Herczegfalvy v Austria* (1993) 15 EHRR 437, para 82.

[129] See further N Mavronicola, '*Güler and Öngel v Turkey*: Article 3 of the European Convention on Human Rights and Strasbourg's Discourse on the Justified Use of Force' (2013) 76 *Modern Law Review* 370.

[130] *Güler* (n 61).

use of force,[131] an aspect of the Court's reasoning which has attracted the comment that the Court has carved out 'exceptions' to Article 3.[132]

The applicants in *Güler* were involved in a demonstration to which numerous police officers had been deployed. At the end of the demonstration a small group of people attacked the police with sticks and stones and the police used truncheons and tear gas to disperse them. The applicants were arrested during this incident and were beaten during and after their arrest. The domestic criminal court acquitted the applicants of charges regarding the demonstrators' attack on the police, finding no evidence that they had attacked the police officers.

The ECtHR accepted that, on the evidence, the applicants' injuries had been sustained at the hands of the police during the demonstration and that the injuries were 'sufficient to bring the applicants' complaints within the scope of Article 3'.[133] It reasoned that 'Article 3 *does not prohibit the use of force in certain well-defined circumstances*', but that 'such force may be used only if indispensable and must not be excessive' (emphasis added).[134] Finding that it could not be shown that the force used against the applicants, who had not been among those attacking the police, was 'justified',[135] the ECtHR concluded that the applicants had been subjected to 'inhuman and degrading treatment'[136] in violation of Article 3.

On the basis of cases such as this, there has been a perception that the Court is carving out qualifications or exceptions to the right enshrined in Article 3 ECHR. For example, a key textbook on the ECHR alludes to 'recognized exceptions to the absolute nature of Article 3' with reference to the justified use of force in defence of self or others.[137] It is not, however, the case that the ECtHR is establishing 'exceptions' to Article 3 or its absolute character – what the Court doing is more complex, and the fact that it finds that certain justified uses of force do not violate Article 3 ECHR does not displace the right or otherwise contradict the right's absolute character. This is because Article 3 does not prohibit the use of force (causing suffering) per se. As argued in this and previous chapters in this book, the wrongs of 'torture or inhuman or degrading treatment or punishment' do not pertain solely and straightforwardly to the use of force or the infliction of a certain intensity of pain, suffering or wounding. Many instances of the use of force may be inhuman, degrading or torturous, but not all are. This is what the ECtHR means when it states that Article 3 'does not prohibit' the use of force in certain circumstances.

[131] ibid paras 28–29.

[132] See DJ Harris, M O'Boyle, E Bates and CM Buckley, *Harris, O'Boyle & Warbrick: Law of the European Convention on Human Rights* (4th edn, Oxford University Press 2018) 237. See also J Christoffersen, *Fair Balance: Proportionality, Subsidiarity and Primarity in the European Convention on Human Rights* (Martinus Nijhoff 2009) 84–87, and 116–17, citing *Rivas v France* App no 59584/00 (ECtHR, 1 April 2004), para 41.

[133] *Güler* (n 61) para 27.

[134] ibid para 28, citing *Rehbock* (n 127) paras 66–78.

[135] *Güler* (n 61) para 29.

[136] ibid para 31.

[137] Harris et al (n 132) 237.

It is in this context that severity's relational and qualitative character takes centre stage. The overarching reasoning of the Court in regard to the use of force emerges in *Muradova*, where, after stating that Article 3 does not prohibit the use of indispensable force in well-defined circumstances, the Court continued: 'Recourse to physical force which has not been made *strictly necessary* by a person's own conduct diminishes human dignity and is in principle an infringement of the right set forth in Article 3 of the Convention' (emphasis added).[138] Through this reasoning, the ECtHR makes transparent the significance of human dignity in the specification of the Article 3 threshold in circumstances involving the use of force.

Human dignity signifies the entitlement of all human persons to – borrowing from the wording of the ECtHR – a minimum level of respect.[139] Respect is called for towards our mutual humanity; and an element, though not an essential one,[140] of our humanity is human agency, that is, the capacity to make choices and enact these choices.[141] The Court's position is that only force which has been made strictly necessary by the individual's actions can potentially be understood as respecting rather than brutalising the person. In a similar vein, Jeremy Waldron has spoken of the prohibition of torture as being archetypal of the rejection of brutality in law, such that '[i]f law is forceful or coercive', it is meant to '[get] its way by non-brutal methods which respect rather than mutilate the dignity and agency of those who are its subjects'.[142] On this account, the strict necessity criterion that the Court employs in cases such as *Muradova* and *Güler* may be read as a means of delineating uses of force which respect rather than mutilate human agency, in that strict necessity sets up the idea of a response directly targeted to repelling the harmful action of the agent and no more. This reasoning, which is premised on human dignity and respect for agency, therefore appears appropriate in delineating inhumanity or degradation. The justificatory reasoning operating here amounts, in principle, to relevant reasoning in specifying the right rather than to distortion or displacement of the right and, accordingly, does *not* offend the absoluteness starting point.

The Court's doctrine on the use of force therefore confirms that the use of force or indeed the infliction of suffering do not amount to the be-all and end-all

[138] *Muradova* (n 55) para 109. See also *Bouyid* [Grand Chamber] (n 21) para 88.

[139] The concept of 'respect' is frequently employed by the ECtHR in relation to human dignity – see, for example, *Bouyid* [Grand Chamber] (n 21) para 87; *Svinarenko* (n 2) para 115. See, in relation to 'respect', R Dworkin, *Justice for Hedgehogs* (Harvard University Press 2011) 335–36; see also Bronsther (n 33). On the related concept of 'regard', see Webster (n 7).

[140] For a rejection of treating agency as essential to human dignity, see J Tasioulas, 'Human Dignity and the Foundations of Human Rights' in C McCrudden (ed), *Understanding Human Dignity* (Oxford University Press 2013).

[141] For an interesting account of agency in the context of the criminal law, see V Chiao, 'Action and Agency in the Criminal Law' (2009) 15 *Legal Theory* 1. But see the complex account of agency in A Bandura, 'Human Agency in Social Cognitive Theory' (1989) 44 *American Psychologist* 1175.

[142] J Waldron, 'Torture and Positive Law: Jurisprudence for the White House' (2005) 105 *Columbia Law Review* 1681, 1726–27.

of concepts such as 'inhuman' or 'degrading' treatment, and that the nature and context of events can be crucial in determining whether a particular treatment is inhuman or degrading. Consider, for example, the shooting of someone in the arm in distinct circumstances. Shooting someone in the arm certainly causes a great deal of physical and probably mental suffering. Shooting someone in the arm when they are strapped onto a chair, and leaving them to suffer long enough to yield some information from them, would probably be considered by the Court to fall within the definition of torture.[143] The shooting of an unarmed peaceful protester in the arm by a police officer will be considered to be inhuman treatment (if not torture).[144] Yet if a police officer shot a person, A, in the arm as a measure of last resort to incapacitate A while A was in the process of shooting the police officer or a third party, such shooting may, if strictly necessary to stop A, not amount to inhuman or degrading treatment.[145]

Crucially, the Court's strict necessity assessment also connotes a sensitivity to relevant context, notably to the power asymmetries at play in situations where persons are confronted by State agents. Its fundamental starting point, as affirmed in *Bouyid*, is that

> in respect of a person who is deprived of his liberty, or, more generally, is confronted with law-enforcement officers, any recourse to physical force which has not been made strictly necessary by his own conduct diminishes human dignity and is, in principle, an infringement of the right set forth in art.3.[146]

This approach has led the Court to adopt a presumption, in respect of *any* recourse to physical force by State agents, of a violation of Article 3, which places an onus on the State to demonstrate the strict necessity of the force used.[147]

As set out above, the Court has stated that Article 3 'does not prohibit' the use of force in narrow, 'well-defined circumstances', where the government proves that such force was strictly necessary – that is, indispensable and not excessive.[148] The Court has included in these 'well-defined' circumstances the use of force 'to effect an arrest'.[149] In this context, the Court's position remains that, in respect of a person facing arrest, 'any recourse to physical force which has not been made strictly necessary by his or her own conduct diminishes human dignity and is,

[143] See the analysis in Ch 4.

[144] As per the analysis above. See *Muradova* (n 55).

[145] See Mavronicola (n 129) 379; see also N Mavronicola and F Messineo, 'Relatively Absolute? The Undermining of Article 3 ECHR in *Ahmad v UK*' (2013) 76 *Modern Law Review* 589, 594. Consider, too, Henry Shue's distinction between the principles relating to lethal force and those relating to *torture*, in H Shue, 'Torture' (1978) 7 *Philosophy & Public Affairs* 124, 125–30.

[146] *Bouyid* [Grand Chamber] (n 21) para 88.

[147] See, in this regard, the Court's reasoning in *Güler* (n 61) paras 28–29; and in *Bouyid* [Grand Chamber] (n 21) para 102.

[148] *Güler* (n 61) para 28. This is the approach in *Rehbock* (n 127) para 72.

[149] *Shchukin* (n 127) para 93. See, among others, *Vasilev* (n 127) para 63; *Rehbock* (n 127) paras 68–78; *Krastanov* (n 112) paras 52–53.

in principle, an infringement of the right set forth in Article 3'.[150] Any force used must be both necessary and proportionate; this is key to determining whether the arrest involved treatment that was 'inhuman' or 'degrading'.[151] Concretely, this entails that substantial force will only be treated as strictly necessary in those rare circumstances where the government can show that a person facing arrest was acting in a way that immediately threatened someone's life or bodily integrity.[152]

Another line of case law concerning circumstances in which force or the invasion of bodily integrity may be considered Article 3-compatible relates to medically necessary treatment.[153] Even where treatment may be medically necessary, where it impinges on bodily integrity, the Court has underlined that 'the *manner* in which the applicant is subjected to [the medically necessary measure must] not trespass the threshold of a minimum level of severity envisaged by the Court's case law under Art.3 of the Convention' (emphasis added).[154] The Court's approach to medical necessity highlights that absence of consent to acts impinging on bodily integrity may not always, in the Court's view, entail inhumanity or degradation. At the same time, while there are recognised limits to autonomous consent in certain medical contexts,[155] it remains in broad terms a canon in healthcare provision[156] alongside the benefit of the patient,[157] and the Court appears to recognise these dynamics in its approach to the issue. With respect to involuntary treatment, the 'minimum level of severity' criterion is superimposed onto the assessment, and the Court is very sensitive to pain, suffering, humiliation or anguish where the treatment that causes it is not urgently necessary or wholly aligned to the purpose

[150] *Kanciał v Poland* App no 37023/13 (ECtHR, 23 May 2019), para 72.

[151] See, for instance, *Shchukin* (n 127) paras 97–100. This delimitation bears resemblance to Art 9 of the French Declaration of the Rights of Man of 1789, which states that 'if arrest shall be deemed indispensable, all harshness not essential to the securing of the prisoner's person shall be severely repressed by law'.

[152] In this regard, a parallel may be drawn to the absolute necessity of potentially lethal force under Art 2 ECHR: as the Court has put it in the context of arrests, for example, 'there can be no such necessity where it is known that the person to be arrested poses no threat to life or limb and is not suspected of having committed a violent offence even if refraining from using lethal force may result in the opportunity to arrest the fugitive being lost' (*Nachova and others v Bulgaria* (2006) 42 EHRR 43, para 95). See, further, the analysis in the Report of the Special Rapporteur on Torture and Other Cruel, Inhuman or Degrading Treatment or Punishment, UN Doc A/72/178, 20 July 2017, para 62.

[153] See, for example, *Nevmerzhitsky* (n 128) para 94; *Herczegfalvy* (n 128) para 82; *Naumenko* (n 128) para 112.

[154] *Nevmerzhitsky* (n 128) para 94.

[155] See J Coggon and J Miola, 'Autonomy, Liberty, and Medical Decision-Making' (2011) 70 *Cambridge Law Journal* 523, 530. For instance, the exercise of a choice to sell one's organs is not respected at law, and human dignity – as it pertains to humanity or the human species – arguably lies at the centre of this prohibition. See S Wheatley, 'Human Rights and Human Dignity in the Resolution of Certain Ethical Questions in Biomedicine' (2001) 3 *European Human Rights Law Review* 312, 323; D Feldman, 'Human Dignity as a Legal Value: Part 1' [1999] *Public Law* 682, 684.

[156] Coggon and Miola (n 155).

[157] See R Gillon, 'Defending the Four Principles Approach as a Good Basis for Good Medical Practice and Therefore for Good Medical Ethics' (2015) 41 *Journal of Medical Ethics* 111.

of preserving the individual's health.[158] In *VC v Slovakia*, which concerned the involuntary sterilisation of a woman who had just given birth, the Court dismissed the government's appeals to necessity, clear that the sterilisation procedure was 'not an imminent necessity from a medical point of view'.[159] Finding the authorities to have acted without the applicant's free and informed consent, the Court denounced their 'gross disregard to her right to autonomy and choice as a patient' in making a finding of an Article 3 violation.[160]

The extent to which coercion can be seen as justified in the name of 'medical necessity' becomes particularly contentious in the practice of force-feeding, notably in the context of hunger strikes, which can be a vital form of protest in circumstances of relative powerlessness. The Court has put forward the following principles on the issue in *Ciorap v Moldova*:

> [A] measure which is of therapeutic necessity from the point of view of established principles of medicine cannot in principle be regarded as inhuman and degrading … The same can be said about force-feeding that is aimed at saving the life of a particular detainee who consciously refuses to take food. The Convention organs must nevertheless satisfy themselves that the medical necessity has been convincingly shown to exist … Moreover, the manner in which the applicant is subjected to force-feeding during the hunger-strike must not trespass the threshold of the minimum level of severity envisaged by the Court's case law under Article 3 of the Convention …[161]

The Court's approach in *Ciorap* discloses, in principle, a careful scrutiny of force-feeding. After a robust overview of the authorities' actions and their failure to prove that they had pursued various procedural guarantees or acted to save the applicant's life, the Court held that the applicant had been subjected to *torture*:

> [T]he Court concludes that the applicant's repeated force-feeding, not prompted by valid medical reasons but rather with the aim of forcing the applicant to stop his protest, and performed in a manner which unnecessarily exposed him to great physical pain and humiliation, can only be considered as torture.[162]

The Court is therefore alert to, and prepared to condemn, abusive practices in this context.[163]

[158] See, for instance, the important judgment on involuntary sterilisation in *VC v Slovakia* (2014) 59 EHRR 29, paras 103–20.

[159] ibid para 117.

[160] ibid para 119. On reproductive freedom and the anti-torture norm more broadly, see R Sifris, *Reproductive Freedom, Torture and International Human Rights: Challenging the Masculinisation of Torture* (Routledge 2013).

[161] *Ciorap v Moldova* App no 12066/02 (ECtHR, 19 June 2007), para 77.

[162] ibid para 89. See also *Nevmerzhitsky* (n 128) para 98.

[163] But see the critical take on the Court's earlier judgment in *Herczegfalvy* (n 128) in P Bartlett, 'Rethinking Herczegfalvy: The Convention and the Control of Psychiatric Treatment' in E Brems (ed), *Diversity and European Human Rights: Rewriting Judgments of the ECHR* (Cambridge University Press 2012). See, too, the nuanced argument on hunger strikes in Y Barilan, 'The Role of Doctors in Hunger Strikes' (2017) 27 *Kennedy Institute of Ethics Journal* 341.

Stijn Smet, observing the operation of proportionality reasoning in delineating the justified use of force, has argued that 'for Article 3 to maintain its absolute nature, considerations of proportionality and balancing against a public interest or the rights of others cannot be brought into the threshold question'.[164] Smet proposes distinguishing between the 'proportionality test' and what he calls 'contextualisation'.[165] From a 'contextualisation' perspective, he argues that 'the proportionality test is … not relevant to the use of non-excessive force to arrest a violent suspect or to subdue a violent detainee'.[166] In his rejection of proportionality in the application of an absolute right, Smet is referring to the proportionality test applicable in relation to qualified rights, which allows for legitimate interference with the right in the pursuit of extraneous legitimate aims, such as national security. This clarification is welcome. At the same time, it does not render irrelevant the application of a distinct set of strict necessity considerations with relation to the use of force. When Smet himself refers to 'non-excessive' force, he is arguably alluding precisely to an assessment of the strict necessity and proportionality of the force employed. In cases like *Güler* and *Muradova* the Court engages in an assessment of the correspondence of the force used to any action by the alleged victims necessitating such force – any excess pushes the use of force into Article 3 territory.[167]

Smet argues that the cases on force-feeding suggest that 'public interests or other (Convention) rights "outweigh" the interest of the applicant'; this, in his view, may be considered contrary to 'the aim of declaring a right to be absolute [which] is precisely to shield it from such balancing'.[168] Such a depiction of the issue nonetheless elides the complexity of the right not to be subjected to torture or inhuman or degrading treatment or punishment: the right does not simply reflect an (inviolable) interest in being free from forceful coercion. Rather, the Court takes the position that the question of whether certain forms of forceful coercion such as force-feeding are inhuman, degrading or torturous can appropriately relate to whether they are strictly targeted and tailored towards saving the individual's life; in other words, whether they are protecting rather than violating one's person.

[164] S Smet, 'The "Absolute" Prohibition of Torture and Inhuman or Degrading Treatment in Article 3 ECHR: Truly a Question of Scope Only?' in E Brems and J Gerards (eds), *Shaping Rights in the ECHR: The Role of the European Court of Human Rights in Determining the Scope of Human Rights* (Cambridge University Press 2013) 276.

[165] ibid.

[166] ibid 279.

[167] For a somewhat diluted version of this strict necessity analysis, see M Nowak, 'Challenges to the Absolute Nature of the Prohibition of Torture and Ill-treatment' (2005) 23 *Netherlands Quarterly of Human Rights* 674, 676–79. On the degradation involved in 'incapacitating [someone] more than necessary' see Costello (n 44) 191, with reference to J Waldron, 'Inhuman and Degrading Treatment: The Words Themselves' (2010) 23 *Canadian Journal of Law & Jurisprudence* 269, 277–78. See also the ECtHR's reasoning in relation to handcuffing, shackling and other forms of restraint in, for example, *Hénaf v France* (2005) 40 EHRR 44, paras 48–53; *Harutunyan v Armenia* (2012) 55 EHRR 12, paras 123–29; *Svinarenko* (n 2) paras 117–39.

[168] Smet (n 164) 281.

Such considerations *can*, at least in principle, amount to relevant reasoning insofar as they relate to whether human dignity has been respected or flouted.[169]

The doctrine indicating that the use of (coercive) force might be justified and, by being respectful of human dignity, not be inhuman or degrading, does not necessarily connote displacement of the right, but rather is capable of amounting to legitimate specification of inhumanity or degradation. Whether the Court appropriately navigates human dignity's application in all such instances is a question that I do not purport to address comprehensively in this study; but it is a question that requires us to reflect critically and with vigilance on the way the Court reasons through the various cases that come before it and that make up the Court's specification of the Article 3 'threshold'.

5.4. '*All* the Circumstances of the Case'(?) and Legitimate Specification

The assessment of whether a treatment may be characterised as inhuman or degrading – or both – operates through consideration of a variety of factors which carry relevance in establishing the pain, suffering, anguish or humiliation experienced, and/or the character of the conduct itself. Through the brief examination of the variables at play offered above, it becomes evident that the ECtHR endeavours to consider *relevant* circumstances in order to pin down whether the *treatment* at issue reaches a minimum level of severity. This 'test' is not purely a matter of establishing a certain quantum or degree of intensity of pain, suffering, anguish or humiliation. Rather, severity is best conceived as being relational and qualitative in character: what the Court is seeking to establish is whether a person has been wronged in a way that strikes at the mutual respect human dignity demands. As argued in Chapter 3, identifying the 'wrongs themselves' involves alternating between specification and abstraction, and sometimes, specification can only be arrived at through abstraction. The Court's doctrine embodies this: the factors it considers, such as age or state of health, map onto broader concerns such as vulnerability and power asymmetry; and human dignity is notably employed to delineate circumstances in which the use of force is, or is not, inhuman or degrading.[170]

[169] See the argument on good care, therapeutic necessity and human dignity in A Hendriks, 'Personal Autonomy, Good Care, Informed Consent and Human Dignity – Some Reflections from a European Perspective' (2009) 28 *Medicine and Law* 469. Note, in this regard, the complexities regarding the force-feeding of anorexic persons refusing food, discussed in F Freyenhagen and T O'Shea, 'Hidden Substance: Mental Disorder as a Challenge to Normatively Neutral Accounts of Autonomy' (2013) 9 *International Journal of Law in Context* 53.

[170] *Bouyid* [Grand Chamber] (n 21) para 88; *Muradova* (n 55) para 109; see, too, *RS v Hungary* App no 65290/14 (ECtHR, 2 July 2019) (on forced catheterisation amounting to inhuman and degrading treatment), para 34.

The Court's endeavour is complex, contentious and open to critique (at the level of the abstract as well as the specific). As I hope the discussion above has shown, relevant context can be critically important, and some justificatory reasoning may in certain contexts be appropriate, in determining inhumanity or degradation. Article 3 does not simply prohibit the use of force, or simply proscribe all interference with an interest in not being forcefully coerced. Accordingly, the idea that uses of force or forceful coercion may be justified such that they are *not* inhuman or degrading does not *in and of itself* amount to displacement or distortion of the prohibition on inhuman or degrading treatment. At the same time, the extent to which the justificatory reasoning that the Court is prepared to accommodate maps onto the *wrongs themselves* or amounts to irrelevant reasoning is open to critical interrogation, and readers are invited to engage in this with vigour. The same is true in respect of the question of what amounts to relevant context, and how far the Court is taking into account relevant factors and dismissing irrelevant factors in specifying the wrongs of inhuman and degrading treatment. With respect to the doctrine's capacity to guide, the 'minimum level of severity' idea poses appreciable challenges for certainty; but the Court's candid engagement in evaluative and principled reasoning as well as in outlining relevant contextual factors, rather than jumping to all-things-considered conclusions, offers the grounding for principled coherence and generalisable parameters of assessment in the endeavour to identify inhumanity and degradation.

5.5. Inhumanity and Degradation in the Context of Punishment

5.5.1. The Court's Reasoning and the Puzzles of Punishment

It may be assumed that 'punishment' can be subsumed within 'treatment', but this can overlook significant conceptual issues that arise in delineating inhumanity and degradation in the context of punishment. Conceptual questions come up in particular because punishment carries the implication of something undesirable or unpleasant in response to a behaviour considered to be unacceptable,[171] but also because State-sponsored punishment is coloured by a perception that it is *legitimately* punitive – that is, that it legitimately (and thus not wrongfully) inflicts suffering.[172] ECtHR case law indicates that these elements impact on how the

[171] See, generally, the nuanced account in A Duff, *Punishment, Communication, and Community* (Oxford University Press 2001). Interestingly, the ECtHR uses the term 'punishment' (rather than retribution) in its outline of the four penological grounds on which imprisonment may legitimately be based: 'punishment, deterrence, rehabilitation and protection of the public', see *Vinter v UK* (2016) 63 EHRR 1 [Grand Chamber], para 40.

[172] Note, however, the wider critical discourse on punishment, traced in J Simon and R Sparks, 'Punishment and Society: The Emergence of an Academic Field' in J Simon and R Sparks (eds), *The SAGE Handbook of Punishment and Society* (SAGE 2013) 1–20.

Court reasons through 'punishment' but also what the ECtHR refers to as 'treatment associated with it' ('it' here being punishment).[173] Two key issues arise in the Court's delineation of inhumanity and degradation in this area: the puzzle of the Court's circular legitimacy-based reasoning (what I refer to as the 'legitimacy loop'); and the significance, and contours, of the Court's justificatory reasoning.[174]

A legitimacy loop arises in the ECtHR's assessment of punishment or 'treatment associated with it'. The legitimacy loop arises as a form of circular reasoning, in the following way. Punishment is conclusively unlawful – or conclusively illegitimate – if it crosses the Article 3 threshold. Yet the Court invokes legitimacy as a criterion on the basis of which a punishment may *not* be inhuman or degrading, indicating that:

> In order for a punishment or treatment associated with it to be "inhuman" or "degrading", the suffering or humiliation involved must go beyond that inevitable element of suffering or humiliation connected with a given form of legitimate treatment or punishment.[175]

The Court has said that, in particular, '[m]easures depriving a person of his liberty may often involve such an element'.[176] The Court thus creates a circular test,[177] which is particularly pronounced in its doctrine on imprisonment. The ECtHR's starting point in the application of Article 3 to imprisonment appears to be that institutional incarceration that is compatible with the right to liberty under Article 5 of the ECHR can be taken to be prima facie legitimate. The Court has cemented this by indicating that, to comply with Article 3, States must ensure that persons are detained 'under conditions which are compatible with respect for [their] human dignity and that the manner and method of the execution of the measure do not subject [them] to distress or hardship *exceeding* the unavoidable level of suffering inherent in detention' (emphasis added).[178] From this stance it is evident that, for the Court, the institutional imposition of imprisonment as punishment entails bounded, rather than potentially boundless, suffering. This goes hand in hand with the idea that persons are sent to prison *as* punishment rather than *for* punishment,[179] and with Liora Lazarus's illustration that imprisonment entails a particular rather than a *total* loss of liberty.[180]

[173] *A v UK* (2009) 49 EHRR 29, para 127.

[174] See N Mavronicola, 'Crime, Punishment and Article 3 ECHR: Puzzles and Prospects of Applying an Absolute Right in a Penal Context' (2015) 15 *Human Rights Law Review* 721.

[175] *A v UK* (2009) (n 173) para 127.

[176] *Kafkaris v Cyprus* (2009) 49 EHRR 35, para 96. See also *Ramirez Sanchez* (n 83) para 119.

[177] Consider also Art 1 of the UNCAT, which provides that torture 'does not include pain or suffering arising only from, inherent in or incidental to lawful sanctions'. This issue is discussed in K Wouters, 'Editorial: How Absolute Is the Prohibition on Torture?' (2006) 8 *European Journal of Migration and Law* 1, 2–3.

[178] *Kafkaris* (n 176) para 96. See also *Ramirez Sanchez* (n 83) para 119.

[179] The idea was put forward by Alexander Paterson, see SK Ruck (ed), *Paterson on Prisons: The Collected Papers of Sir Alexander Paterson* (Muller 1951) 13.

[180] L Lazarus, 'Conceptions of Liberty Deprivation' (2006) 69 *Modern Law Review* 738.

The Court's position of principle signals that conduct which causes suffering that goes beyond what is inherent in the deprivation of liberty may amount to inhuman or degrading treatment or punishment; the question of what is 'the unavoidable level of suffering *inherent* in detention' accordingly becomes key to Article 3's application in the prison context. While the Court does not provide a definitive generalisable answer to this question, the Court's case law offers various examples of the infliction of suffering that it considers to go beyond the unavoidable level of suffering inherent in detention. Physical, sexual and mental abuse of detainees, for example, is not considered to be inherent in detention and would be incompatible with Article 3, and indeed may well amount to torture.[181] Uses of force or invasions of bodily integrity that exceed what is strictly necessary or which intentionally humiliate or demean are considered incompatible with Article 3. A striking example of treatment 'associated with [punishment]'[182] which exceeded the 'unavoidable level of suffering inherent in detention'[183] and reached the level of severity encompassed in the Article 3 threshold was the intentionally humiliating strip search of a male detainee in the presence of a female prison officer in *Valašinas v Lithuania*. As the Court put it:

> [W]hile strip-searches may be necessary on occasions to ensure prison security or prevent disorder or crime, they must be conducted in an appropriate manner. Obliging the applicant to strip naked in the presence of a woman, and then touching his sexual organs and food with bare hands showed a clear lack of respect for the applicant, and diminished in effect his human dignity. It must have left him with feelings of anguish and inferiority capable of humiliating and debasing him. The Court concludes, therefore, that the search … amounted to degrading treatment within the meaning of Article 3 of the Convention.[184]

At the same time, the unavoidable level of suffering inherent in detention may be exceeded where context-specific factors, such as a person's age, state of health or disability exacerbate the suffering experienced through detention. In *Farbtuhs v Latvia*,[185] for example, the Court concluded that the detention of a disabled 79-year-old applicant was in breach of Article 3 on account of his age, infirmity and state of health.[186]

The Court has recognised that 'detention *per se* inevitably affects prisoners suffering from serious disorders'.[187] Underlining 'the right of all prisoners to conditions of detention which are compatible with human dignity',[188] this led the Court

[181] See, for example, *Selmouni* (n 36); *Aydin* (n 93); *Karabet v Ukraine* App nos 38906/07 and 52025/07 (ECtHR, 17 January 2013).

[182] *A v UK* (2009) (n 173) para 127.

[183] ibid para 128; *Kafkaris* (n 176) para 96. See also *Ramirez Sanchez* (n 83) para 119.

[184] *Valašinas* (n 90) para 117; but see *Wainwright v UK* (2007) 44 EHRR 40.

[185] *Farbtuhs v Latvia* App no 4672/02 (ECtHR, 2 December 2004).

[186] ibid para 61 (available in French only – my translation).

[187] *Yermolenko v Ukraine* App no 49218/10 (ECtHR, 15 November 2012), para 59.

[188] *Mouisel v France* App no 67263/01 (ECtHR, 14 November 2002), para 40.

to find, in *Mouisel v France*, that after a certain point the continued imprisonment of a person with cancer 'undermined his dignity and entailed particularly acute hardship that caused suffering beyond that inevitably associated with a prison sentence and treatment for cancer', and was therefore inhuman and degrading.[189]

As the Court has established in cases such as *Kulikowski v Poland*, in its assessment of whether imprisonment may be incompatible with Article 3 in light of the individual's state of health, it considers: '(a) the medical condition of the prisoner, (b) the adequacy of the medical assistance and care provided in detention and (c) the advisability of maintaining the detention measure in view of the state of health of the applicant'.[190] The Court is particularly conscious, in this context, of the vulnerability experienced by mentally ill persons in prison, and their potential inability to complain 'coherently' about their treatment.[191] There is a substantial body of cases in which the state of health of an individual has rendered the particular – often 'standard' – form of detention incompatible with Article 3.[192]

A similar context-specific assessment takes place in relation to disability.[193] Disability lay at the heart of the issue in *Price*,[194] where the incarceration of a person with disabilities in a cell without appropriate facilities to accommodate her needs was found to amount to degrading treatment. In *Zarzycki v Poland*, the Court affirmed that '[w]here the authorities decide to place and maintain in detention a person with disabilities, they should demonstrate special care in guaranteeing such conditions as correspond to his special needs resulting from his disability'.[195] The Court confirmed its readiness to examine whether, in view of all the circumstances, detention per se is (in)compatible with a person's disability.[196] It made it clear that detaining persons with disabilities in inappropriate conditions in relation to their disability or state of health, or leaving them to rely on cellmates for vital activities such as relieving themselves, bathing, dressing and undressing, can be degrading.[197] Noting the proactive stance of the prison authorities and the provision of a level of care and assistance to the applicant – who had amputated forearms – while in detention, the Court's ultimate conclusion in *Zarzycki* was that

[189] ibid para 48.

[190] *Kulikowski v Poland (No 2)* App no 16831/07 (ECtHR, 9 October 2012), para 64, citing *Mouisel* (n 188) paras 40–42. See also *Rooman v Belgium* App no 18052/11 (ECtHR, 31 January 2019), paras 142–48.

[191] See, for example, *Rooman* (n 190) para 145; *Keenan* (n 18) para 110.

[192] See, among many examples, *Barilo v Ukraine* App no 9607/06 (ECtHR, 16 May 2013), paras 78–84; *Khudobin v Russia* App no 59696/00 (ECtHR, 26 October 2006), paras 90–97; *Raffray Taddei v France* App no 36435/07 (ECtHR, 21 December 2010), paras 52–63.

[193] See, for example, *Grori v Albania* App no 25336/04 (ECtHR, 7 July 2009), paras 124–33; *Butrin v Russia* App no 16179/14 (ECtHR, 22 March 2016), paras 46–67.

[194] *Price* (n 79) para 33.

[195] *Zarzycki v Poland* App no 15351/03 (ECtHR, 12 March 2013), para 102.

[196] ibid para 105. See also *Helhal v France* App no 10401/12 (ECtHR, 19 February 2015), para 49.

[197] *Zarzycki* (n 195) para 104, citing *Price* (n 79) para 30; *Engel v Hungary* App no 46857/06 (ECtHR, 20 May 2010), paras 27–30; and *Vincent v France* App no 6253/03 (ECtHR, 24 October 2006), paras 94–103. See also *Helhal* (n 196) para 52.

'even though a prisoner with amputated forearms is more vulnerable to the hardships of detention', the applicant's detention did not violate Article 3.[198]

In contrast to *Zarzycki*, the Court found a violation of Article 3 in the case of *DG v Poland*,[199] a case which illustrates the need for prison conditions to be adapted from the ableist 'norm' in order to be compatible with Article 3 when imposed on disabled persons. The case concerned the detention of a paraplegic prisoner in 'standard' detention. The Court found that 'detaining him … in a prison that was unsuitable for the incarceration of persons with physical disabilities and not making sufficient efforts to reasonably accommodate his special needs raises a serious issue under the Convention'.[200] In this instance, the Court concluded that detaining a paraplegic person in conditions where he was 'unable to keep clean without the greatest of difficulty' reached the minimum level of severity and constituted degrading and inhuman treatment contrary to that provision.[201] In *Semikhvostov v Russia*, the Court held that the restrictions on mobility experienced by a disabled person in prison 'must have had a dehumanising effect' and amounted to inhuman and degrading treatment.[202]

The ECtHR's line-drawing in this area therefore comes with substantial demands. The Court requires that the State 'ensure that a person is detained in conditions which are compatible with respect for [their] human dignity', that they are not subjected, in the context of detention, 'to distress or hardship of an intensity exceeding the unavoidable level of suffering inherent in detention' and that '[their] health and well-being are adequately secured by, among other things, providing [them] with the requisite medical assistance'.[203] Authorities are expected to demonstrate 'special care' in providing prison conditions that correspond to disabled persons' particular needs.[204]

Besides the particular vulnerability that may be faced in detention by certain persons in certain situations (notably in ableist 'ordinary' prison settings), other circumstances may bring a detention situation to the Article 3 threshold. The Court has frequently found a violation of Article 3 on account of a lack of personal space afforded to persons in detention,[205] with the recognition that sometimes

[198] *Zarzycki* (n 195) para 125.

[199] *DG v Poland* App no 45705/07 (ECtHR, 12 February 2013).

[200] ibid para 176.

[201] ibid para 177.

[202] *Semikhvostov v Russia* App no 2689/12 (ECtHR , 6 February 2014), paras 85–86.

[203] *Kudla* (n 59) paras 92–94. The outcome in *Kudla* has, however, been criticised – see IE Koch, *Human Rights as Indivisible Rights: The Protection of Socio-Economic Demands Under the European Convention on Human Rights* (Martinus Nijhoff 2009) 101; and Bedford (n 87) 75.

[204] *Butrin* (n 193) para 49.

[205] See, among many, *Verdeș v Romania* App no 6215/14 (ECtHR, 24 November 2015), paras 73–82; *Vladimir Belyayev v Russia* App no 9967/06 (ECtHR, 17 October 2013), paras 27–36; *Generalov v Russia* App no 24325/03 (ECtHR, 9 July 2009), para 103; *Khudoyorov v Russia* (2007) 45 EHRR 5, paras 105–09; *Labzov v Russia* App no 62208/00 (ECtHR, 16 June 2005), paras 44–49; *Novoselov v Russia* App no 66460/01 (ECtHR, 2 June 2005), paras 41–46; *Mayzit v Russia* (2006) 43 EHRR 38, paras 39–43; *Kalashnikov v Russia* (2003) 36 EHRR 34, paras 97–103. See the principles set out in *Muršić v Croatia* (2017) 65 EHRR 1, paras 91–177.

these problems are of a systemic or 'structural nature'[206] and may require the State to adapt its penal practices towards reducing the number of people in prison.[207] Furthermore, the Court has often considered the imposition of restrictive carceral regimes, such as solitary confinement, to fall foul of Article 3 ECHR.[208] It has indicated that '[i]n assessing whether a restrictive regime may amount to treatment contrary to Article 3 in a given case, regard must be had to the particular conditions, the stringency of the regime, its duration, the objective pursued and its effects on the person concerned'.[209] The Court's doctrine on restrictive prison regimes is discussed further, in relation to the justificatory reasoning employed by the Court, below.

As the account above highlights, the legitimacy loop can be elucidated, if not eliminated. The ECtHR's doctrine indicates that while lawfully ordained imprisonment and its attendant suffering are considered prima facie legitimate, a number of factors may augment the severity involved so that imprisonment in the particular circumstances crosses the Article 3 threshold. These factors do not stray significantly from the variables most frequently cited by the Court in its severity assessment. Nonetheless, the idea that a degree of suffering is a 'normal' aspect of imprisonment and that it is only aberrations from this norm that bring the experience(s) of imprisonment over the Article 3 threshold not only begs the question, but also suggests that aspects of imprisonment may be unduly immunised from scrutiny. An enduring question is the extent to which the ECtHR may come ultimately to break the legitimacy loop and to question prison itself, even apart from prison's particularly detrimental impact on persons who are ill, disabled or otherwise in a situation of heightened vulnerability. While the ECtHR seems prepared to engage only in circumscribed questioning of the 'ordinary' prison experience, its case law on prison conditions may be chipping away at the legitimacy of the prison in a way that holds radical potential.

Besides the legitimacy loop, another important feature of the Court's doctrine on punishment and 'treatment associated with it' is the application of justificatory reasoning. Justification is built into the legitimacy loop, particularly in the context of imprisonment, given that the suffering 'inherent' in imprisonment is generally seen as a *warranted* ill, but also because various aspects of the prison regime are tied to certain penological grounds – for instance, public protection or rehabilitation – or, more widely, the requirements of prison administration. Justificatory

[206] See, for example, *Generalov* (n 205) para 103.

[207] See, for example, *Orchowski v Poland* App no 17885/04 (ECtHR, 22 October 2009), para 153, noted in L-A Sicilianos, 'The European Court of Human Rights at a Time of Crisis in Europe' (2016) 2 *European Human Rights Law Review* 121, 123–24.

[208] See, for example, *Simeonovi v Bulgaria* (2018) 66 EHRR 2, paras 88–91; *Mathew v Netherlands* (2006) 43 EHRR 23, paras 197–205, 217.

[209] *Gavazov v Bulgaria* App no 54659/00 (ECtHR, 6 March 2008), para 104, citing *Kehayov v Bulgaria* App no 41035/98 (ECtHR, 18 January 2005), para 65, and *Iovchev v Bulgaria* App no 41211/98 (ECtHR, 2 February 2006), para 128.

reasoning may also be applicable in determining whether the punishment imposed, including the term of imprisonment, is compatible with Article 3. This is so in spite of the Court's assertion that '[a]s the prohibition of torture and of inhuman or degrading treatment or punishment is absolute, irrespective of the victim's conduct, the nature of any offence allegedly committed by the applicant is therefore irrelevant for the purposes of Article 3'.[210] This delineation of the irrelevance of the victim's conduct reflects the applicability parameter of absoluteness, clarifying that everyone is unconditionally entitled to Article 3 protection; but the idea that 'any offence … committed by the applicant is … irrelevant' may be unhelpful in some aspects of the specification of inhuman or degrading *punishment*. Nonetheless, as the account offered below illustrates, much of the Court's justificatory reasoning in this context is premised on and shaped by an emphasis on respect for human dignity.

The Court's case law indicates that the *penal* proportionality of a sentence can be relevant in determining whether it amounts to inhuman or degrading punishment.[211] The Court has said that a grossly disproportionate sentence may cross the Article 3 threshold.[212] This approach can be traced back to the ECtHR's assessment, before the death penalty was deemed conclusively unlawful in *Al Saadoon v UK*,[213] of the compatibility of the death penalty with Article 3. In *Öcalan v Turkey*, the Court had indicated that 'the manner in which the death penalty is imposed or executed, the personal circumstances of the condemned person and a *disproportionality to the gravity of the crime committed*, as well as the conditions of detention awaiting execution' (emphasis added) may bring the treatment or punishment received by the condemned individual 'within the proscription under Art.3'.[214]

Moreover, the penological justification(s) for imprisonment have been relevant in assessing the compatibility of Article 3 ECHR with the imposition of life imprisonment without parole ('LWP').[215] This is best illustrated by examining the ECtHR's Grand Chamber judgment in the case of *Vinter v UK*,[216] which concerned the compatibility of Article 3 with the imposition of whole life 'orders' – also known as 'tariffs', and signifying the period before an individual can be considered for release on parole – on persons who had committed murder(s) with significant aggravating factors.

According to the ECtHR in *Vinter*, the imposition of a life sentence on adult offenders for particularly grave crimes is not in itself incompatible with Article 3

[210] *Al Saadoon and Mufdhi v UK* (2010) 51 EHRR 9, para 122.

[211] For an overview of proportionality in penology, see A Ristroph, 'Proportionality as a Principle of Limited Government' (2005) 55 *Duke Law Journal* 263.

[212] See, notably, *Vinter* [Grand Chamber] (n 171) para 102; *Murray v Netherlands* (2017) 64 EHRR 3, para 99.

[213] *Al Saadoon* (n 210) paras 120, 138 and 144.

[214] *Öcalan v Turkey* (2005) 41 EHRR 45, para 168, citing *Soering* (n 60) para 104. See also the pre-*Vinter* assessment of life imprisonment without parole in *Ahmad v UK* (2013) 56 EHRR 1.

[215] See, for instance, *Kafkaris* (n 176); *Vinter* [Grand Chamber] (n 171).

[216] *Vinter* [Grand Chamber] (n 171). See the account of *Vinter* in N Mavronicola, 'Inhuman and Degrading Punishment, Dignity, and the Limits of Retribution' (2014) 77 *Modern Law Review* 292.

or any other Convention Article.[217] Nonetheless, as the Grand Chamber proceeded to acknowledge, the imposition of an *irreducible* life sentence would raise an issue under Article 3, a principle based on *Kafkaris v Cyprus*.[218] Building on *Kafkaris*, the Grand Chamber in *Vinter* established that an irreducible life sentence violates Article 3 ECHR, finding that the denial of any meaningful prospect – hope[219] – of release and of re-entering society was contrary to human dignity.[220]

At the same time, the Grand Chamber in *Vinter* emphasised that a life sentence does not become irreducible simply on account of the fact that it may be served in full, as long as it is reducible de jure as well as de facto.[221] The Court underlined that if a life prisoner had the right to be considered for release 'but was refused on the ground that he or she continued to pose a danger to society',[222] this would not make the sentence irreducible. It also clarified that the reducibility requirement, which demands that prisoners have a prospect of release, entails the possibility of 'review of a life sentence with a view to its commutation, remission, termination or the conditional release of the prisoner'.[223] According to the Court, reducibility via review by the domestic authorities means that the authorities must assess whether 'changes in the life prisoner are so significant, and such progress towards rehabilitation has been made in the course of the sentence, as to mean that continued detention can no longer be justified on legitimate penological grounds'.[224] While the penological grounds the Court was referring to included 'punishment, deterrence, public protection' as well as 'rehabilitation',[225] the Court indicated that emphasis should shift away from retribution and towards rehabilitation and public protection over time.[226] Ultimately, the ECtHR made rehabilitation central to its demand of a meaningful prospect of release, on the understanding that (life) prisoners should be offered 'the possibility of rehabilitation and the prospect of release if that rehabilitation is achieved'.[227]

[217] *Vinter* [Grand Chamber] (n 171) para 106. See also *Kafkaris* (n 176) para 97.

[218] *Kafkaris* (n 176) paras 97–98, cited in *Vinter* [Grand Chamber] (n 171) paras 107–08.

[219] See *Vinter* [Grand Chamber] (n 171), Concurring Opinion of Judge Power-Forde, and the extensive reference in the majority judgment (paras 69–71, 113) to the German Federal Constitutional Court's *Life Imprisonment Case*, BVerfGE 45, 187. See also *Harakchiev and Tolumov v Bulgaria* App nos 15018/11 and 61199/12 (ECtHR, 8 July 2014), para 262: 'It necessarily follows from paragraph 122 of the Grand Chamber's judgment in Vinter … that in this type of case the breach of Article 3 of the Convention consists of depriving the prisoner, for any period of time, of any *hope* of release, however tenuous that hope may be' (emphasis added). See, further, *Matiošaitis and others v Lithuania* App nos 22662/13, 51059/13, 58823/13, 59692/13, 59700/13, 60115/13, 69425/13 and 72824/13 (ECtHR, 23 May 2017), para 180.

[220] See *Vinter* [Grand Chamber] (n 171) para 113; see, subsequently, *Harakchiev* (n 219) para 245; *Murray* (n 212) para 101.

[221] *Vinter* [Grand Chamber] (n 171) para 108.

[222] ibid.

[223] ibid para 109.

[224] ibid para 119.

[225] ibid para 111.

[226] ibid paras 112–19; see the analysis in Mavronicola (n 216).

[227] *Vinter* [Grand Chamber] (n 171) paras 114 and 119; see also the Court's analysis in *Harakchiev* (n 219) para 245; *Murray* (n 212) para 101; *Marcello Viola v Italy (No 2)* App no 77633/16 (ECtHR, 13 June 2019), para 113.

The primacy of rehabilitation in *Vinter* emerged through a focus on human dignity,[228] and with the aid of comparative materials,[229] notably the judgment of the German Federal Constitutional Court (FCC) in the 1977 *Life Imprisonment Case*, which found that it would be incompatible with human dignity for a person to be deprived of freedom without any chance to regain it some day, and underlined that prison authorities had the duty to pursue a life sentenced prisoner's rehabilitation and potential reintegration into society.[230] The ECtHR transposed the findings of the FCC on the basis that '[s]imilar considerations must apply under the Convention system, the very essence of which, as the Court has often stated, is respect for human dignity'.[231] *Vinter*, and the ECtHR's approach to irreducible life imprisonment, discloses an understanding of human dignity that demands respect for egregious wrong-doers' personhood and sociability,[232] concretised through an entitlement to hope to re-enter society. To deny that hope, the Court has explained subsequently, 'would be to deny a fundamental aspect of their humanity',[233] or – as Judge Pinto de Albuquerque has put it – to treat them as 'human waste'.[234]

Vinter stands as authority that imprisoning individuals for their whole life on purely retributive grounds is contrary to Article 3 ECHR,[235] as it was the elimination of the prospect of rehabilitation triggering release that rendered whole life orders incompatible with Article 3. Nonetheless, public protection concerns, if subsisting at the point(s) of the requisite review, may be sufficient to justify what might ultimately amount to life imprisonment. These findings are tied to the primacy of rehabilitation in the Court's implicit ranking of 'legitimate penological grounds', and to the Court's (not unproblematic) drawing of a connection between the rehabilitation of a convicted offender and the goal of public protection: that is, linking rehabilitation to the elimination of dangerousness,[236] and thereby to the prospect of 'safe' return to society.[237]

The emphasis placed by the Court on rehabilitation in *Vinter* carries significance beyond the assessment of particular sentences' compatibility with Article 3,

[228] See the analysis in D van Zyl Smit, P Weatherby and S Creighton, 'Whole Life Sentences and the Tide of European Human Rights Jurisprudence: What Is to Be Done?' (2014) 14 *Human Rights Law Review* 59, 65–71.

[229] See *Vinter* [Grand Chamber] (n 171) paras 113–18 (and the expository account in paras 60–64, 76).

[230] See *Vinter* [Grand Chamber] (n 171) para 113, referring to the *Life Imprisonment Case*, BVerfGE 45, 187.

[231] *Vinter* [Grand Chamber] (n 171) para 113.

[232] On the centrality of sociability to the human person, see A Sangiovanni, *Humanity without Dignity* (Harvard University Press) 6ff.

[233] *Matiošaitis* (n 219) para 180. Robert Spano has spoken of 'paying heed to the human being's, the [criminal] perpetrator's, humanity': R Spano, 'Deprivation of Liberty and Human Dignity in the Case-Law of the European Court of Human Rights' (2016) 4 *Bergen Journal of Criminal Law and Criminal Justice* 150, 154.

[234] *Murray* (n 212), Partly Concurring Opinion of Judge Pinto de Albuquerque, para 21.

[235] This reflects a prediction issued in D Van Zyl Smit, 'Outlawing Irreducible Life Sentences: Europe on the Brink?' (2010) 23(1) *Federal Sentencing Reporter* 39, 46.

[236] Mavronicola (n 174) 739.

[237] The Court's concern about the protection of the public is evident in *Matiošaitis* (n 219) para 180.

and indeed beyond the Court's backtracking in *Hutchinson v UK*[238] on the specifics of the UK's compliance with the demands of *Vinter*.[239] Rehabilitation's significance in relation to the experience of imprisonment as well as the prospect of release is evident in *Murray v Netherlands*, where the Court found that the lack of necessary psychiatric treatment and support towards rehabilitation for a whole life prisoner rendered his life term de facto irreducible in violation of Article 3 ECHR.[240] In other case law, the Court has underlined that 'the regime and conditions [of imprisonment] … need to be such as to make it possible for the life prisoner to endeavour to reform himself, with a view to being able one day to seek an adjustment of his or her sentence',[241] and has denounced restrictive or 'impoverished' regimes of imprisonment which undermine, or provide inadequate opportunities for, rehabilitation.[242] In establishing that the treatment of prisoners must be guided primarily by principles of rehabilitation, the judgment in *Vinter* has made rehabilitation central in determining the Article 3 compatibility of elements of prison administration.[243] Accordingly, the Court's doctrine in this area of application of Article 3 provides an underpinning, premised on human dignity, for how we might understand – and question – justifications for imprisonment, and for what persons (are to be expected to) experience and endure within imprisonment.

Justificatory reasoning has also featured prominently in the ECtHR's assessment of solitary confinement or forms of segregation or isolation within the prison. The Court's stance on solitary confinement can be summarised as follows:

> [C]omplete sensory isolation, coupled with total social isolation can destroy the personality and constitutes a form of inhuman treatment which cannot be justified by the requirements of security or any other reason … While prolonged removal from association with others is undesirable, whether such a measure falls within the ambit of Article 3 of the Convention depends on the particular conditions, the stringency

[238] *Hutchinson v UK* App no 57592/08 (ECtHR, 17 January 2017).

[239] Lewis Graham suggests, I think rightly, that *Hutchinson* may be isolated 'to its own factual situation', rather than signalling a fundamental change in Strasbourg's Art 3 doctrine on life imprisonment without parole: see L Graham, 'From Vinter to Hutchinson and Back Again? The Story of Life Imprisonment Cases in the European Court of Human Rights' (2018) 3 *European Human Rights Law Review* 258, 266. I do not propose to dwell here on the problematic application of the reducibility requirement by the ECtHR in *Hutchinson*, but see the appropriately critical accounts in K Dzehtsiarou, 'Guest Post on Grand Chamber Judgment in Hutchinson', *ECHR Blog*, 19 January 2017, available at: http://echrblog.blogspot.com/2017/01/guest-post-on-grand-chamber-judgment-in.html (accessed 3 January 2020); and B Çalı, 'Coping with Crisis: Whither the Variable Geometry in the Jurisprudence of the European Court of Human Rights' (2018) 35 *Wisconsin International Law Journal* 237; see, too, the scathing Dissenting Opinion of Judge Pinto de Albuquerque in *Hutchinson*, above.

[240] *Murray* (n 212). See the discussion of *Murray* in Spano (n 233) 159–61. On de facto reducibility and rehabilitation opportunities, see also *Harakchiev* (n 219); *Matiošaitis* (n 219).

[241] *Matiošaitis* (n 219) para 177.

[242] See, for example, *Harakchiev* (n 219) para 266; *Matiošaitis* (n 219) para 179.

[243] Mavronicola (n 174) 736, 740.

of the measure, its duration, the objective pursued and its effects on the person concerned ...[244]

The Court has accordingly established that *total* sensory and social isolation is incompatible with Article 3 per se,[245] while '[o]ther forms of solitary confinement which fall short of complete sensory isolation'[246] call for a more fact-specific assessment, the extent of sensory and social isolation being a significant factor in such assessment.[247]

Justificatory reasoning can become prominent in this more fact-specific assessment of certain forms of confinement or segregation within the prison. The ECtHR frequently acknowledges and appears to accept that stringent security measures which restrict interaction with others, with a view to preventing the risk of escape, attack or violent disturbance of the prison community, may be put in place to address particular dangers posed by particular prisoners.[248] At the same time, the Court has tended to view with suspicion restrictions placed on prisoners who have not behaved in a violent or 'disorderly' manner,[249] restrictions which cannot be reasonably related to or are not demonstrated to be necessary for achieving the purported objective of isolation,[250] and restrictions which remain in place after the person no longer poses the relevant risks.[251] In its assessment, the Court has on occasion made its justificatory reasoning transparent by alluding to a 'legitimate aim': according to the Court, 'the measures taken must ... be necessary to attain the legitimate aim pursued'.[252] At the same time, a study of the Court's reasoning in cases concerning solitary confinement and other restrictive prison regimes makes it clear that the 'legitimate aims' are not open ended. For example, the Court does not consider further punishment to be a basis on which a restrictive prison regime can be justified so as to be compatible with Article 3. Rather, the Court refers to the security risk posed by the prisoner and to measures strictly necessary for, and tailored to, the purpose of containing the risk.[253] The Court has also underlined that 'substantive reasons must be given when a protracted period of solitary confinement is extended' and that the expected 'statement of reasons will need to be increasingly detailed and compelling the more time goes by'.[254]

[244] *Onoufriou v Cyprus* App no 24407/04 (ECtHR, 10 December 2009), para 69.
[245] ibid; *Ahmad* (n 214) para 206.
[246] *Ahmad* (n 214) para 207.
[247] See, for instance, *Ramirez Sanchez* (n 83) para 135; *Ahmad* (n 214) para 222.
[248] See, for example, *Ramirez Sanchez* (n 83) para 138; *Alboreo v France* App no 51019/08 (ECtHR, 20 October 2011), para 110.
[249] See, for example, *AB v Russia* (2012) 55 EHRR 4, para 105; *Csüllög v Hungary* App no 30042/08 (ECtHR, 7 June 2011), para 36; *Harakchiev* (n 219) paras 206–07.
[250] *Csüllög* (n 249) para 34; *Karwowski v Poland* App no 29869/13 (ECtHR, 19 April 2016), para 43.
[251] See, for example, *Khider v France* App no 39364/05 (ECtHR, 9 July 2009), paras 118–19.
[252] *Ramirez Sanchez* (n 83) para 119. See also *Piechowicz v Poland* (2015) 60 EHRR 24, para 178.
[253] See, for example, *Karykowski v Poland* App no 653/12 (ECtHR, 12 January 2016), paras 29–40; see, further, Mavronicola (n 174) 731, 734–40.
[254] *Piechowicz* (n 252) para 165.

It transpires quite clearly from the doctrine that the particular nature of solitary confinement, causing as it does significant distress, renders it a prima facie suspect measure in the view of the Court[255] – just as non-consensual physical force is also prima facie suspect. Yet the ECtHR maintains that restrictive prison regimes may be applied in a way which remains respectful of human dignity, insofar as they are orientated and tailored solely towards averting risks posed by the acts of the person subjected to them and with due safeguards for that person's health and well-being,[256] including their 'mental and physical stimulation'.[257] Following *Vinter*, the importance of rehabilitation is already playing and bound to continue to play a vital role in the Court's appraisal of the implications for human dignity of solitary confinement and other restrictive prison regimes. In *Petukhov v Ukraine*, for example, the ECtHR underlined States' 'positive obligation to secure prison regimes to life prisoners which are compatible with the aim of rehabilitation and enable such prisoners to make progress towards their rehabilitation'[258] and found that a regime whereby life prisoners are 'segregated from other prisoners and spend up to twenty-three hours per day in their cells … with little in terms of organised activities and association' was incompatible with the aim of rehabilitation and therefore with the requirement of reducibility under Article 3.[259]

Another example of the application of justificatory reasoning in the context of punishment which illustrates that further punishment is not a 'legitimate aim' of prison administration can be found in *Yankov v Bulgaria*.[260] In this case, the Court found that the forced shaving of a detainee's hair and beard, in the context of a punishment imposed on him for writing critical and offensive remarks about prison warders, affected 'human dignity'[261] and 'constituted an unjustified treatment of sufficient severity to be characterised as degrading within the meaning

[255] The ECtHR understands solitary confinement as an 'exceptional' measure: see *Ramirez Sanchez* (n 83) para 139; *Csüllög* (n 249) para 34. For a consideration of the problematic nature of solitary confinement more generally, see, among many works on the subject, S Shalev, *A Sourcebook on Solitary Confinement* (LSE: Mannheim Centre for Criminology 2008) available at: http://eprints.lse.ac.uk/24557/1/SolitaryConfinementSourcebookPrint.pdf (accessed 3 January 2020); S Grassian, 'Psychiatric Effects of Solitary Confinement' (2007) 22 *Washington University Journal of Law & Policy* 325. On understanding solitary confinement as torture, see A Conley, 'Torture in US Jails and Prisons: An Analysis of Solitary Confinement Under International Law' (2017) 7 *Vienna Journal on International Constitutional Law* 415.

[256] *Ramirez Sanchez* (n 83) para 139. But note the criticised judgment in *Lindström and Mässeli v Finland* App no 24630/10 (ECtHR, 14 January 2014), discussed in L Lavrysen, 'Defecating in "closed" overall not "degrading" according to Strasbourg Court', *Strasbourg Observers*, 10 February 2014, available at: https://strasbourgobservers.com/2014/02/10/shitting-in-closed-overall-not-degrading-according-to-strasbourg-court/ (accessed 3 January 2020).

[257] *Piechowicz* (n 252) para 173.

[258] *Petukhov v Ukraine (No 2)* App no 41216/13 (ECtHR, 12 March 2019), para 181.

[259] ibid paras 182–87. On the relevance of rehabilitation in respect of the socialisation of prisoners in the context of the right to family life, see *Khoroshenko v Russia* App no 41418/04 (ECtHR, 30 June 2015).

[260] *Yankov v Bulgaria* (2005) 40 EHRR 36.

[261] ibid para 114.

of Art.3 of the Convention'.[262] The treatment at issue amounted to an invasion of bodily integrity with the intent of degradation and further punishment, rather than a motive related to maintaining hygiene in prison, and was accordingly not respectful of the applicant's human dignity.[263]

5.5.2. Interrogating Legitimate Specification in the Context of Punishment

The absoluteness starting point entails that Article 3 ECHR proscribes torture as well as inhuman or degrading treatment or punishment without exception, without the possibility of lawful derogation, and irrespective of the victim's conduct; and the legitimate specification requirements for absolute norms comprise: (1) the capacity to guide; (2) relevant reasoning; and (3) non-displacement. The Court's delineation of the Article 3 threshold in relation to inhuman or degrading punishment 'or treatment associated with it' may be perceived as contradicting the absoluteness starting point. This is because it may appear as though the Court is assessing Article 3 compliance in light of legitimate aims akin to those pursued in the context of qualified rights, such as suppressing crime; and as though the protection of Article 3 depends on the good or bad character of the (alleged) victim of ill-treatment.[264]

Yet, once again, such a perception can be reconsidered. In the Court's jurisprudence, attributing the label 'inhuman' or 'degrading' to punishment or treatment associated with punishment hinges on a complex assessment within which the crime committed by the individual or the particular risk of harm they pose at a given time to themselves or others may be relevant, in some instances, in some way. The ECtHR views punishment which 'matches' the offence committed by the individual and which is not excessive in this regard as respectful, in principle, of human dignity, reflecting the limits on individual autonomy and the recognition of individual responsibility embodied in the criminal law and criminal justice system more broadly.[265] This is subject to the conclusive incompatibility with Article 3 of judicially enforced corporal punishment,[266] including the death penalty,[267]

[262] ibid para 120. See also the ECtHR's reasoning in relation to shackling in *Hénaf* (n 167) paras 48–53; and in relation to withholding a prisoner's glasses in *Slyusarev v Russia* (2013) 57 EHRR 33, paras 43–44.

[263] There were repeated references to (human) dignity in the judgment, see *Yankov* (n 260) paras 104, 107, 110, 113–14.

[264] See, for instance, Smet (n 164) 279–81.

[265] See the analysis in J Tasioulas, 'Justice and Punishment' in J Skorupski (ed), *The Routledge Companion to Ethics* (Routledge 2010). For a critical perspective on this, see SB Lutz, 'The Eighth Amendment Reconsidered: A Framework for Analyzing the Excessiveness Prohibition' (2005) 80 *New York University Law Review* 1862, 1873.

[266] *Tyrer* (n 13). See, further, Mavronicola (n 174) 728, 740.

[267] *Al Saadoon* (n 210) paras 120 and 144. See also D van Zyl Smit, 'Punishment and Human Rights' in Simon and Sparks (eds) (n 172) 395.

and of total sensory and social isolation,[268] and the limits placed on whole life imprisonment without parole in *Vinter*.[269] The complex assessment that may be necessitated (and the justificatory reasoning it may accommodate) in the context of punishment does not mean that the individual's 'bad character' operates to *displace* Article 3's protection. Indeed, it is clear from the vast array of findings of breach of Article 3 in cases concerning persons who are in prison that Article 3 protection pertains to *all*, and that Article 3 may offer substantial protection in such circumstances of power asymmetry.[270] Moreover, the Court's assessment of situations involving punishment or treatment 'associated with it' display significant sensitivity to relevant context, notably general and particular vulnerabilities arising in the prison environment. At the same time, it remains important to question whether the Court concedes too much in its 'legitimacy loop' to the historically contingent 'given' of the prison, and whether it should more deeply question the 'ought' – the deontic humanity – of the prison (experience).

The above is only a snapshot of the Court's specification of inhuman and/or degrading punishment or treatment associated with punishment. The question of whether the doctrine occupies the optimal space in the abstraction–specification spectrum endures, and there is good reason to suggest that the requisite *ex ante* guidance is still, to some degree, lacking. In particular, and even though inhuman and/or degrading punishment or treatment associated with punishment are the subject of ever-increasing case-by-case concretisation,[271] the Court would do well to spell out more clearly its idea of what is legitimate in the context of punishment,[272] and what is 'inherent in detention', not only so that the doctrine's key facets may be effectively applied, but also so that they may be further interrogated and, indeed, challenged.

5.6. Conclusion

The Article 3 'threshold' concepts of inhuman and/or degrading treatment, as well as inhuman and/or degrading punishment 'or treatment associated with it', are complex, contestable and context-sensitive in their application. As I argue, it is possible to reconcile attention to relevant contextual factors as well as some forms

[268] *Onoufriou* (n 244) para 69.

[269] *Vinter* [Grand Chamber] (n 171).

[270] Mavronicola (n 174) 740.

[271] But see the forceful critique by Laurens Lavrysen in L Lavrysen, 'The Court could provide more guidance in prisoner cases', *Strasbourg Observers*, 30 May 2013, available at: https://strasbourgobservers.com/2013/05/30/the-court-could-provide-more-guidance-in-prisoner-cases/ (accessed 3 January 2020).

[272] This can also contribute to confronting the concept of 'lawful sanctions' in Art 1 UNCAT, on which see Wouters (n 177); CEF Coracini, 'The Lawful Sanctions Clause in the State Reporting Procedure before the Committee Against Torture' (2006) 24 *Netherlands Quarterly of Human Rights* 305.

of justificatory reasoning in the specification of these concepts with the absoluteness starting point. A fundamental aspect of such reconciling is an appreciation of the relational and qualitative nature of the 'severity' test, which is not – and cannot sensibly be – attached purely to a quantum of suffering. In key case law, the ECtHR has explicitly tied its reasoning on the wrong(s) at issue to human dignity, describing inhuman or degrading acts as attacks on or interferences with human dignity. The endeavour of establishing inhumanity or degradation can involve alternating between abstraction and specification, concretising the abstract commitment encapsulated by human dignity in an array of different circumstances.

This chapter does not aim to offer an exhaustive account of the Article 3 threshold or answers to every difficult question its specification raises – such an enterprise must after all be considered a constant, and always incomplete, one. Far from simplifying the specification of the Article 3 threshold, the above analysis serves to illuminate the complexity of identifying inhumanity and degradation in various forms of treatment and punishment. Nonetheless, I hope it elucidates that this specification is, and ought to be, premised on a meaningful interpretive endeavour which encompasses consideration of relevant circumstances, rather than an unbridled, all-things-considered moral choice.[273] The chapter serves as a critical reflection on some of the doctrine's key puzzles, and an invitation for further meaningful engagement in specifying the contours of inhumanity and degradation.

There is considerable scope, in such engagement, for critiquing how the ECtHR has reasoned through the specification of the Article 3 threshold, and on whether and how its reasoning could be incrementally or drastically reshaped. For example, the strict delimitation of justified use of force can compel rethinking of prevailing understandings of necessity and proportionality in the use of force, including the use of weapons, by law enforcement authorities; and the human dignity-based delineation of inhuman or degrading *punishment* might ultimately hold the radical promise of questioning the legitimacy of the prison itself.

[273] N Mavronicola, 'Is the Prohibition against Torture and Cruel, Inhuman and Degrading Treatment Absolute in International Human Rights Law? A Reply to Steven Greer' (2017) 17 *Human Rights Law Review* 479, 493–96.

6

The Specification of Positive Obligations under Article 3 ECHR

6.1. Introduction

There are question marks surrounding the positive obligations States bear under Article 3 ECHR. Particular controversy may be seen to stem from what can be viewed as two incompatible dimensions of Article 3. On the one hand, Article 3 is said to enshrine an absolute right, which 'must be fulfilled without any exceptions'.[1] On the other hand, positive obligations under Article 3 ECHR cannot sensibly be limitless.[2] The latter aspect of Article 3 might be taken to contradict the absolute character of the right: absoluteness entails that all correlative obligations are to be fulfilled without any exceptions, and some might view the limits of positive obligations as *exceptions*.

The account of positive obligations offered in this chapter contests the idea that Article 3's demanding, but bounded, positive obligations contradict the absolute character of the right. The ECtHR's specification of positive obligations under Article 3 is examined through an appraisal of the circumstances in which positive obligations arise and of the considerations shaping the substantive scope of such obligations.[3] While the account offered in this chapter broadly defends the criteria which shape the substantive scope of positive obligations under Article 3 in light

[1] A Gewirth, 'Are There Any Absolute Rights?' (1981) 31 *The Philosophical Quarterly* 1, 2.

[2] See the discussion in Chs 2 and 3; see also N Mavronicola, 'Is the Prohibition against Torture and Cruel, Inhuman and Degrading Treatment Absolute in International Human Rights Law? A Reply to Steven Greer' (2017) 17 *Human Rights Law Review* 479, 483. For Miles Jackson, this entails that (certain) positive obligations under Art 3 ECHR are not absolute: M Jackson, 'Amnesties in Strasbourg' (2018) 38 *Oxford Journal of Legal Studies* 451, 453.

[3] While some of the analysis in this chapter touches on the issue, the chapter does not provide a comprehensive examination of the justification(s) for recognising positive obligations within the Convention in general, or under Art 3 in particular. But see the analysis in D Xenos, *The Positive Obligations of the State under the European Convention of Human Rights* (Routledge 2012) 19–22. See, too, the pithy remarks in B Dickson, 'Positive Obligations and the European Court of Human Rights' (2010) 61 *Northern Ireland Legal Quarterly* 203. On positive obligations more generally, see L Lavrysen, *Human Rights in a Positive State: Rethinking the Relationship between Positive and Negative Obligations under the European Convention on Human Rights* (Intersentia 2016). On positive obligations under Art 3 as the law stood in 2004, see A Mowbray, *The Development of Positive Obligations Under the European Convention on Human Rights by the European Court of Human Rights* (Hart Publishing 2004) 42–65.

of the absoluteness starting point, it also calls for more clarity and transparency on the socio-economic dimension of positive obligations, and strikes a note of caution regarding the coercive 'sting'[4] of the ECtHR's specific demands.

6.2. What Are Positive Obligations?

In his monograph on positive obligations under the Convention,[5] Alastair Mowbray invokes a statement by Judge Martens describing positive obligations as 'requiring member states to … take action'.[6] Understood as such, positive obligations transcend the often opaque distinction drawn between negative and positive *rights*, which can yield confusion by 'branding' particular rights enshrined in provisions of human rights treaties as negative or positive even though human rights provisions frequently tend to encompass a multitude of negative and positive correlative duties.[7] The ECtHR often ties positive obligations to Article 1 of the ECHR,[8] which requires States to 'secure' the rights enshrined in the Convention, but this also indicates their immanence within the rights enshrined in the ECHR, not least Article 3.[9] An overarching principle that shapes positive obligations under the ECHR is that 'the object and purpose of the Convention as an instrument for the protection of individual human beings require that its provisions be interpreted and applied so as to make its safeguards practical and effective';[10] positive obligations therefore require measures capable of offering 'practical and effective protection'.[11]

At the same time, it must be acknowledged that the line between acts and omissions is not a bright one in all cases disclosing a human rights issue. Circumstances raising human rights concerns may stem from a combination of acts and omissions where the two are closely interlinked: for instance, licensing a dangerous activity and failing to regulate it or adopt the necessary safeguards to protect those exposed to risk,[12] or placing a person in a place of detention and

[4] L Lazarus, 'Positive Obligations and Criminal Justice: Duties to Protect or Coerce?' in L Zedner and J Roberts (eds), *Principles and Values in Criminal Law and Criminal Justice* (Oxford University Press 2012) 145.

[5] Mowbray (n 3) 2.

[6] *Gul v Switzerland* (1996) 22 EHRR 93, Dissenting Opinion of Judge Martens, para 7.

[7] Indeed, Henry Shue maintains that the negative and positive rights distinction can be harmful, because it may result in the neglect of necessary duties: H Shue, *Basic Rights: Subsistence, Affluence and U.S. Foreign Policy* (2nd edn, Princeton University Press 1996) chs 1–2. See also I Koch, 'Dichotomies, Trichotomies or Waves of Duties?' (2005) 5 *Human Rights Law Review* 81, 83–84, 99.

[8] See, for instance, *Z and others v UK* (2002) 34 EHRR 3, para 73. Art 1 ECHR provides that the Contracting Parties 'shall secure to everyone within their jurisdiction' the rights and freedoms contained in the Convention.

[9] See, for instance, *MC v Bulgaria* (2005) 40 EHRR 20, paras 148–53.

[10] *Svinarenko and Slyadnev v Russia* App nos 32541/08 and 43441/08 (ECtHR, 17 July 2014), para 118; *Ali and Ayşe Duran v Turkey* App no 42942/02 (ECtHR, 8 April 2008), para 59.

[11] *Valiulienė v Lithuania* App no 33234/07 (ECtHR, 26 March 2013), para 75; *Rantsev v Cyprus and Russia* (2010) 51 EHRR 1, para 284.

[12] See the Art 2 case of *Öneryildiz v Turkey* (2005) 41 EHRR 20.

failing to provide them with the healthcare they need and could otherwise have accessed.[13] In the socio-economic context, there are circumstances where the law and policy of a Contracting State's government, in what it provides for, what it omits and what it takes away, can be said to *inflict* suffering – 'policy-induced suffering', as Lutz Oette puts it[14] – rather than fail to alleviate it. The ECtHR has long held that

> suffering which flows from naturally occurring illness, physical or mental, may be covered by Article 3, where it is, or risks being, exacerbated by treatment, whether flowing from conditions of detention, expulsion or other measures, for which the authorities can be held responsible.[15]

Nonetheless, the delimitation of States' duties to take positive measures to safeguard rights can be informed by these dynamics without entirely abandoning the distinction between negative and positive obligations.[16]

6.3. The Circumstances in Which Positive Obligations Arise under Article 3 ECHR

The two planes of analysis conducted by the ECtHR in the specification of positive obligations are illustrated in its delineation of the duty to take operational measures to protect a victim of domestic violence in *Opuz v Turkey*:

> The Court observes ... that the violence suffered by the applicant, in the form of physical injuries and psychological pressure, were [*sic*] sufficiently serious to amount to ill-treatment within the meaning of Article 3 of the Convention.
>
> ... Therefore, the Court must next determine whether the national authorities have taken all reasonable measures to prevent the recurrence of violent attacks against the applicant's physical integrity.[17]

Typically, if not always explicitly, as in *Opuz*, the Court first considers whether the circumstances disclose(d) ill-treatment or a risk of ill-treatment falling within Article 3, and proceeds to assess whether the national authorities had taken 'all reasonable measures' to prevent or address it.[18] A similar approach was adopted

[13] See, for example, *Wenner v Germany* (2017) 64 EHRR 19.

[14] L Oette, 'Austerity and the Limits of Policy-induced Suffering: What Role for the Prohibition of Torture and Other Ill-treatment?' (2015) 15 *Human Rights Law Review* 669.

[15] *Pretty v UK* (2002) 35 EHRR 1, para 52.

[16] For an important discussion of the continuum 'from "negative" to more "positive" obligations' (at 86) and more broadly on moving from the negative/positive dichotomy and the tripartite – respect, protect, fulfil – typology to conceptualising 'waves' of obligations, see Koch (n 7).

[17] *Opuz v Turkey* (2010) 50 EHRR 28, paras 161–62.

[18] See also, for example, *Bălşan v Romania* App no 49645/09 (ECtHR, 23 May 2017), paras 60–61. On the 'bifurcation' between 'scope' and (de)limitation, see L Lavrysen, 'The Scope of Rights and the Scope of Obligations: Positive Obligations' in E Brems and J Gerards (eds), *Shaping Rights in the ECHR:*

in the domestic violence case of *Volodina v Russia*, where the Court separated its analysis into the question of '(a) Whether the applicant was subjected to treatment contravening Article 3' and '(b) Whether the authorities discharged their obligations under Article 3'.[19]

A number of observations may be made in relation to the ECtHR's doctrine on the circumstances in which positive obligations arise under Article 3 ECHR. The first relates to actualities and probabilities. Positive obligations can be triggered by the incidence of ill-treatment *as well as* by the risk of ill-treatment. Where the ill-treatment at issue is a future possibility, general as well as particular risks (beyond the negligible) of such ill-treatment can trigger *some* positive obligations under Article 3.[20] The risk involved can be general to the entire jurisdiction, specific to particular groups of persons in particular contexts, or particular to an individual in a specific situation. In *Opuz*, for example, the applicant's risk lay generally in 'the vulnerable situation of women in south-east Turkey',[21] as well as more particularly in the threat of repeated violence by her husband.

While generic risks can generate positive obligations under Article 3 ECHR, the nature and degree of the risk involved shapes the nature and substantive scope of positive obligations triggered. For instance, positive obligations to establish a sufficiently protective legal framework are triggered by a general risk of ill-treatment; on the other hand, operational measures to protect a specific person are required in circumstances of a real and immediate risk that is known or ought to be known by the authorities.[22] As explained below, the substantive scope of positive obligations varies according to the context and circumstances surrounding the trigger.

Torture, inhuman or degrading treatment, or risk thereof, by non-State actors will trigger positive obligations incumbent on the State under Article 3 (whose substantive delimitation is discussed below),[23] and, indeed, the State also bears positive obligations to act to alleviate risks of, and appropriately respond to, ill-treatment involving *State* actors.[24] A more complex question is to what extent

The Role of the European Court of Human Rights in Determining the Scope of Human Rights (Cambridge University Press 2013).

[19] *Volodina v Russia* App no 41261/17 (ECtHR, 9 July 2019), paras 73–102.

[20] This was a position developed persuasively in the England and Wales Court of Appeal Art 2 case of *R (Bloggs 61) v Secretary of State for the Home Department* [2003] EWCA Civ 686, [2003] 1 WLR 2724, [61] (Auld LJ).

[21] *Opuz* (n 17) para 160.

[22] On the parameters of the knowledge criterion, see generally Lavrysen (n 3) 131–37. On the distinct trigger and scope between the generic and operational obligations, see B Conforti, 'Exploring the Strasbourg Case-Law: Reflections on State Responsibility for the Breach of Positive Obligations' in M Fitzmaurice and D Sarooshi (eds), *Issues of State Responsibility before International Judicial Institutions* (Hart Publishing 2004) 134.

[23] See, for example, *Z v UK* (n 8); *MC v Bulgaria* (n 9); *Opuz* (n 17); *Volodina* (n 19).

[24] That positive obligations include the obligation 'to take measures to protect individuals from suffering [ill-treatment] at the hands of the state' is noted in E Webster, *Dignity, Degrading Treatment and Torture in Human Rights Law: The Ends of Article 3 of the European Convention on Human Rights*

suffering of which no particular human agency can be said to be the immediate cause gives rise to positive obligations under Article 3. The ECtHR's doctrine in this area oscillates between 'teasing promise' and 'doctrinal reality', as Colm O'Cinneide put it in 2008.[25] While the Court has recognised positive obligations in certain circumstances involving illness and/or socio-economic deprivation, its position has been characterised by a degree of reticence and a shortfall in clarity.[26] The Court has appeared largely to confine positive obligations in such circumstances to contexts where other laws independently impose relevant obligations on the State,[27] where the State exerts substantial control over the individual (notably in circumstances of custody[28]) or the individual is, in the circumstances, wholly dependent on State support,[29] and/or where the State's involvement exacerbates or risks exacerbating their suffering.[30]

The Court has indicated, for example, that Article 3 'entails a positive obligation on the part of the State to protect the individual from acute ill-treatment, whether physical or mental, whatever its source', and that 'if the source … is a naturally occurring illness, *the treatment for which could involve the responsibility of the State*, but is not forthcoming or patently inadequate, an issue may arise under [Article 3]' (emphasis added).[31] In *RR v Poland*, the ECtHR underlined that 'it cannot be excluded that the acts and omissions of the authorities in the field of

(Routledge 2017) 35. See, among many examples, *Myumyun v Bulgaria* App no 67258/13 (ECtHR, 3 November 2015).

[25] C O'Cinneide, 'A Modest Proposal: Destitution, State Responsibility and the European Convention on Human Rights' (2008) 5 *European Human Rights Law Review* 583, 590.

[26] The uncertainty characterising the doctrine may be partly attributed to the fact that some key case law consists of admissibility decisions, meaning that the reasoning of the Court is sparse and underdeveloped. See ibid 589; I Leijten, 'The German Right to an Existenzminimum, Human Dignity, and the Possibility of Minimum Core Socioeconomic Rights Protection' (2015) 16 *German Law Journal* 23, 26–27. See, for example, *Larioshina v Russia* (Admissibility) App no 56869/00 (ECtHR, 23 April 2002); *Pančenko v Latvia* (Admissibility) App no 40772/98 (ECtHR, 28 October 1999).

[27] Such laws can include EU Regulations and Directives, as was the case in *MSS v Belgium and Greece* (2011) 53 EHRR 2, with Council Directive 2003/9/EC of 27 January 2003 laying down minimum standards for the reception of asylum seekers [2003] OJ L31/18. See *MSS* para 263.

[28] See, for example, *Rooman v Belgium* App no 18052/11 (ECtHR, 31 January 2019). The 'absolute control' over persons in detention is noted in Oette (n 14) 681, while Stephanie Palmer comments that 'when an individual is in the custody of the State, State authorities have a pre-existing and special responsibility for that individual's welfare': S Palmer, 'A Wrong Turning: Article 3 ECHR and Proportionality' (2006) 65 *Cambridge Law Journal* 438, 450. See, further, E Palmer, 'Protecting Socio-economic Rights through the European Convention on Human Rights: Trends and Developments in the European Court of Human Rights' (2009) 2 *Erasmus Law Review* 397, 410–12; I Koch, *Human Rights as Indivisible Rights: The Protection of Socio-Economic Demands under the European Convention on Human Rights* (Brill 2009) 90–102.

[29] See *Budina v Russia* (Admissibility) App no 45603/05 (ECtHR, 18 June 2009), para 3; *MSS* (n 27) para 253; *Shioshvili and others v Russia* App No 19356/07 (ECtHR, 20 December 2016), para 81.

[30] See text to n 15 above; see also *Hristozov and others v Bulgaria* App nos 47039/11 and 358/12 (ECtHR, 13 November 2012), para 111.

[31] *L v Lithuania* (2008) 46 EHRR 22, para 46. Xenos hailed *L* as a 'notable' step in clarifying that the reference to 'treatment' in Art 3 does not exclude positive obligations arising in respect of suffering – Xenos (n 3) 143–44.

healthcare policy may in certain circumstances engage their responsibility under art.3 by reason of their failure to provide appropriate medical treatment'.[32] It found that denying a pregnant woman timely access to genetic tests to ascertain whether her foetus faced severe genetic abnormalities violated Article 3.[33] Yet the Court in *RR* relied heavily on the pre-existing domestic legal framework establishing obligations for antenatal testing and related treatment, to which the authorities had blatantly failed to adhere.[34] At the same time, the Court has recognised substantial duties on the State to provide adequate healthcare to persons that the State has placed in detention.[35]

The Court's stance in respect of socio-economic conditions is that 'the Convention does not guarantee, as such, the right to a certain living standard', but that 'a complaint about a *wholly insufficient* amount of pension and the other social benefits may, in principle, raise an issue under Article 3 of the Convention' (emphasis added).[36] The Court has also indicated that 'State responsibility could arise for "treatment" where an applicant, in circumstances wholly dependent on State support, found herself faced with official indifference when in a situation of serious deprivation or want incompatible with human dignity'.[37] In spite of the acknowledgement that a situation of serious deprivation or want may be incompatible with human dignity, the Court has not tended to make a finding of an Article 3 violation *purely* on the basis of insufficient socio-economic support outside of circumstances of pre-existing responsibility, control or default on the part of the State.[38] Writing in 2008, O'Cinneide observed that obligations to 'provide' in the context of socio-economic need had been recognised only in situations where State involvement could be pinpointed as exposing individuals to degradation, either by driving them into poverty or failing to support them 'where the State could be said to be under a distinct and specific responsibility'[39] to do so. In 2009 Ellie Palmer argued that the principle emerging from the ECtHR is one

> whereby states may be held responsible for extreme socio-economic deficits in circumstances where it can be shown that there are direct and verifiable links between the

[32] *RR v Poland* (2011) 53 EHRR 31, para 152. For an interesting take on the negative–positive obligation divide in relation to the findings in this case, see A Timmer, 'R.R. v. Poland: of reproductive health, abortion and degrading treatment', *Strasbourg Observers*, 31 May 2011, available at: http://strasbourgobservers.com/2011/05/31/r-r-v-poland-of-reproductive-health-abortion-and-degrading-treatment/ (accessed 3 January 2020). In relation to reproductive healthcare and Art 3, see also *P and S v Poland* App no 57375/08 (ECtHR, 30 October 2012). But see the very brief assessment and dismissal of the Art 3 claim in *A, B and C v Ireland* (2011) 53 EHRR 13, paras 160–65.

[33] *RR* (n 32) paras 151–62.

[34] ibid paras 156–57.

[35] See, among many, *Rooman* (n 28); *Salakhov and Islyamova v Ukraine* App no 28005/08 (ECtHR, 14 March 2013); *McGlinchey v UK* (2003) 37 EHRR 41. See the discussion in Koch (n 28) 90–102.

[36] *Kutepov and Anikeyenko v Russia* App no 68029/01 (ECtHR, 25 October 2005), para 62; *Larioshina* (n 26) para 3; *Budina* (n 29) para 3.

[37] *Budina* (n 29) para 3; see also *MSS* (n 27) para 253; *Tarakhel v Switzerland* (2015) 60 EHRR 28, para 98.

[38] The landmark case of *MSS* (n 27), for example, involved such circumstances; see the analysis below.

[39] O'Cinneide (n 25) 589.

> conduct of the state or its agents and the origins or continuation of conduct that has caused intolerable harm.[40]

A combination of pre-existing responsibility and fault as well as a degree of control over the situation at issue was notably at play in the landmark case of *MSS v Belgium and Greece*, decided in 2011.[41] The Greek authorities had failed to process an asylum seeker's application promptly and had exposed him to destitution – 'living in a state of the most extreme poverty, unable to cater for his most basic needs: food, hygiene and a place to live'[42] – during the processing period. The Grand Chamber in *MSS* emphasised that Article 3 'cannot be interpreted as obliging the high contracting parties to provide everyone within their jurisdiction with a home' or 'to give refugees financial assistance to enable them to maintain a certain standard of living'.[43] Nonetheless, it found that 'what is at issue in the instant case cannot be considered in those terms' because the obligation 'to provide accommodation and decent material conditions to impoverished asylum seekers has now entered into positive law and the Greek authorities are bound to comply with their own legislation' (which transposed relevant EU law).[44] The Court also attached significance 'to the applicant's status as an asylum seeker and, as such, a member of a particularly underprivileged and vulnerable population group in need of special protection',[45] and ultimately found that the Greek authorities had not had 'due regard to the applicant's vulnerability as an asylum seeker'.[46] It held the Greek authorities responsible, because of their inaction, 'for the situation in which he has found himself for several months, living in the street, with no resources or access to sanitary facilities, and without any means of providing for his essential needs'.[47] Finding this situation to 'have attained the level of severity required to fall within the scope of art.3 of the Convention',[48] the Grand Chamber concluded that 'through the fault of the authorities, the applicant has found himself in a situation incompatible with art.3 of the Convention'.[49] Since *MSS*, the Court has continued chiefly to recognise positive obligations in circumstances of socio-economic deprivation and health-related suffering where the State has pre-existing responsibility or control over the individual and the individual's situation, including where the State has foreclosed alternative means of protection.[50]

[40] E Palmer (n 28) 414.
[41] *MSS* (n 27) paras 249–64.
[42] ibid para 254.
[43] ibid para 249.
[44] ibid para 250.
[45] ibid para 251.
[46] ibid para 263.
[47] ibid.
[48] ibid.
[49] ibid para 264; see also *VM v Belgium* App no 60125/11 (ECtHR, 7 July 2015), paras 162–63; *Rahimi v Greece* App no 8687/08 (ECtHR, 5 April 2011), paras 93–94.
[50] See, in this regard, V Stoyanova, 'Causation between State Omission and Harm within the Framework of Positive Obligations under the European Convention on Human Rights' (2018) 18 *Human*

Academic commentators have noted the frequent dismissal by the Court of Article 3 complaints regarding deprivation of basic socio-economic provision,[51] which may also be partly attributed to a typically reserved stance on the part of the Court, which signals that a finding of violation in this area is – and should be – unlikely or aberrant. This is evident in the Court's reiteration that Article 3 'cannot be interpreted' as guaranteeing everyone certain socio-economic fundamentals,[52] as well as the language the Court employs to characterise circumstances attracting positive obligations of socio-economic provision, such as 'very special circumstances', as the Court put it in *Shioshvili v Russia*.[53] The Court described its reasoning in the following terms in the healthcare-related case of *Hristozov v Bulgaria*: 'the threshold in such situations is high, because the alleged harm emanates not from acts or omissions of the authorities but from the illness itself'.[54]

The element of vulnerability can sometimes play a crucial role in pushing the relevant circumstances over the 'threshold' or triggering the State's responsibility: the applicant's vulnerability was underlined in *MSS*,[55] for example, as well as in other relevant case law in which the Court has been prepared to recognise positive obligations to provide socio-economic protection, notably case law concerning children and other vulnerable persons in irregular migration contexts.[56] As Dimitris Kagiaros has noted, the criterion of vulnerability may operate in an exclusionary way in this context,[57] by being treated as an 'extra' condition that needs to be met for positive obligations to be generated in the first place, rather than as a factor that may augment and tailor the particular protection called for.

The 'high threshold' and tendency to look for additional sources of responsibility or fault on the part of the State may also be tied to a merging, in socio-economic contexts, of the question of whether an overarching duty to take protective action under Article 3 arose at all, with the question of whether the State violated this duty

Rights Law Review 309, 329–32. Note the commentary in F de Londras and K Dzehtsiarou, *Great Debates on the European Convention on Human Rights* (Palgrave 2018) 154–56.

[51] See L Thornton, 'The European Convention on Human Rights: A Socio-Economic Rights Charter?' in S Egan, L Thornton and J Walsh (eds), *Ireland and the European Convention on Human Rights: 60 Years and Beyond* (Bloomsbury 2014).

[52] See, for example, *MSS* (n 27) para 249; *Shioshvili* (n 29) para 80.

[53] *Shioshvili* (n 29) para 86.

[54] *Hristozov* (n 30) para 111. The high threshold in Art 3's socio-economic application is noted in Thornton (n 51).

[55] *MSS* (n 27) paras 251, 259, 263.

[56] See, for example, *Rahimi* (n 49); *VM v Belgium* (n 49); *Shioshvili* (n 29); *Khan v France* App no 2267/16 (ECtHR, 28 February 2019).

[57] D Kagiaros, 'Vulnerability as a Path to a "Social Minimum"? An Analysis of ECtHR Jurisprudence' in T Kotkas, I Leijten and F Pennings (eds), *Specifying and Securing A Social Minimum in the Battle Against Poverty* (Hart Publishing 2019) 255–56. The Court has, in distinct contexts, indicated that the protection provided by positive obligations 'calls for reasonable and effective measures, *including* with regard to children and other vulnerable individuals' (*Members of the Gldani Congregation of Jehovah's Witnesses v Georgia* (2008) 46 EHRR 30, para 96); 'including' here should be taken to connote that positive obligations' protection is not limited to vulnerable persons.

by not taking reasonable and adequate action.[58] Such an elision may be observed in *Shioshvili*, for example. The case concerned the exposure of a heavily pregnant woman, accompanied by her four young children, to very poor living conditions in the context of a process of collective expulsion. The ECtHR reasoned that the applicants' situation had been 'caused by the conduct of the Russian authorities', that 'the Russian authorities showed indifference towards the applicant's extremely difficult situation', and that *therefore* 'the very special circumstances of the present case are sufficient to accept a positive obligation under Article 3 of the Convention'.[59]

The ECtHR's doctrine in this area is therefore indicative of a certain reluctance to 'extend' Article 3's positive obligations' reach into the socio-economic sphere, and the willingness to do so only in limited – or 'special'[60] – circumstances.[61] The idea that a heightened threshold applies in socio-economic contexts is substantively suspect, suggestive of a distortion or partial displacement – likely on the basis of pragmatic concerns – of the right in its socio-economic application. After all, the same argument as in *Hristozov* – that the harm did not emanate (directly) from acts or omissions of the authorities[62] – could be made about ill-treatment at the hands of non-State actors. Insofar as the doctrine represents an unwillingness to 'over'-extend the ECHR's reach into the socio-economic sphere,[63] it sits uneasily with the ECtHR's position in *Airey v Ireland*, reiterated in relation to Article 3 ECHR in *Budina v Russia*, that 'the mere fact that an interpretation of the Convention may extend into the sphere of social and economic rights should not be a decisive factor against such an interpretation', as 'there is no water-tight division separating that sphere from the field covered by the Convention'.[64] One could argue that the distinct approach the Court takes in the socio-economic context might reflect a concern that 'treatment' remains a key term of Article 3.[65]

[58] See the critical commentary on this aspect of the reasoning in *MSS* in Lavrysen (n 18) 180–81.

[59] *Shioshvili* (n 29) para 86. See also the reasoning of the ECtHR in the case of an unaccompanied foreign minor who spent six months in dire conditions on the Calais heath in France, *Khan* (n 56) paras 93–94; see, further, the reasoning in cases such as *Budina* (n 29) para 3; *MSS* (n 27) paras 249–64; and *Said Good v Netherlands* (Admissibility) App no 50613/12 (ECtHR, 23 January 2018), para 23.

[60] See *Shioshvili* (n 29) para 86.

[61] See also the discussion of the 'medical cases' concerning the Art 3 duty against removal in Ch 7.

[62] *Hristozov* (n 30) para 111.

[63] See Lavrysen (n 3) 107.

[64] *Airey v Ireland* (1979–80) 2 EHRR 305, para 26, cited in *Budina* (n 29) para 3. But see the critical discussion in C Warbrick, 'Economic and Social Interests and the European Convention on Human Rights' in M Baderin and R McCorquodale (eds), *Economic, Social and Cultural Rights in Action* (Oxford University Press 2007); and the analysis in de Londras and Dzehtsiarou (n 50) 148–56.

[65] Indeed, this could be coupled with an emphasis on the term 'subjected', as was done in the Court's assertion in *Nicolae Virgiliu Tănase v Romania* App no 41720/13 (ECtHR, 25 June 2019) that 'bodily injuries and physical and mental suffering experienced by an individual following an accident which is merely the result of chance or negligent conduct cannot be considered as the consequence of "treatment" to which that individual has been "subjected" within the meaning of Article 3'. But note the Partly Dissenting Opinion of Judge Kūris, para 63.

Yet this would elide the reality that any wrong involved in the experience of suffering related to health or socio-economic conditions is fundamentally shaped by the way that such suffering is treated, including by way of official *indifference*, a point the ECtHR itself has acknowledged.[66] Indifference, in this context, may be understood as inaction; in dismissing allegations of an Article 3 violation in respect of a person in poverty in *Hunde v Netherlands*, the Court indicated that the domestic authorities had not been shown to 'have fallen short of their obligations under Article 3 by having remained inactive or indifferent'.[67] In order for the State not to demonstrate 'indifference' to a situation of acute hardship, it must take *some* positive measure(s) to alleviate it.

Ultimately, therefore, any setting apart of circumstances emanating 'not from' acts or *omissions* of the authorities begs the question. The reality is that indifference (in the sense of inaction) in respect of ill-treatment at the hands of non-State actors as well as indifference towards suffering stemming from illness or socio-economic hardship amounts to a failure to protect from suffering occurring other than at the hands of the State. What should then become critical to establish is whether the State has been 'indifferent' towards the individual's plight in that it failed to take the requisite steps to address the relevant situation or risk thereof: this is to be determined through the specification of the positive obligations at issue.

It is hard to dispute that (a risk of) grave suffering, anguish, and/or humiliation arises in circumstances where a person's 'most basic needs'[68] are not being met,[69] and that indifference to these falls foul of Article 3 ECHR. As Jeremy Waldron has argued, inhumanity may encompass the disregard of or 'failure in sensitivity' towards 'the most basic needs … of a human life'.[70] Such basic needs arguably map onto certain aspects of the 'minimum core' of key socio-economic rights, including essential sustenance, healthcare and shelter.[71] Responding to such needs may necessitate the provision of basic subsistence. As Lutz Oette posits, where a

[66] See text to n 37 and n 59 above. For an expansive account of 'treatment', see Webster (n 24) ch 5. See also her nuanced account of *O'Rourke v UK* App no 39022/97 (ECtHR, 26 June 2001) and the contours of individual and State responsibility in ibid ch 6.

[67] *Hunde v Netherlands* (Admissibility) App no 17931/16 (ECtHR, 5 July 2016), para 59. See also *Ndikumana v Netherlands* (Admissibility) App no 4714/06 (ECtHR, 6 May 2014), para 47.

[68] Emphasis is placed on catering for one's 'most basic needs' in the Court's application of Art 3 in *MSS* (n 27) para 254.

[69] See, in this regard, F Tulkens, 'Implementing the European Convention on Human Rights in times of economic crisis', *Seminar to mark the opening of the judicial year of the European Court of Human Rights* (Strasbourg, January 2013), available at: www.echr.coe.int/Documents/Speech_20130125_Tulkens_ENG.pdf (accessed 3 January 2020).

[70] J Waldron, *Torture, Terror and Trade-offs: Philosophy for the White House* (Oxford University Press 2012) 308. William Twining, too, sees the concept of 'inhuman and degrading treatment' as providing 'a direct link to the idea of basic human needs': W Twining, 'Have Concepts, Will Travel: Analytical Jurisprudence in a Global Context' (2005) 1 *International Journal of Law in Context* 5, 10.

[71] Committee on Economic, Social and Cultural Rights (CESCR), General Comment No 3: The nature of States parties' obligations, UN Doc E/1991/23, 14 December 1990, para 10.

subsistence minimum is not provided, 'an inherent risk of intolerable suffering is present'.[72] Ingrid Leijten argues that when the understanding of 'treatment' is nuanced, Article 3 can, accordingly, be linked to 'the provision of basic means of subsistence needed for living a human life'.[73] This perspective is bolstered by the centrality of human dignity within Article 3, and the ECtHR's recognition that 'a situation of serious deprivation or want' can be 'incompatible with human dignity'.[74] That lacking vital subsistence undermines human dignity is also reflected in the German Constitutional Court's affirmation that Article 1 of Germany's Basic Law, which provides that human dignity is inviolable, requires the State to guarantee a subsistence minimum for every individual to maintain an existence in human dignity.[75]

Taking seriously the idea that Article 3 is violated in circumstances of 'official indifference' towards 'a situation of serious deprivation or want incompatible with human dignity'[76] can therefore bring the Court to view any situation, or risk thereof, in which a person's most basic needs are cognisably not being met as generating obligations on the State to take positive measures to alleviate it. While such a situation may not be clear-cut to ascertain in all cases, this approach has the capacity to avoid the opacity and exclusionary potential attached to the idea of a heightened threshold or 'special' circumstances. The delineation of State responsibility in circumstances of (risk of) such hardship can then turn on the substantive scope of positive obligations at issue, which can be delimited through an assessment of what can reasonably be expected of State authorities in the particular circumstances, duly taking into account relevant contextual elements such as the particular vulnerability of the person in need.[77]

6.4. The Substantive Scope of Positive Obligations under Article 3

6.4.1. A Typology of Obligations

The ECtHR has established that a range of positive obligations emerge from Article 3 ECHR. A dominant way of categorising such obligations is by reference to the measures required.[78] General, or framework, duties require States to set

[72] Oette (n 14) 688.

[73] I Leijten, *Core Socio-Economic Rights and the European Court of Human Rights* (Cambridge University Press 2018) 218.

[74] See, among others, *Budina* (n 29) para 3; see also *MSS* (n 27) para 253; *Tarakhel* (n 37) para 98.

[75] See the discussion of relevant case law in Leijten (n 26).

[76] See text to n 37 above.

[77] See, in this regard, the path proposed in Kagiaros (n 57) 259–60.

[78] But see the somewhat distinct typology adopted in V Stoyanova, *Human Trafficking and Slavery Reconsidered: Conceptual Limits and States' Positive Obligations in European Law* (Cambridge University Press 2017) ch 8; and the typologies identified in Lavrysen (n 3) ch 2.

up adequate legal provisions, implementation mechanisms, and other relevant structures towards preventing and protecting individuals from ill-treatment.[79] Operational duties require States to protect persons at real and immediate risk of suffering ill-treatment where this risk is known – in the sense of actual or constructive knowledge – by the authorities.[80] Investigative duties require States to investigate credible complaints or suspected incidents of ill-treatment,[81] and the accompanying duties of redress require States to provide for and/or pursue redress for individuals who have suffered the proscribed treatment.[82] A brief overview of the parameters of these duties can help illuminate the ECtHR's delineation of the substantive scope of positive obligations under Article 3 ECHR.

The State's general, or framework, obligations to protect persons within its jurisdiction arise out of the general incidence and possibility of ill-treatment. These obligations may be found to be breached by subsisting systems of law or enforcement practices in Contracting States,[83] and they also function as a fundamental bulwark against regressive developments in States' laws or enforcement practices.[84] Where these obligations are at issue, the Court assesses the reasonableness and adequacy of the State's relevant legal and administrative framework and the mechanisms and structures giving effect to it in protecting individuals from ill-treatment.

The case of *O'Keeffe v Ireland* demonstrates the significance and potency of these obligations, which, while general, are responsive to relevant context. In *O'Keeffe*, the Court made clear that Article 3 demands substantial safeguards to be established by the State to provide effective protection for schoolchildren against the risk of sexual abuse.[85] In the context of the 'provision of an important public service such as primary education', the Court reasoned, education authorities are 'obliged to protect the health and well-being of pupils and, in particular, of young children who are especially vulnerable and are under the exclusive control of those authorities'.[86] Accordingly,

> when relinquishing control of the education of the vast majority of young children to non-State actors, the State should … have been aware, given its inherent obligation to protect children in this context, of potential risks to their safety if there was no

[79] See, for example, *MC v Bulgaria* (n 9) paras 167–87; *Volodina* (n 19) paras 78–85.

[80] See, for example, *Z v UK* (n 8) paras 69–75; *E v UK* (2003) 36 EHRR 31, paras 88–101; *Volodina* (n 19) paras 86–91.

[81] See, for example, *Assenov v Bulgaria* (1999) 28 EHRR 652, paras 101–06; *Volodina* (n 19) paras 92–101.

[82] See, for example, *Gäfgen v Germany* (2011) 52 EHRR 1, paras 116–19.

[83] See, for instance, *MC v Bulgaria* (n 9); *Volodina* (n 19).

[84] Phedon Vegleris has argued that many of these obligations have underpinned criminal and civil law even before human rights treaties. See P Vegleris, '"Twenty Years" Experience of the Convention and Future Prospects' in AH Robertson (ed), *Privacy and Human Rights* (Manchester University Press 1973) 382.

[85] *O'Keeffe v Ireland* (2014) 59 EHRR 15, para 152.

[86] ibid para 145.

> appropriate framework of protection. This risk should have been addressed through the adoption of commensurate measures and safeguards. Those should, at a minimum, have included effective mechanisms for the detection and reporting of any ill-treatment by and to a State-controlled body, such procedures being fundamental to the enforcement of the criminal laws, to the prevention of such ill-treatment and, more generally therefore, to the fulfilment of the positive protective obligation of the State.[87]

The Court found a violation of Ireland's positive obligations under Article 3 on account of the State's failure to put in place 'any mechanism of effective State control against the risks of such abuse occurring'.[88]

In its elaboration of these general positive obligations, the Court has tended to place significant emphasis on the criminal law – to the concomitant exclusion or sidelining of other tools – as a (purported) means of protection from, and redress for, ill-treatment. For example, in its discussion of the State's general obligations in the domestic violence case of *Volodina v Russia*, the Court began by stating that 'comprehensive legal *and other measures* are necessary to provide victims of domestic violence with effective protection and safeguards' (emphasis added),[89] to then focus primarily on the adequacy of criminal law provisions in respect of domestic violence in Russia.[90] The Court has underlined that penal sanctions should attach to various forms of ill-treatment that fall within the reach of Article 3 ECHR; it has stipulated, for example, that Article 3 requires 'the penalisation and effective prosecution of any non-consensual sexual act, including in the absence of physical resistance by the victim'.[91] In its judgment in *Cestaro v Italy*, the Court made a statement tying the investigation of (alleged) Article 3 ill-treatment to the criminalisation of such ill-treatment and indicating that all practices contrary to Article 3 should be criminalised:

> For an investigation to be effective in practice it is a prerequisite that the State has enacted *criminal-law provisions penalising practices that are contrary to Article 3* … The absence of criminal legislation capable of preventing and effectively punishing the perpetrators of acts contrary to Article 3 can prevent the authorities from prosecuting violations of that fundamental value of democratic societies, assessing their gravity, imposing adequate penalties and precluding the implementation of any measure likely to weaken the penalty excessively, undermining its preventive and dissuasive effect … (citations omitted, emphasis added).[92]

These elements of the Court's doctrine highlight the interconnections between investigative and general obligations, and the implications of these interconnections for duties of redress. Besides the Court's (somewhat sweeping[93]) demand

[87] ibid para 162.
[88] ibid para 168.
[89] *Volodina* (n 19) para 78.
[90] ibid paras 78–85. But note the Court's reference to protective orders at para 82. See also the emphasis on criminal law provisions in *O'Keeffe* (n 85) para 148.
[91] *MC v Bulgaria* (n 9) para 166; see also ibid paras 170–87.
[92] *Cestaro v Italy* App no 6884/11 (ECtHR, 7 April 2015), para 209.
[93] This is highlighted in N Mavronicola, 'Coercive Overreach, Dilution, Diversion: Potential Dangers of Aligning Human Rights Protection with Criminal Law (Enforcement)' in L Lavrysen and

for the criminalisation of *all* practices contrary to Article 3, States are required to establish and make effectively available civil remedies in respect of all instances of Article 3 breach,[94] which should encompass 'compensation for the pecuniary and non-pecuniary damage flowing from the breach'.[95] At the same time, the Court has underlined that 'in cases of wilful ill-treatment a violation of Articles 2 or 3 cannot be remedied exclusively through an award of compensation to the victim',[96] and that criminal redress should be available and pursued in respect of such incidents to avoid 'impunity'.[97]

The Court particularises the reasonable measures required when the risk itself is particular and in the actual or constructive knowledge of the authorities. In a similar vein to Article 2 cases since the approach elaborated in *Osman v UK*,[98] the Court has demanded operational measures to protect a particular person in circumstances where State authorities knew or ought to have known of a real and immediate risk of ill-treatment.[99] The element of constructive knowledge in these operational duties – 'ought to have known' – entails an obligation on the authorities to take measures that enable them to be apprised of or to ascertain a risk or ongoing situation of ill-treatment,[100] including by means of adequate mechanisms of 'detection and reporting',[101] and by '[a]ctive anticipation' of foreseeable (general or particular) risks.[102] In assessing and acting on the relevant risk, authorities are duty-bound 'to take account of … [the individual's] particular psychological and physical vulnerability and to assess the situation accordingly by taking immediate and appropriate protective measures'.[103]

The measures required can vary according to the circumstances of the (potential) victim(s), and the position that the relevant State institution or agent holds in relation to the victim(s) or potential victim(s), encompassing many factors, including the organ's function as well as its proximity[104] to the victim(s). The operation of these factors can account for the extensive operational duties arising in imprisonment contexts, given the relationship of proximity and control between the relevant State organs and imprisoned individuals.[105] Importantly, the

N Mavronicola (eds), *Coercive Human Rights: Positive Duties to Mobilise the Criminal Law under the ECHR* (Hart Publishing 2020).

[94] *Gäfgen* (n 82) paras 115–18.

[95] *Aleksakhin v Ukraine* App no 31939/06 (ECtHR, 19 July 2012), para 60. See, also, in relation to Art 2, the Court's approach in *Tarariyeva v Russia* App no 4353/03 (ECtHR, 14 December 2006), para 75.

[96] *Aleksakhin* (n 95) para 60; see also *Gäfgen* (n 82) paras 116, 119.

[97] *Gäfgen* (n 82) para 119.

[98] *Osman v UK* (2000) 29 EHRR 245.

[99] See, for example, *Z v UK* (n 8) para 73; *Tautkus v Lithuania* App no 29474/09 (ECtHR, 27 November 2012), para 53.

[100] See, for example, *E v UK* (n 80) para 97.

[101] *O'Keeffe* (n 85) para 162.

[102] Lavrysen (n 3) 135; see also Stoyanova (n 78) 328.

[103] *VC v Italy* (2019) 69 EHRR 13, para 110.

[104] On proximity and positive obligations, see Lavrysen (n 3) 137–46.

[105] This is highlighted in PJ Duffy, 'Article 3 of the European Convention on Human Rights' (1983) 32 *International & Comparative Law Quarterly* 316, 323. See, further, J Gerards, 'The ECtHR's Response to

operational measures required are meant to be responsive and tailored to the individual's particular circumstances and the nature of the risk faced. For example, in respect of a medical condition of a person in detention, relevant authorities are required 'to ensure, in particular, that diagnosis and care have been prompt and accurate, and that supervision by proficient medical personnel has been regular and systematic and involved a comprehensive therapeutic strategy', with the Court examining whether 'the relevant domestic authorities have in a timely fashion provided all reasonably available medical care in a conscientious effort to hinder development of the disease in question'.[106] The Court has also clarified that, where a person in detention is suffering from mental ill-health that may raise a risk of self-harm, the authorities must offer medical care as well as take 'precautionary measures in order to diminish the opportunities for self-harm'.[107] The powerlessness experienced in detention, but also particular factors that may amplify the vulnerable situation in which persons in custody find themselves, contribute to shaping the measures required.[108] Of course, these obligations operate in conjunction with negative obligations to refrain from taking action that may exacerbate a situation, such as placing a mentally ill person in solitary confinement.[109]

The relationship between operational and general positive obligations illuminates the layered manifestation of positive obligations. While on a generic level legislative action may be demanded of central government in the case of, for example, an endemic shortcoming in the law whereby it falls short of effectively protecting individuals from ill-treatment,[110] direct preventative action is required where State bodies have or ought to have knowledge of an actual or potential Article 3 violation in respect of a specific person or person(s).[111] There may be *layers* of obligation pertaining to a particular risk of ill-treatment: for example, a woman who faces a real and immediate risk of ill-treatment at the hands of her partner is entitled not only to operational measures, but also to the general measures to which any person facing a risk of domestic violence is entitled.[112]

At the same time, the Court is often asked to consider only whether a *particular* (often operational) obligation arises under Article 3 and whether it has been breached by the State. This can mean that the Court makes a narrow finding without fully specifying other positive obligations that may be applicable in the context at hand. For example, in *Pretty v UK*, which concerned Diane Pretty's wish to secure assisted suicide, the Court found that

Fundamental Rights Issues Related to Financial and Economic Difficulties – the Problem of Compartmentalisation' (2015) 33 *Netherlands Quarterly of Human Rights* 274, 283–86.

[106] *Jashi v Georgia* App no 10799/06 (ECtHR, 8 January 2013), para 61.

[107] ibid para 62.

[108] See the analysis on inhumanity and degradation in the context of punishment in Ch 5.

[109] See, for example, *Keenan v UK* (2001) 33 EHRR 38.

[110] See, for example, the reasoning in *Cestaro* (n 92) paras 243–46; *Volodina* (n 19) paras 78–85.

[111] See, for example, *Volodina* (n 19) paras 86–91.

[112] See ibid paras 78–91.

> no positive obligation arises under Article 3 of the Convention to require the respondent State either to give an undertaking not to prosecute the applicant's husband if he assisted her to commit suicide or to provide a lawful opportunity for any other form of assisted suicide.[113]

Such a finding – that the State did not bear a positive duty to provide a 'lawful opportunity' for assisted suicide – need not be read as meaning that no other general or specific positive obligations were at play requiring the State to protect Diane Pretty and other persons in a similar situation from inhumanity or degradation.[114] Similarly, as I argue in Chapter 2, in the kidnap case of *Gäfgen*,[115] there were multiple positive obligations at play to take measures towards saving the kidnapped child, Jakob, even as a positive obligation of ill-treating the child's kidnapper, Magnus Gäfgen, did *not* arise.[116]

The duty of investigation, which arises in the context of an arguable allegation or suspicion of ill-treatment,[117] aptly embodies the tailoring of obligations to context. At the same time, the parameters of the investigative obligation have been the subject of a substantial body of case law encompassing significant generalisable statements of principle.[118] The investigative duty requires 'that the investigation be independent, impartial and subject to public scrutiny, and that the competent authorities act with exemplary diligence and promptness'.[119] These requirements map onto concerns of efficacy and effectiveness – for instance, lack of independence can compromise the investigation's rigour, and delays can entail the deterioration of relevant evidence. In order for an investigation to be considered effective, the authorities must take 'whatever reasonable steps they can to secure the evidence concerning the incident, including, inter alia, a detailed statement concerning the allegations from the alleged victim, eyewitness testimony, forensic evidence and, where appropriate, additional medical reports'.[120] It is now well established that

[113] *Pretty* (n 15) para 56.

[114] The UN Special Rapporteur on Torture, for example, has underlined the importance of provision of pain relief and palliative care in giving effect to the prohibition of torture and other cruel, inhuman or degrading treatment or punishment: Report of the Special Rapporteur on Torture and Other Cruel, Inhuman or Degrading Treatment or Punishment, UN Doc A/HRC/22/53, 1 February 2013, paras 55, 86.

[115] *Gäfgen* (n 82).

[116] See the (unwarranted, in my view) critique by Steven Greer on this aspect of the Grand Chamber's reasoning in S Greer, 'Is the Prohibition against Torture, Cruel, Inhuman and Degrading Treatment Really "Absolute" in International Human Rights Law?' (2015) 15 *Human Rights Law Review* 101, 124; *cf* Mavronicola (n 2) 483–84.

[117] *M and others v Italy and Bulgaria* App no 40020/03 (ECtHR, 31 July 2012), para 100. See also *Volodina* (n 19) para 93; *K.Ö. v Turkey* App no 71795/01 (ECtHR, 11 December 2007), para 43; *Erdem v Turkey* App no 42234/02 (ECtHR, 17 July 2008), para 26.

[118] See U Erdal and H Bakirci, *Article 3 of the European Convention on Human Rights: A Practitioner's Handbook* (OMCT Handbook Series 2006) 219–26; A Morawa, N Bürli, P Coenen and L Ausserladscheider Jonas, *Article 3 of the European Convention on Human Rights: A Practitioner's Handbook* (2nd edn, OMCT Handbook Series 2014) 222–24.

[119] *M and others v Italy and Bulgaria* (n 117) para 100.

[120] ibid para 100. See, further, *Çelik and İmret v Turkey* App no 44093/98 (ECtHR, 26 October 2004), para 55; *Batı and others v Turkey* App nos 33097/96 and 57834/00 (ECtHR, 3 June 2004), para 134.

authorities must act with speed, diligence and transparency (incorporating an element of public scrutiny) with a view to establishing what occurred, determining whether it involved a violation of Article 3 and/or a criminal offence or other legal wrong, and identifying those responsible,[121] and must involve the victim – or, where relevant, their next of kin – within the investigation, to the extent necessary to safeguard their legitimate interests.[122]

The investigative duty has been expressly tied to redress; according to the ECtHR:

> Where an individual has an arguable claim that he has been ill-treated by agents of the State, the notion of an 'effective remedy' entails, in addition to the payment of compensation where appropriate, a thorough and effective investigation capable of leading to the identification and punishment of those responsible.[123]

The emphasis on the capacity of the investigation to lead to the identification *and punishment* of those responsible[124] in the delineation of the investigative duty has tied the investigative duty to individual-responsibility-apportioning justice processes, notably the criminal justice process.[125] When examining whether a State has discharged its positive obligations in respect of the investigation and suppression of what the ECtHR sees as Article 3 'offences',[126] the Court often places emphasis on domestic courts themselves and the extent to which, in their interpretation and application of the law, domestic courts engage in a 'scrupulous examination' of (alleged) incidents of ill-treatment and 'maintain the deterrent power of the judicial system'.[127] The Court has also indicated that it is prepared to 'intervene in cases of manifest disproportion between the gravity of the act and the punishment imposed'.[128] It has embedded this approach and made findings of such 'manifest disproportion' in its investigative duty jurisprudence.[129] The ECtHR views this as part of its role in ensuring 'that national authorities do not allow such treatment to go unpunished',[130] which also entails an opposition –

[121] *El-Masri v FYROM* (2013) 57 EHRR 25, paras 182–94.

[122] See *Rantsev* (n 11) para 288, referring to the investigative duty under Arts 2, 3 and 4 ECHR; see, further, *Zontul v Greece* App no 12294/07 (ECtHR, 17 January 2012), paras 110–11; *El-Masri* (n 121) para 185.

[123] *El-Masri* (n 121) para 255, with reference to Art 13 ECHR.

[124] See ibid para 182; *O'Keeffe* (n 85) para 172.

[125] See, for example, the recent child sexual abuse case of *A and B v Croatia* App no 7144/15 (ECtHR, 20 June 2019), paras 105–30.

[126] On 'human rights offences', see K Kamber, *Prosecuting Human Rights Offences: Rethinking the Sword Function of Human Rights Law* (Brill 2017).

[127] *Cestaro* (n 92) para 206; see also *Myumyun* (n 24) paras 66–67.

[128] See *Gäfgen* (n 82) para 123.

[129] See, for example, *Beganović v Croatia* App no 46423/06 (ECtHR, 25 June 2009), para 78; *Myumyun* (n 24) paras 67, 75; *Voroshilov v Russia* App no 59465/12 (ECtHR, 17 July 2018), para 26. See the discussion of the 'manifest disproportion' case law in L Lavrysen, 'Positive Obligations and the Criminal Law: A Bird's-Eye View on the Case Law of the European Court of Human Rights' in Lavrysen and Mavronicola (eds) (n 93).

[130] *Myumyun* (n 24) para 67.

as a matter of principle – by the Court to amnesties, pardons or limitation periods in respect of Article 3 'offences'.[131]

The Court's extensive elaboration of the investigative duty's parameters has not entailed an absence of controversy or uncertainty, not least in terms of the implications of the coercive and carceral dimensions of the duty,[132] as well as the tensions between the pursuit of (historical) truth and the pursuit of justice in delineating and discharging the duty.[133] These tensions, and accompanying questions of process and substance, have persisted in relation to Article 2 as well as Article 3 ECHR, particularly in the aftermath of conflict and widespread violence across the Council of Europe.[134] As I argue below, a re-centring of the protective character of positive obligations may entail a reconsideration of the parameters of this as well as other positive duties.

6.4.2. Delimiting Positive Obligations: The Criteria of Reasonableness and Adequacy

The ECtHR's approach in determining what is required on the basis of positive obligations arising under Article 3 is encapsulated in its references to 'reasonable measures'[135] and 'reasonable steps',[136] as well as to 'adequate' measures[137] and safeguards.[138] Reference to 'reasonable steps' and 'reasonable measures', in particular, abounds in the ECtHR's case law on positive obligations.[139] The term 'reasonable'

[131] The ECtHR has underlined that 'when an agent of the State is accused of crimes that violate Article 3, any ensuing criminal proceedings and sentencing must not be time-barred and the granting of amnesty or pardon should not be permissible': *Ateşoğlu v Turkey* App no 53645/10 (ECtHR, 20 January 2015), para 25; *Derman v Turkey* (2015) 61 EHRR 27, para 27. See the discussion on amnesties in Jackson (n 2).

[132] See, for example, K Pitcher, 'Coercive Human Rights and Unlawfully Obtained Evidence in Domestic Criminal Proceedings' in Lavrysen and Mavronicola (eds) (n 93).

[133] See Jackson (n 2).

[134] On the Art 2 and Art 3 ECHR issues arising in relation to the legacy of the Troubles in Northern Ireland, for example, see L Mallinder, L Moffett, K McEvoy and G Anthony, *Investigations, Prosecutions, and Amnesties under Articles 2 & 3 of the European Convention on Human Rights* (Queen's University Belfast 2015). See, more generally, B Dickson, 'The Limitations of a Criminal Law Approach in a Transitional Justice Context' in Lavrysen and Mavronicola (eds) (n 93). On Art 2 ECHR in the context of European conflicts, see H Russell, *The Use of Force and Article 2 of the ECHR in Light of European Conflicts* (Hart Publishing 2017).

[135] See for example, *Opuz* (n 17) para 162.

[136] See, for example, *Z v UK* (n 8) para 73.

[137] See, for example, *Opuz* (n 17) para 165. See, too, on the provision of 'adequate' medical treatment, *Rooman* (n 28) para 147. For a thorough account of terms and principles employed by the ECtHR to delimit positive obligations, see Lavrysen (n 3) ch 3, particularly at 158–66.

[138] See, for example, *Volodina* (n 19) paras 77–78, referring to the requirement of an 'adequate legal framework' and 'adequate legal mechanisms'.

[139] See, among a vast array of case law, *Volodina* (n 19) para 87; *M v Italy and Bulgaria* (n 117) para 99; *Muradova v Azerbaijan* (2011) 52 EHRR 41, paras 101, 124.

carries the implication that positive obligations are bounded by what may reasonably be expected of State authorities in the particular context at issue. At the same time, the term 'adequate' conveys that, although not boundless, the State's positive obligations must still reach a level of effort and efficacy that can be considered adequate in view of the imperative of securing 'practical and effective protection'[140] and in light of the importance of what Article 3 is meant to safeguard.

As mentioned above, positive obligations under Article 3 are not boundless. The Court has repeatedly highlighted, in determining the scope of operational duties in particular, that

> [b]earing in mind the difficulties in policing modern societies, the unpredictability of human conduct and the operational choices which must be made in terms of priorities and resources, the scope of this positive obligation must … be interpreted in a way which does not impose an impossible or disproportionate burden on the authorities.[141]

Tom Hickman has observed that, in relation to positive obligations under Article 3 (as well as Article 2) ECHR, 'a standard of reasonableness appropriately accommodates conflicting concerns and constraints on state action'.[142] Indeed, a number of limiting factors can be ascertained in the delimitation of positive obligations through the 'reasonableness' criterion, including competing claims to limited resources, as well as negative obligations under the Convention. Considerations of (im)possibility[143] (ought implies can) and good faith[144] are also at play in the Court's specification of positive obligations.

When potential positive acts to protect individuals from Article 3 ill-treatment involve the utilisation of limited resources, competing claims to these limited resources, including claims arising from other rights or *others'* rights, are relevant in delimiting the scope of what action can appropriately be required of the State in the particular circumstances. Accordingly, when positive action that may protect individuals has significant resource implications, the Court is prepared to make concessions to proportionality or 'fair balance'[145] considerations in the allocation of scarce resources. In this way, the Court acknowledges the challenges and limits involved even in efforts to maximise protection in the context of limited resources,

[140] *Valiulienė* (n 11) para 75.

[141] *Đorđević v Croatia* App no 41526/10 (ECtHR, 24 July 2012), para 139. See also *Galotskin v Greece* App no 2945/07 (ECtHR, 14 January 2010), para 36. See, similarly, in relation to Art 2, *Opuz* (n 17) para 129; *Edwards v UK* (2002) 35 EHRR 19, para 55.

[142] TR Hickman, 'The Reasonableness Principle: Reassessing Its Place in the Public Sphere' (2004) 63(1) *Cambridge Law Journal* 166, 189. See also Lavrysen (n 18) 172. But see the nuanced discussion in V Stoyanova, 'Common Law Tort of Negligence as a Tool for Deconstructing Positive Obligations under the European Convention on Human Rights' (2020) 24 *International Journal of Human Rights* 632, 646–47 (accessed online, 3 January 2020).

[143] This is evident in the 'impossible or disproportionate burden' narrative (text to n 141).

[144] See, for example, *MP and others v Bulgaria* App no 22457/08 (ECtHR, 15 November 2011), para 113; *Talpis v Italy* App no 41237/14 (ECtHR, 2 March 2017), para 128.

[145] Lavrysen (n 3) 172–79.

as well as the complex character of polycentric decision making.[146] The Court applies both substantive and institutional restraint, acknowledging the limits of what is possible and appropriate as well as the limits of its own competence in determining this in a context of polycentric demands, when it declares that it must refrain from imposing an 'impossible or disproportionate burden' on State authorities.[147]

Cases relating to healthcare are indicative of the Court's sensitivity to the challenges raised by limited resources and polycentricity.[148] For example, in its assessment of the merits in *RR v Poland*, where the applicant successfully argued that the failure to provide her with relevant pre-natal testing and lawful abortion access violated Article 3, the Court noted:

> [It] has not been argued, let alone *shown*, that at the material time genetic testing as such was unavailable for lack of equipment, medical expertise or funding. On no occasion was the applicant told that it was impossible to carry out the tests for any kind of technical or material reasons (emphasis added).[149]

Two things appear implicit in the Court's reasoning. One is that the Court may be prepared to entertain considerations such as lack of equipment or other technical or material constraints in delimiting the scope of the positive obligations in a given case. The other clear implication, however, is that relevant medical measures will be expected where such constraints have not been shown to be present. This means that there is an onus on the State to show that it has made adequate efforts, and any omission in requisite healthcare was reasonable in the circumstances. The relevant circumstances should arguably encompass any other reasonable measures that were pursued or in place.

It is noteworthy, however, that the Court takes a firmer stance in the prison context, where control and proximity are heightened, and where the line between subjection to, and failure to protect from, inhumanity and degradation is more difficult to draw. The Court demands that imprisoned individuals are held in conditions that are 'compatible with human dignity',[150] delineates robust requirements by way of medical provision,[151] and has indicated that 'lack of resources

146 For some arguments against undue judicial restraint in the context of polycentricity, see J King, 'The Pervasiveness of Polycentricity' [2008] *Public Law* 101.

147 See text to n 141 above.

148 The polycentric nature of healthcare-related decisions is highlighted in D Feldman, 'The Contribution of Human Rights to Improving Public Health' (2006) 120 *Public Health* 61, 67. Keith Syrett points to the need for rationing in healthcare decision-making: 'In view of the fact of scarcity, [rationing] will necessarily carry the consequence that some individuals will only secure access to the resource in question after others have already done so, and may not obtain access at all if the resources has already been exhausted', K Syrett, *Law, Legitimacy and the Rationing of Health Care: A Contextual and Comparative Perspective* (Cambridge University Press 2007) 16.

149 *RR v Poland* (n 32) para 155.

150 See, for example, *Mouisel v France* App no 67263/01 (ECtHR, 14 November 2002), para 48.

151 See, for example, *Rooman* (n 28) paras 142–48; Koch (n 28) 90–102.

cannot in principle justify prison conditions which are so poor as to reach the threshold of treatment contrary to Article 3 of the Convention'.[152]

Indicating its application of a degree of institutional restraint, the Court has mentioned the margin of appreciation in a number of Article 3 positive obligations cases,[153] though without fully elaborating what it entails in this area.[154] For example, in *Valiulienė v Lithuania*, a case concerning the prosecution of domestic violence, the Court stated that

> within the limits of the Convention, the choice of the means to secure compliance with Article 3 in the sphere of the relations of individuals between themselves is in principle a matter that falls within the domestic authorities' margin of appreciation, provided that criminal-law mechanisms are available to the victim.[155]

Yet although the Court may not always readily dictate the particular means by which the State is to secure protection from ill-treatment,[156] it does not tend to use the margin of appreciation as a basis on which to refrain from rigorous scrutiny of the adequacy of measures taken and thus to carve out a space in which positive obligations are simply left to the judgement or sovereign will of the State.[157] In *Valiulienė*, for example, it underlined the need for criminal law mechanisms, undertook an assessment of the adequacy of the measures taken, and found the State action lacking. It highlighted that it

> cannot accept that the purpose of effective protection against acts of ill-treatment is achieved where the criminal proceedings are discontinued owing to the fact that the

[152] See, for example, *Orchowski v Poland* App no 17885/04 (ECtHR, 22 October 2009), para 153, noted in L-A Sicilianos, 'The European Court of Human Rights at a Time of Crisis in Europe' (2016) 2 *European Human Rights Law Review* 121, 123–24.

[153] See, for instance, *Beganović* (n 129) para 80; *Valiulienė* (n 11) para 85; *Wenner* (n 13) para 61.

[154] Leijten (n 73) 292.

[155] *Valiulienė* (n 11) para 85.

[156] On the operation of the margin of appreciation in this manner in positive obligations case law, see J Kratochvíl, 'The Inflation of the Margin of Appreciation by the European Court of Human Rights' (2011) 29 *Netherlands Quarterly of Human Rights* 324, 333–34. The nuanced operation (encompassing merits reasoning and non-merits reasoning) of the margin of appreciation in such contexts is considered in OM Arnardóttir, 'Rethinking the Two Margins of Appreciation' (2016) 12 *European Constitutional Law Review* 27, 44–45, citing *Beganović* (n 129) para 80. See, too, the consideration of the margin's application and the operation of deference in relation to positive obligations under Arts 2 and 3 ECHR in J Gerards, 'Margin of Appreciation and Incrementalism in the Case Law of the European Court of Human Rights' (2018) 18 *Human Rights Law Review* 495, 501.

[157] Indeed, this leads Jan Kratochvíl to suggest that reference to the margin of appreciation in such case law may even be redundant: Kratochvíl (n 156) 334. On the broader function of the margin of appreciation in ECtHR doctrine see, among many, HC Yourow, *The Margin of Appreciation Doctrine in the Dynamics of European Human Rights Jurisprudence* (Martinus Nijhoff 1996); Y Arai-Takahashi, *The Margin of Appreciation Doctrine and the Principle of Proportionality in the Jurisprudence of the ECHR* (Intersentia 2002); A Legg, *The Margin of Appreciation in International Human Rights Law* (Oxford University Press 2012). But note the nuanced account of the margin of appreciation in Arnardóttir (n 156).

> prosecution has become time-barred and where this has occurred … as a result of the flaws in the actions of the relevant State authorities,[158]

concluding that the State had not provided 'adequate protection to the applicant against acts of violence'.[159] This shows that any latitude allowed is ultimately subject to a robust adequacy check by the Court.

The Court completely refrained from mentioning the margin of appreciation in the more recent domestic violence case of *Volodina*, where it conducted a methodical assessment of the State's discharge of its general, operational and investigative obligations, and found Russian authorities' actions inadequate on all fronts.[160] In *Wenner v Germany*, where the Court held that refusing to provide drug-substitution therapy to a prisoner violated Article 3, it indicated that while a margin of appreciation applied to the determination of appropriate therapeutic treatment, the Court 'has to determine whether the respondent State has provided credible and convincing evidence proving that the applicant's state of health and the appropriate treatment were adequately assessed and that the applicant subsequently received comprehensive and adequate medical care in detention'.[161]

Although the ECtHR may therefore allow States some leeway in determining the particular measures to be taken, it conducts a robust check on effort, procedure and (potential as well as actual) effectiveness – as well as, often implicitly, good faith – under the reasonableness and adequacy criteria. There is, moreover, an additional and crucial dimension to the Court's assessment of States' efforts: the overarching imperative of non-discrimination requires that States discharge their positive obligations without discrimination.[162] Indeed, the ECtHR has found violations of Article 14 ECHR in conjunction with Article 3 ECHR in circumstances where discrimination – or 'large-scale structural bias'[163] – could be attached to shortcomings in protective measures,[164] or where the ill-treatment's (suspected) discriminatory motive has been inadequately investigated.[165]

[158] *Valiulienė* (n 11) para 85.
[159] ibid para 86.
[160] *Volodina* (n 19) paras 76–102; see also *Talpis* (n 144).
[161] *Wenner* (n 13) para 62.
[162] See Art 14 ECHR: 'The enjoyment of the rights and freedoms set forth in this Convention shall be secured without discrimination on any ground such as sex, race, colour, language, religion, political or other opinion, national or social origin, association with a national minority, property, birth or other status'. On the requirement to discharge positive obligations without discrimination, see J-F Akandji-Kombe, *Positive obligations under the European Convention on Human Rights: A guide to the implementation of the European Convention on Human Rights* (Council of Europe 2007) 58.
[163] *Volodina* (n 19) para 114.
[164] See, for example, the domestic violence cases of *Opuz* (n 17) paras 177–202; *Talpis* (n 144) paras 133–49; *Volodina* (n 19) paras 103–33; see also the Court's findings in respect of a religiously motivated attack in *Members of the Gldani Congregation of Jehovah's Witnesses* (n 57) paras 138–42.
[165] See, for example, *Petropoulou-Tsakiris v Greece* (2009) 48 EHRR 47, paras 56–66; *Škorjanec v Croatia* (2018) 66 EHRR 14, paras 50–72; *Identoba and others v Georgia* (2018) 66 EHRR 17, paras 75–81.

What the Court requires States to do on the basis of the Convention must also be within the bounds of what is lawful under the Convention.[166] The Court has, in this regard, indicated that a 'relevant consideration' in delimiting operational duties is

> the need to ensure that the police exercise their powers to control and prevent crime in a manner which fully respects the due process and other guarantees which legitimately place restraints on the scope of their action to investigate crime and bring offenders to justice, including the guarantees contained in arts 5 and 8 of the Convention.[167]

Negative obligations – that is, what is prohibited – under the ECHR therefore limit what can fall within positive obligations under Article 3, although this is not always clearly articulated by the Court. The limit of intra-Convention lawfulness has two key implications. First, as argued in Chapters 2 and 3, positive obligations do not include duties to act in ways that are conclusively unlawful under the ECHR, such as inflicting torture or inhuman or degrading treatment or punishment.[168] For example, purporting to protect a kidnap victim by means of torturing a kidnap suspect, or purporting to protect prisoners from interpersonal violence by means of a blanket policy of total social isolation, would not be lawful under the Convention. Second, with respect to rights that may be lawfully infringed or derogated from, positive obligations may only extend to measures that amount to necessary and proportionate infringements on those rights, or that are strictly required by the exigencies of the emergency situation in circumstances of lawful derogation.

Regarding negative obligations under qualified rights, the proportionality test applicable in relation to interference with qualified rights may operate in line with the strong imperative of protecting persons under Article 3 in order to determine what positive action would be unlawful under the Convention, and accordingly to delimit positive obligations under Article 3. The terms 'rights of others' or 'rights and freedoms of others' best capture the legitimate aim applicable.[169] While the imperative of practical and effective protection under Article 3 ECHR is rightly recognised as forceful, the Court appears to be careful not to require States to take measures which disproportionately trespass on qualified rights under the ECHR.[170]

[166] See the analysis in Ch 3. See also N Mavronicola, 'What Is an "Absolute Right"? Deciphering Absoluteness in the Context of Article 3 of the European Convention on Human Rights' (2012) 12 *Human Rights Law Review* 723, 732; Mavronicola (n 2) 484.

[167] *Đorđević* (n 141) para 139; *Talpis* (n 144) para 101. See also the acknowledgement of the 'countervailing principle of respecting and preserving family life' in the child abuse case of *Z v UK* (n 8) para 73.

[168] See also Mavronicola (n 166) 732; Mavronicola (n 2) 483–85.

[169] See Lavrysen (n 3) 173.

[170] Nonetheless, there is controversy regarding the interplay between positive obligations' punitive edge and the right to a fair trial: see Pitcher (n 132).

Contemplating conflicts between absolute rights, including a conflict between the negative and positive obligations under Article 3 ECHR, Stijn Smet has also acknowledged the limits negative obligations set in the specification of positive obligations, suggesting that 'in cases of conflicts between absolute rights, negative obligations principally trump positive obligations'.[171] The terms 'conflict' and 'trump' can mislead, however: while the overarching duty to protect may be distilled into an extensive range of demands in respect of Article 3, these do not include a duty to ill-treat. Accordingly, there is no conflict of duties, and therefore no displacement.[172]

6.5. The Specification of Positive Obligations under Article 3 in Light of the Absoluteness Starting Point

The positive obligations arising under Article 3 are obligations to employ 'reasonable' and 'adequate' measures of protection and redress,[173] and it is understood that these may not guarantee that no ill-treatment takes place or that applicants' desired redress is always achieved.[174] However, the idea that Article 3 gives rise to positive obligations 'not of result, but of means',[175] as the Court puts it, does not entail *displacement* of the right or of the overarching requirement to take reasonable and adequate positive measures in respect of ill-treatment. As I argue in this section, the specification of positive obligations under Article 3 through the criteria of reasonableness and adequacy is not incompatible with the absolute character of the right.

The Court has indicated that

> [positive] obligations shall not, however, be interpreted as meaning that the State shall *guarantee* that ill-treatment is *never* inflicted or that criminal proceedings should necessarily lead to a sanction … Nevertheless the State shall be held liable in a situation if the domestic legal system fails to provide effective protection against violation of the rights enshrined by Article 3 … (emphasis added).[176]

Statements like this underline that the State is not automatically deemed responsible for every instance of ill-treatment suffered within its jurisdiction and that

[171] S Smet, 'Conflicts between Absolute Rights: A Reply to Steven Greer' (2013) 13 *Human Rights Law Review* 469, 469ff.

[172] See further Mavronicola (n 2) 482–85.

[173] See, for example, *Opuz* (n 17) paras 162 and 165.

[174] See, notably, the idea that, in respect of the duty to investigate and pursue redress, there is 'no absolute obligation for all prosecutions to result in conviction or in a particular sentence' put forward in *Ali and Ayşe Duran v Turkey* App no 42942/02 (ECtHR, 8 April 2008), para 61. In the application of Art 14 in conjunction with Art 3 ECHR in respect of the duty to investigate the discriminatory dimension(s) of an incident of ill-treatment, the Court has referred to the duty as 'not absolute', alongside indications that it is one of 'best endeavours': see *Beganović* (n 129) para 93.

[175] See, for example, *Cestaro* (n 92) para 215.

[176] *JL v Latvia* App no 23893/06 (ECtHR, 17 April 2012), para 67.

positive obligations under an absolute right do not – and cannot – guarantee that torture, inhumanity or degradation never occur or that relevant proceedings in response to suspected ill-treatment bring about the victim's desired result. At the same time, the Court is by no means suggesting that the State is absolved of its overarching duties to take adequate protective measures, such as maintaining a sufficiently effective legal framework for protection, in respect of inhumanity or degradation suffered within its jurisdiction. Accordingly, the right is not displaced by the delimitation of positive obligations through the criteria of reasonableness and adequacy. Rather, the right's correlative obligations – the precise contours of what one is entitled to by way of positive protective measures – are *specified* through these criteria.

The Court, therefore, holds the position that positive obligations are not boundless and cannot guarantee the desired outcome in all cases. At the same time, actual, alleged or potential victims maintain a non-displaceable entitlement to a reasonable and adequate level of protection mapping onto a typology of relevant duties. An attempt by a State to *extinguish* investigative duties in claims of ill-treatment in the context of immigration detention, for example, would not – and should not – survive ECtHR assessment. The criterion of reasonableness does not displace the duty to take protective action; rather, it delimits how far the State is obligated to go in its actions and, accordingly, serves to specify some actions as falling within the State's positive obligations, and others as falling outside the State's positive obligations in the case at hand.[177]

The specification of positive duties under Article 3 involves delimiting what States ought to do – and, in turn, the wrong of omitting to do it – by taking into account what States can, lawfully and reasonably, do.[178] The criterion of reasonableness acknowledges the limits on what may be appropriately demanded of States, not least by acknowledging the bounds of what is possible.[179] The Court also appears to acknowledge the polycentric nature of decisions involving the allocation of limited resources. At the same time, these considerations are subject to the Court's adequacy check, which places the onus on States to show robust good faith efforts that employ effective tools to secure the right. In this way, the ECtHR is effectively assessing, through relevant reasoning, whether State omissions amount to wrongful failings. In the reasoning of the Court, such wrongful failings arise where the State fails to take reasonable measures that are within its capacity and are capable of effectively protecting persons from ill-treatment. As highlighted

[177] See also Stoyanova (n 78) 325, fn 28; and ibid 281.
[178] S Palmer (n 28) 449.
[179] Patricia Smith comments that 'it is not reasonable to expect A to do s if A has no opportunity to do s, has no ability to do s, or has no way to know or no reason to believe that doing s is a possibility': P Smith, 'Feinberg and the Failure to Act' (2005) 11 *Legal Theory* 237, 239.

above, the extent of the positive measures demanded is appropriately layered and determined in a context-sensitive manner,[180] whereby obligations are heightened on the basis of control, proximity or vulnerability. Applied with significant emphasis being accorded to the imperative of effectively protecting individuals from torture, inhumanity and degradation, the limiting standard of reasonableness in conjunction with a rigorous check on adequacy can serve to specify positive obligations under Article 3 in an appropriate manner. While one might, and might rightly, disagree with the Court's concrete assessment, findings and conclusions in particular cases, the criteria of reasonableness and adequacy that it applies may be seen in principle as compatible with the legitimate specification requirements of relevant reasoning and non-displacement.

In respect of the capacity to guide, the specification of positive obligations combines the certainty challenges associated with the specification of torture and inhuman or degrading treatment or punishment with concerns surrounding the inevitably varied operation of the criteria of reasonableness and adequacy in delineating the context-sensitive measures demanded from case to case. Nonetheless, while the concepts of adequacy and reasonableness generally frame an *ex post facto* contextual assessment in the case law of the Court, they necessitate (and ought to be treated as necessitating) considerable *ex ante* efforts and vigilance on behalf of States. Inaction or inertia in respect of (risks of) Article 3 ill-treatment is not an option.[181] Moreover, as the case law on Article 3 continues to grow, the general parameters of different types of obligations are unpacked, concrete obligations in particular contexts are elucidated, and the 'teachability' of the Court's specification of positive obligations is strengthened. Furthermore, the Court's adoption of a methodical analysis in cases such as *Volodina*—discretely addressing distinct types of measures[182] – helps boost the doctrine's capacity to guide.

A key aspect of the Court's specification of positive obligations nonetheless amplifies concerns pertaining to uncertainty in the specification of Article 3 and raises questions regarding how far the particular positive duties the Court tends to recognise cohere with the spirit of Article 3 ECHR and the Convention more broadly: the obligations' coercive and carceral slant. The extent to which the Court ought to reconsider its enduring prioritisation of criminal law measures as a means of protection is therefore addressed briefly below.

[180] The context-sensitive operation of positive obligations is noted in H Keller and R Walther, 'Evasion of the International Law of State Responsibility? The ECtHR's Jurisprudence on Positive and Preventive Obligations under Article 3' (2019) *International Journal of Human Rights* (advance online access) 3.

[181] Indeed, the Court recognises that systemic 'passivity' may create a climate conducive to ill-treatment: see, on domestic violence and gender-based discrimination: *Talpis* (n 144) para 141.

[182] *Volodina* (n 19) paras 73–102.

6.6. Rethinking Positive Obligations' Coercive Orientation

There is considerable concern, voiced by Liora Lazarus and other authors, regarding positive obligations' tendency to operate as 'coercive duties', demanding the mobilisation of criminal law (enforcement) and indeed often equating such mobilisation with effective protection.[183] The coercive 'sting'[184] of positive obligations under Article 3 is evidenced in a substantial body of case law where the general positive duties are taken to pertain chiefly to the criminal law and its enforcement, the operational duties are taken to attach to police operations, and the investigative duty is taken to require a criminal investigation (capable of) leading to prosecution and, if appropriate, to punishment.[185]

The ECtHR's coercive focus in delineating positive obligations under Article 3 ECHR, tying them frequently and often exclusively to the mobilisation of criminal law (enforcement), raises several concerns. One key concern is the possibility of 'coercive overreach':[186] that the Court's doctrine may be read as demanding the penalisation of acts or omissions which might, as a matter of principle or policy, not necessarily warrant penal sanction. Consider, for example, the principle that for an investigation to be effective it is a 'prerequisite' for the State to have put in place criminal law provisions penalising 'practices that are contrary to Article 3'.[187] This is a sweeping stance, given that there are practices and situations that are contrary to Article 3 that may lack a criminal intent,[188] or which are part of diffuse and/or systemic problems within a particular domain of State law or policy, such as prison conditions.[189] Although there may be many instances of such situations where the culpability of an individual or individuals involved may reach a level that warrants civil and/or criminal liability, this is not necessarily so in all cases.[190] Moreover, we know that excessive use of force by law enforcement

[183] Lazarus (n 4). See also M Pinto, 'Sowing a "Culture of Conviction": What Shall Domestic Criminal Justice Systems Reap from Coercive Human Rights?' in Lavrysen and Mavronicola (eds) (n 93). For a critical examination of coercive duties also looking beyond the ECHR, see K Engle, 'Anti-Impunity and the Turn to Criminal Law in Human Rights' (2015) 100 *Cornell Law Review* 1069. See also the landmark article by Judge Tulkens, describing the 'sword' and 'shield' function of human rights law in the field of criminal justice as a paradox that one must come to terms with: F Tulkens, 'The Paradoxical Relationship between Criminal Law and Human Rights' (2011) 9 *Journal of International Criminal Justice* 577.

[184] Lazarus (n 4).

[185] See the discussion in Mavronicola (n 93).

[186] Lazarus (n 4) 145.

[187] *Cestaro* (n 92) para 209 (citations omitted).

[188] Intent to harm or inflict suffering or humiliation is not a necessary element of inhuman or degrading treatment or punishment. See, for example, *Korneykova and Korneykov v Ukraine* (2017) 64 EHRR 24, para 111; *MSS* (n 27) para 220; see also *V v UK* (2000) 30 EHRR 121, para 71.

[189] See Ch 5.

[190] Vladislava Stoyanova suggests that this speaks to a deeper problem, which she pithily captures in the following way: 'criminal law and international human rights law rest on two contradictory interpretative approaches: while the first forbids an expansive interpretation of norms, the second celebrates such expansions': Stoyanova (n 78) 336.

authorities – that is, force that was not indispensable in the circumstances – may be (rightly) found to be inhuman or degrading.[191] Although such excess may frequently involve a criminal level of culpability, this might not always be the case – the excessive force used may have stemmed from a genuine and reasonable mistake, general under-preparedness, lack of equipment,[192] or another factor that might reasonably be considered a basis for an exculpatory defence or mitigation of sentence in a State's criminal law.[193]

An additional concern in relation to the obligations' coercive reach relates to the implications of uncertainty for the autonomy of those persons who stand to be impacted upon by positive obligations' coercive slant. The element of uncertainty surrounding the delimitation of Article 3 ECHR, which may be broadly acceptable if not optimal as regards the regulation of *State* (in)action, becomes considerably more problematic where this delimitation has implications for individual criminal liability. If all wrongs proscribed under Article 3 are treated as criminal wrongs, such that Article 3 violations *align* with criminal liability, the uncertainty concerns raised in previous chapters deepen substantially. Insofar as the Court may mitigate its sweeping approach to alignment by focusing on 'wilful ill-treatment',[194] which seems to necessitate the mobilisation of mechanisms for establishing criminal liability, it is again not entirely clear – at least not to a standard of certainty that generally applies with respect to criminal offences – what is the *mens rea* that characterises what the ECtHR deems 'wilful ill-treatment'.

Most worryingly, the coercive approach to positive obligations has the potential to be damaging to protection against Article 3 ill-treatment. It can be damaging in a number of ways. First, given that the coercive approach to positive obligations often proceeds on the basis of aligning violations of the negative obligation with criminal liability, it raises the troubling prospect that Article 3 wrongs will be interpreted through a criminal lens, and thereby interpreted *narrowly*, potentially limiting the circumstances in which States are held to have violated Article 3 ECHR to circumstances encompassing criminal culpability.[195] In other words, treating Article 3 wrongs as necessarily involving criminally wrongful conduct raises a risk of under-inclusion. Alignment therefore gives rise to the concern that the Court may become more reluctant to recognise Article 3 violations in circumstances lacking criminally culpable behaviour. Should this path be followed, it is capable of eroding much of Article 3's protection in a range of contexts where inhumanity or degradation may be inflicted unintentionally, by virtue of a legal regime, or as a result of structural, systemic or diffuse problems, failings or errors.

[191] See, for example, *Güler and Öngel v Turkey* App nos 29612/05 and 30668/05 (ECtHR, 4 October 2011), paras 25–31.

[192] See, for example, *Boukrourou v France* App no 30059/15 (ECtHR, 16 November 2017) paras 87–88.

[193] For a related discussion on Art 2 ECHR, see N Mavronicola, 'Taking Life and Liberty Seriously: Reconsidering Criminal Liability under Article 2 of the ECHR' (2017) 80 *Modern Law Review* 1026.

[194] See, for example, *Gäfgen* (n 82) paras 116, 119.

[195] See the more widely applicable argument made in B Roth, 'Just Short of Torture: Abusive Treatment and the Limits of International Criminal Justice' (2008) 6 *Journal of International Criminal Justice* 215, 235; see also Mavronicola (n 93).

An example of this danger transpiring may arguably be found in the reasoning employed by the ECtHR in *Nicolae Virgiliu Tănase v Romania*, in which the Grand Chamber held that the duty to investigate under Article 3 was inapplicable to a negligent car accident involving private individuals. To arrive at this conclusion, the majority of the Grand Chamber reasoned that the factors contributing to the Article 3 threshold being reached 'presuppose that the treatment to which the victim was "subjected" was the consequence of an intentional act'[196] and held that

> bodily injuries and physical and mental suffering experienced by an individual following an accident which is merely the result of chance or negligent conduct cannot be considered as the consequence of 'treatment' to which that individual has been 'subjected' within the meaning of Article 3.[197]

The troubling implications of this reasoning are evident. In his vigorous criticism of the majority's reasoning in this case, Judge Kūris pointed specifically to prison conditions as a situation in which ill-treatment is not 'the consequence of an intentional act'.[198]

A second damaging aspect of the coercive orientation of positive obligations is the problem of diversion. In particular, a focus on criminal law tools in the delineation of positive obligations may wrongly overshadow or divert from practical and effective protective measures beyond the criminal law and its enforcement, not least measures capable of dismantling or alleviating the effects, systems and structures of abuse and victimisation. Such measures would include, for example, effective access to shelter, and to divorce, property, inheritance and child custody rights and related legal proceedings for (potential) victims of domestic violence.[199] An assessment of protective measures which solely homes in on criminal law mechanisms implicitly treats such non-coercive measures as peripheral, in spite of their protective potency. Additionally, delineating the investigative duty under Article 3 through a focus on identifying and *punishing* those responsible risks obscuring wider systemic issues – the 'rotten orchard',[200] as distinct from the 'bad apples'[201] – that may be relevant

[196] *Nicolae Virgiliu Tănase* (n 65) para 121.

[197] ibid para 123. For a forceful criticism of the majority's reasoning, see ibid, Partly Dissenting Opinion of Judge Kūris.

[198] ibid, Partly Dissenting Opinion of Judge Kūris, para 52. See also the critical analysis in N Bürli, 'Grand Chamber limits the scope of Article 3 for non-state ill-treatment', *Strasbourg Observers*, 3 September 2019, available at: https://strasbourgobservers.com/2019/09/03/grand-chamber-limits-the-scope-of-article-3-for-non-state-ill-treatment/ (accessed 3 January 2020).

[199] Report of the Special Rapporteur on Torture and Other Cruel, Inhuman or Degrading Treatment or Punishment, UN Doc A/74/148, 12 July 2019, para 73.

[200] M Punch, 'Rotten Orchards: "Pestilence", Police Misconduct and System Failure' (2003) 13 *Policing and Society* 171. For an important development of this idea with a focus on torture, see Danielle Celermajer's account of the 'ecology' of torture and the production of 'worlds of torture' in D Celermajer, *The Prevention of Torture: An Ecological Approach* (Cambridge University Press 2018), especially chs 3 and 4.

[201] But for an important argument on redressing the practices and structures of inhumanity at the border through *international* criminal law that partly responds to the 'bad apples' issue, see I Kalpouzos and I Mann, 'Banal Crimes against Humanity: The Case of Asylum Seekers in Greece' (2015) 16 *Melbourne Journal of International Law* 1.

to the violation at issue but also key to shaping practical and effective prevention efforts and guarantees of non-recurrence.[202]

Lastly, the coercive and carceral approach to positive obligations raises questions about the integrity of Article 3 ECHR. In particular, it requires us to interrogate how far such a firm alliance with coercive and carceral mechanisms coheres with the essence of Article 3 and the ECHR more broadly, given the centrality of human dignity and human freedom to the ECHR edifice,[203] and the multiple and pervasive ways in which States' penal systems often challenge these fundamentals. The specification of Article 3 ECHR makes clear some of these challenges: from the excessive use of force inflicted all too regularly by law enforcement officials, to the undue punitiveness located in life imprisonment without the possibility of parole, and the degradation that is rife in many prison systems across the Council of Europe and beyond. There is therefore a profound tension, if not contradiction, between the interventions made on the basis of Article 3 and human dignity to soften the edge of State penality, and the coercive push, in positive obligations doctrine, to sharpen it.

Upholding Article 3's integrity requires the Court to employ greater caution against both undue coercion through Article 3 and the undue narrowing of Article 3. It also calls for the ECtHR to acknowledge that, while the mobilisation of the criminal law may be partly effective towards preventing torture and other forms of criminally culpable ill-treatment,[204] criminalisation and criminal redress may in some circumstances not be necessary, and will in most if not all circumstances not be *sufficient* for preventing ill-treatment or indeed more generally protecting (potential) victims of ill-treatment.[205] Indeed, criminalisation, criminal law enforcement and criminal redress may address only a fraction of what are often substantial obstacles or shortcomings in protecting persons from ill-treatment. Accordingly, a fundamentally protective (re-)orientation is warranted in the specification of Article 3's positive obligations, looking beyond the criminal law and criminal process in identifying reasonable and adequate safeguards against ill-treatment, and delivering accountability and redress in a manner that addresses the structural and systemic backdrop against which the violation(s) occurred. It is to be hoped that both litigants and the Court seek such a protective (re-)orientation in the specification of Article 3's positive obligations.

[202] See, on this, the Report of the Special Rapporteur on Torture and Other Cruel, Inhuman or Degrading Treatment or Punishment, UN Doc A/HRC/19/61, 18 January 2012, para 52.

[203] As the ECtHR has put it, 'the very essence of the Convention is respect for human dignity and human freedom': *Pretty* (n 15) para 65.

[204] See R Carver and L Handley, *Does Torture Prevention Work?* (Liverpool University Press 2016) ch 3; F Laguardia, 'Deterring Torture: The Preventive Power of Criminal Law and its Promise for Inhibiting State Abuses' (2017) 39 *Human Rights Quarterly* 189.

[205] On the insufficiency of the criminal law approach to prevention, see Celermajer (n 200) 320–21. See, too, the discussion in V Stoyanova, 'Separating Protection from the Exigencies of the Criminal Law: Achievements and Challenges under Article 4 ECHR' in Lavrysen and Mavronicola (eds) (n 93).

6.7. Conclusion

Although positive obligations under Article 3 are not, and cannot be, boundless, they make considerable demands of States in an array of contexts, requiring the pursuit, in good faith, of practical and effective measures, which are delimited by a context-sensitive application of criteria of reasonableness and adequacy, yielding distinct requirements in different circumstances. As argued in this chapter, applying criteria of reasonableness and adequacy in a context-specific manner is, in principle, an appropriate approach to determining the wrongfulness of State omissions under Article 3, and does not displace the right to which these obligations correspond. Moreover, the constraint of lawfulness within the ECHR clarifies that human rights such as Article 3 ECHR are not, through the flawed notion of allegedly unbounded positive obligations, to become a rhetorical vehicle for their own destruction: there is no duty, therefore, to torture a kidnap suspect even as there are manifold duties to take measures protective of his victim.

While the criteria of reasonableness and adequacy shaping the ECtHR's delimitation of positive obligations do not, in my view, contradict the absoluteness starting point, there are troubling elements in significant 'pockets' of the Court's doctrine. In particular, the ECtHR can further elucidate its doctrine in relation to positive obligations in circumstances of socio-economic need, and can do so through a greater preparedness to recognise State 'indifference' – that is, refusal or failure to take reasonable and adequate protective action – towards the hardship endured in circumstances where persons' most basic needs are not being met as being contrary to Article 3 ECHR. Moreover, integrity demands that the ECtHR reconsider, and re-orientate, the often coercive and carceral slant of its positive obligations doctrine, in the spirit of human dignity and of the 'practical and effective' protection that positive obligations are meant to provide.

7

Specifying the *Non-Refoulement* Duty under Article 3 ECHR

7.1. Introduction

The (specification of the) ban on expelling or removing – whether by deportation, extradition, pushback or otherwise – individuals to places where they face a real risk of torture or inhuman or degrading treatment or punishment under Article 3 ECHR has attracted both political discontent[1] and academic critique.[2] The *non-refoulement* duty's significance for those on Europe's periphery (of concern) and its concurrent contestation by powerful forces make its examination an important element of this study. While this chapter does not purport to offer a complete justification or comprehensive analysis of the obligation against expulsion (taken to encompass extradition for the purposes of this chapter[3]) – which will also be referred to as the *non-refoulement* duty – under Article 3 ECHR, it seeks to elucidate the central obligation at issue and to assess its specification in light of the absolute character of the right and the legitimate specification criteria. As jurisdiction is not a focal point of the book, this chapter does not delve into questions surrounding jurisdiction, focusing on the delineation of the obligation against expulsion in circumstances where jurisdiction is established.[4]

[1] Such discontent has been longstanding. See, for example, BBC News, 'Blair "to amend human rights law"', 14 May 2006, available at: http://news.bbc.co.uk/1/hi/uk/4770231.stm (accessed 3 January 2020); M Elliott, 'Torture, Deportation and Extra-judicial Detention: Instruments of the "War on Terror"' (2009) 68 *Cambridge Law Journal* 245, 245.

[2] See, for example, J Finnis, 'Absolute Rights: Some Problems Illustrated' (2016) 61 *The American Journal of Jurisprudence* 195; M Bossuyt, 'The Court of Strasbourg Acting as an Asylum Court' (2012) 8 *European Constitutional Law Review* 203; H Battjes, 'In Search of a Fair Balance: The Absolute Character of the Prohibition of *Refoulement* under Article 3 ECHR Reassessed' (2009) 22 *Leiden Journal of International Law* 583. See also the nuanced critical reflections in K Greenman, 'A Castle Built on Sand? Article 3 ECHR and the Source of Risk in Non-Refoulement Obligations in International Law' (2015) 27 *International Journal of Refugee Law* 264.

[3] In this chapter, I employ the terms 'expulsion' and 'removal' interchangeably and take both to encompass extradition. But see the nuance underlined in F de Weck, *Non-Refoulement under the European Convention on Human Rights and the UN Convention against Torture: The Assessment of Individual Complaints by the European Court of Human Rights under Article 3 ECHR and the United Nations Committee against Torture under Article 3 CAT* (Brill 2016) 9.

[4] On *non-refoulement* and jurisdiction under the ECHR, see C Costello, *The Human Rights of Migrants and Refugees in European Law* (Oxford University Press 2015) 238–49. See also N Markard, 'The Right to Leave by Sea: Legal Limits on EU Migration Control by Third Countries' (2016) 27 *European Journal of International Law* 591.

7.2. The Nature of the Central Obligation

The *Soering* case forms the starting point of the application of Article 3 ECHR to the proposed removal of an individual to a State where that person faces a real risk of Article 3 ill-treatment. The real risk of ill-treatment in *Soering v UK* lay in the prospect of conviction for murder, capital punishment, and the devastating experience of the 'death row phenomenon'.[5] According to the ECtHR,

> the decision by a Contracting State to extradite a fugitive may give rise to an issue under Article 3, and hence engage the responsibility of that State under the Convention, where substantial grounds have been shown for believing that the person concerned, if extradited, faces a real risk of being subjected to torture or to inhuman or degrading treatment or punishment in the requesting country. The establishment of such responsibility inevitably involves an assessment of conditions in the requesting country against the standards of Article 3 of the Convention. Nonetheless, there is no question of adjudicating on or establishing the responsibility of the receiving country, whether under general international law, under the Convention or otherwise. In so far as any liability under the Convention is or may be incurred, it is liability incurred by the extraditing Contracting State by reason of its having taken action which has as a direct consequence the exposure of an individual to proscribed ill-treatment.[6]

The Court in *Soering* considered the express obligation under Article 3 of the UN Convention Against Torture not to expel, return or extradite a person to another State where there are substantial grounds for believing that he would be in danger of being subjected to torture, and found that the fact that a specialised treaty spelled out such an obligation 'does not mean that an essentially similar obligation is not already inherent in the general terms of Article 3 [ECHR]'.[7] It suggested that 'were a Contracting State knowingly to surrender a fugitive to another State where there were substantial grounds for believing that he would be in danger of being subjected to torture, however heinous the crime allegedly committed', this 'would plainly be contrary to the spirit and intendment' of Article 3 ECHR.[8] According to the Court, 'this inherent obligation not to extradite also extends to cases in which the fugitive would be faced in the receiving State by a real risk of exposure to inhuman or degrading treatment or punishment'.[9] Since *Soering*, the obligation against expulsion – including extradition – where substantial grounds have been shown for believing that the person concerned faces a real risk of torture or inhuman or degrading treatment or punishment in the destination State,

[5] *Soering v UK* (1989) 11 EHRR 439. See the discussion of the roots of the obligation in A Cassese, 'Prohibition of Torture and Inhuman or Degrading Treatment or Punishment' in RSJ MacDonald (ed), *The European System for the Protection of Human Rights* (Martinus Nijhoff 1993) 225.

[6] *Soering* (n 5) para 91.

[7] ibid para 88.

[8] ibid.

[9] ibid.

including ill-treatment at the hands of non-State actors, has come to be cemented in Article 3 case law.[10]

As *Soering* indicates, the basis for Article 3's engagement in expulsion decisions is that Article 3 protects individuals who are within a Contracting State's jurisdiction from the proscribed treatment, irrespective of whether the actual treatment occurs in the territory of the Contracting State or somewhere else at a later date.[11] In this context 'liability [is] incurred … by reason of … having taken action which has as a direct consequence the exposure of an individual to proscribed ill-treatment'.[12] The crux of the obligation is therefore a negative duty to refrain from action which places an individual at a particular, augmented risk of torture or inhuman or degrading treatment or punishment. The Court has stated that 'what is in issue here is the negative obligation not to expose persons to a risk of ill-treatment proscribed by Article 3'.[13] Kees Wouters has underlined that duties 'not to expel, deport, return, extradite or in any other way forcibly remove a person to a country where he will face a real risk of being subjected to proscribed ill-treatment' are all 'negative obligations on the State as they require the responsible State to refrain from acting'.[14] The central wrong at issue consists of taking coercive action which knowingly (encompassing actual or constructive knowledge, including by failure to ascertain risk) places someone at real risk of either torture or inhuman or degrading treatment or punishment. Because there is a knowledge dimension to the wrong at issue, the central obligation against removal entails, as Cathryn Costello highlights, 'various positive duties to assess the risk posed to the individual on removal'.[15]

A fundamental challenge involved in delineating and applying this obligation is that it encompasses establishing *prospective* ill-treatment. This was an important and novel aspect of the Court's *Soering* judgment. Taking the step of establishing prospective ill-treatment was justified by the ECtHR with reference to the imperative of averting serious and irreparable harm:

> It is not normally for the Convention institutions to pronounce on the existence or otherwise of potential violations of the Convention. However, where an applicant

[10] See the account provided in M-B Dembour, *When Humans Become Migrants: Study of the European Court of Human Rights with an Inter-American Counterpoint* (Oxford University Press 2015) ch 7. On the applicability of the *non-refoulement* duty to ill-treatment carried out by non-State actors see, for example, *HLR v France* (1998) 26 EHRR 29, para 40. The *non-refoulement* duty pertains both to the prospect of torture and to that of inhuman or degrading treatment or punishment: see, for example, *GS v Bulgaria* App no 36538/17 (ECtHR, 4 April 2019), para 81.

[11] K Wouters, *International Legal Standards for the Protection from Refoulement* (Intersentia 2009) 326–27.

[12] *Soering* (n 5) para 91. See also the recognition of 'indirect' consequence in cases such as *MSS v Belgium and Greece* (2011) 53 EHRR 2 and *Hirsi Jamaa v Italy* (2012) 55 EHRR 21.

[13] *Paposhvili v Belgium* App no 41738/10 (ECtHR, 13 December 2016), para 188.

[14] Wouters (n 11) 316 (citations omitted); *cf* Battjes (n 2). See the nuanced account in Costello (n 4) 191–92.

[15] Costello (n 4) 191. See, notably, *MA v Lithuania* App no 59793/17 (ECtHR, 11 December 2018), paras 103, 113–15; *Amerkhanov v Turkey* App no 16026/12 (ECtHR, 5 June 2018), paras 57–58.

> claims that a decision to extradite him would, if implemented, be contrary to Article 3 by reason of its foreseeable consequences in the requesting country, a departure from this principle is necessary, in view of the serious and irreparable nature of the alleged suffering risked, in order to ensure the effectiveness of the safeguard provided by that Article.[16]

The significance of effective protection rightly underpins this approach and underlines the importance of *ex ante* guidance on the substantive scope of Article 3 ECHR for the benefit of right-holders and norm-appliers.

Nonetheless, the conceptual basis or tenability of the relevant obligation(s) has been questioned. Hemme Battjes has suggested, for example, that the ECHR 'does not forbid expulsion' because, as a departure from 'the established principle that a state may control entry and residence of aliens on its territory', such a prohibition 'should be laid down *expressis verbis*'.[17] In a critical appraisal of the judgment in *Soering*, Battjes has also argued that 'Article 1 ECHR limits responsibility to "acts to persons within the territory" of the UK', and that accordingly the ECHR 'could not possibly apply to Soering's treatment in the USA'.[18]

There are various problems with the arguments put forward by Battjes. To begin with, the State's power to control the entry and residence of 'aliens' on its territory is, along with much else that the State is otherwise empowered to do, subject to human rights standards. As the Court has made clear, 'Contracting States have the right, as a matter of well-established international law and *subject to their treaty obligations including the Convention*, to control the entry, residence and expulsion of aliens' (emphasis added).[19] Furthermore, in respect of Article 1 ECHR, the wording of the Article entails responsibility to secure the rights of 'everyone within [a Contracting State's] jurisdiction' – not territory.[20] The obligation against expulsion operates in relation to individuals who *are* – at the point when the duty 'bites' – within a Contracting State's jurisdiction. Somewhat perplexingly, Battjes proceeds to acknowledge this.[21]

Along with Battjes, Kathryn Greenman has also interrogated the *implied* nature of the obligation against expulsion under Article 3 ECHR, suggesting that its foundations are thereby shaky: that it is a 'castle built on sand'.[22] The ECtHR has itself referred to the obligation as 'implied':

> [I]t is well established in the case law of the Court that expulsion by a Contracting State may give rise to an issue under Article 3, and hence engage the responsibility of that State under the Convention, where substantial grounds have been shown for

[16] *Soering* (n 5) para 90.

[17] H Battjes, 'Landmarks: Soering's Legacy' (2008) 1 *Amsterdam Law Forum* 139, 140.

[18] ibid 141.

[19] *Chahal v UK* (1997) 23 EHRR 413, para 73.

[20] Art 1 ECHR provides as follows: 'The High Contracting Parties shall secure to everyone within their jurisdiction the rights and freedoms defined in Section I of this Convention'.

[21] Battjes (n 17) 142.

[22] Greenman (n 2) 265. See also the discussion of purposive interpretation of Art 3 ECHR in Greenman (n 2) 277–78.

> believing that the person in question, if expelled, would face a real risk of being subjected to treatment contrary to Article 3 in the receiving country. In these circumstances, Article 3 *implies* the obligation not to expel the person in question to that country (emphasis added).[23]

Yet the significance of the fact that the obligation against expulsion is not expressly stipulated in Article 3 ECHR is overstated. Previous chapters have highlighted that distilling concrete rules and findings out of this overarching norm inevitably involves the specification of obligations which are not expressly 'enumerated' in its text. Expelling persons to places where they face a real risk of ill-treatment is one particular type of State wrong proscribed by Article 3. Consider, in a different context, obligations relating to the imposition of restrictive incarceration measures such as solitary confinement; in such cases, the Court has established that authorities are obligated to refrain from placing someone in a situation where they face a real risk of grave suffering or distress. This was the case in *Keenan v UK*, for example, where the Court assessed that forcibly placing a mentally ill person in solitary confinement 'may well have threatened his physical and moral resistance' and accordingly violated Article 3.[24] Indeed, the imperative of refraining from such action is heightened in circumstances where the act of placing persons in harm's way carries the element of irreversibility that expulsion does.

John Finnis has challenged the absolute character of the *non-refoulement* duty under Article 3 ECHR, arguing that absolutely proscribing action with reference to its 'unintended effects' is 'morally incoherent'.[25] Finnis sees an absolute ban on causing foreseeable but unintended side-effects as both logically and morally unsustainable, suggesting that it is capable of pulling the State in conflicting directions. He focuses particularly on the ECtHR's clarification in cases such as *Chahal v UK* that 'the activities of the individual in question, however undesirable or dangerous, cannot be a material consideration' towards displacing the obligation against expulsion.[26] His argument contemplates circumstances in which 'choosing non-removal imposes on citizens of the would-be removing state real risks of inhuman treatment or death broadly equivalent to or greater than the risks of inhuman treatment imposed on the persons removed',[27] and he concludes that this exposes the moral incoherence of the risk-based *non-refoulement* duty. This is a misleading argument. It miscasts the obligation at issue, given that the *non-refoulement* duty is a very specific obligation not to coercively place a person at a particular risk of ill-treatment of which the authorities know, or ought to know (or are indifferent to find out), with the attendant wrongfulness of such an act. On the other hand, while the State bears positive obligations to legislate and act against various risks of torture

[23] *Chahal* (n 19) para 74.
[24] *Keenan v UK* (2001) 33 EHRR 38, para 115.
[25] Finnis (n 2) 195.
[26] *Chahal* (n 19) para 80.
[27] Finnis (n 2) 206.

or ill-treatment, these obligations would not reasonably extend to duties to expel persons on the basis of a diffuse risk *supposedly* inhering in not expelling them. In terms of the logic of Finnis's argument in relation to persons who have in fact committed violent criminal offences, the supposed binary of choices he presents obscures the actions available to the State in respect of a person who has committed or is suspected of having committed serious criminal acts, and in relation to the prevention of criminal violence more broadly. Finally, and crucially, Finnis's argument relies on ascribing a general, augmented risk of violence to non-citizens. This renders his argument fundamentally dehumanising – elsewhere, he has alluded to this risk as relating to 'the importation of ebola or other plague, or of uncountable numbers of terrorists, or others, intent on overthrowing by force, or numbers, the state and the Convention'.[28] His argument is built on normatively setting apart – othering – those who stand to be protected from the *non-refoulement* duty under Article 3 ECHR. It is therefore not only unpersuasive, but starkly contradictory to the absolute and therefore unconditional character of Article 3 ECHR, and embodies a form of othering which is characteristic of the wrongs Article 3 proscribes.[29]

7.3. The *Non-Refoulement* Duty Seen Through the Applicability Parameter

The *non-refoulement* duty under Article 3 ECHR admits of no exceptions according to the ECtHR and pertains to every individual within a Contracting State's jurisdiction, including a suspected 'terrorist' or other allegedly 'undesirable' individual. This was clarified by the Court in *Chahal v UK*, which concerned the UK's attempts to deport a man considered to be a Sikh separatist to India, where he faced a real risk of Article 3 ill-treatment:

> The Court is well aware of the immense difficulties faced by States in modern times in protecting their communities from terrorist violence. However, even in these circumstances, the Convention prohibits in absolute terms torture or inhuman or degrading treatment or punishment, irrespective of the victim's conduct. Unlike most of the substantive clauses of the Convention … Article 3 makes no provision for exceptions and no derogation from it is permissible under Article 15 even in the event of a public emergency threatening the life of the nation …
>
> The prohibition provided by Article 3 against ill-treatment is equally absolute in expulsion cases. Thus, whenever substantial grounds have been shown for believing that an individual would face a real risk of being subjected to treatment contrary to Article 3 if

[28] J Finnis, 'Judicial Power: Past, Present and Future', 20 October 2015, 24–25, available at: http://judicialpowerproject.org.uk/wp-content/uploads/2015/10/John-Finnis-lecture-20102015.pdf (accessed 3 January 2020).

[29] See N Mavronicola, 'Torture and Othering' in B Goold and L Lazarus (eds), *Security and Human Rights* (Hart Publishing 2019).

> removed to another State, the responsibility of the Contracting State to safeguard him or her against such treatment is engaged in the event of expulsion. In these circumstances, the activities of the individual in question, however undesirable or dangerous, cannot be a material consideration.[30]

Chahal therefore reflects the three key elements of the absolute character of Article 3 ECHR as repeatedly affirmed by the ECtHR: Article 3 makes no provision for lawful exceptions – in contrast to many other provisions within the ECHR, there is no possibility of lawful interference that is 'necessary in a democratic society' for the fulfilment of a legitimate aim; Article 15 ECHR does not allow for any derogation from Article 3 even in the event of a public emergency threatening the life of the nation; and the protection of Article 3 applies irrespective of the victim's conduct.[31]

In the subsequent case of *Saadi v Italy*[32] (concerning the proposed deportation of a man suspected of involvement in international terrorism) the UK, as an intervening party, argued for a distinction to be made between treatment inflicted by a Contracting State's authorities and treatment inflicted by a non-Contracting State's authorities outside of a Contracting State's jurisdiction, suggesting the latter should be assessed through a balancing of interests. The UK attempted to import balancing into the *non-refoulement* parameter of Article 3 in two ways: by arguing in favour of weighing the risk of ill-treatment against the 'weighty' reasons for expulsion; and suggesting that stronger evidence of risk should be required where the person facing expulsion represents a threat to national security.[33] The Grand Chamber dismissed the UK government's arguments, affirming a clarification made in *Chahal*[34] that 'it is not possible to weigh the risk of ill-treatment against the reasons put forward for the expulsion in order to determine whether the responsibility of a state is engaged under art.3' and that accordingly 'the conduct of the person concerned, however undesirable or dangerous, cannot be taken into account' for such purposes.[35] The Court found the idea of balancing inapposite, indicating that the concept of 'risk' of ill-treatment on the one hand and the individual's dangerousness on the other 'do not lend themselves to a balancing test because they are notions that can only be assessed independently of each other', and underlining that an individual's dangerousness in no way reduces the risk that they will be ill-treated upon expulsion.[36]

[30] *Chahal* (n 19) paras 79–80 (citations omitted).

[31] See the analysis in Ch 2.

[32] *Saadi v Italy* (2009) 49 EHRR 30. The judgment attracted considerable commentary. See, for example, D Feldman, 'Deporting Suspected Terrorists to Face Torture' (2008) 67 *Cambridge Law Journal* 225; F de Londras, 'Saadi v Italy' (2008) 102 *American Journal of International Law* 616; D Moeckli, '*Saadi v Italy*: The Rules of the Game Have *Not* Changed' (2008) 8 *Human Rights Law Review* 534; G Gentili, 'European Court of Human Rights: An Absolute Ban on Deportation of Foreign Citizens to Countries where Torture or Ill-treatment is a Genuine Risk' (2010) 8 *International Journal of Constitutional Law* 311.

[33] *Saadi* (n 32) paras 117–23.

[34] *Chahal* (n 19) para 81.

[35] *Saadi* (n 32) para 138.

[36] ibid para 139.

The ECtHR in *Saadi* also rejected the argument that stronger evidence should be required to substantiate the risk of ill-treatment where the person at risk represents a national security threat, observing that 'such an approach is not compatible with the absolute nature of the protection afforded by art.3'.[37] It affirmed that an increase in the 'terrorist' threat after 9/11 could not modify the prohibition on expelling persons where substantial grounds have been shown that they face a real risk of proscribed ill-treatment in the destination State.[38] In a Concurring Opinion, Judge Zupančič suggested that a concession to the UK government's argument could only take place by maintaining that 'such individuals [as the applicant in *Saadi*] do not deserve human rights – the third-party intervener is unconsciously implying just that to a lesser degree – because they are less human'.[39]

The non-displaceable character of the *non-refoulement* obligation under Article 3, as affirmed in *Chahal* and *Saadi*, can be contrasted with the equivalent obligation under a qualified right such as Article 8 ECHR. Article 8 ECHR may be engaged in cases on expulsion which impact upon an individual's right to family life, for instance, but the State can bring forward justifications under Article 8(2) that fulfil the proportionality test under that provision and may thereby render expulsion lawful under the Convention.[40]

The absolute prohibition on *refoulement* under Article 3 ECHR has also been applied to removals occurring within the Council of Europe, in cases such as *MSS v Belgium and Greece*.[41] Given the dire conditions faced by asylum seekers in Greece, which were considered to breach Article 3 ECHR and of which the Belgian authorities were or ought to have been aware, the return by the Belgian authorities of an asylum seeker from Belgium to Greece under the Dublin II Regulation scheme of the European Union was found to be in breach of the prohibition on *refoulement* under Article 3 ECHR.[42]

[37] ibid para 140.

[38] ibid para 141.

[39] ibid, Concurring Opinion of Judge Zupančič.

[40] See, for instance, *Boultif v Switzerland* (2001) 33 EHRR 50, paras 39–56; see also *Üner v Netherlands* (2007) 45 EHRR 14, paras 54–67. Compare with the Art 3 case of *Ahmed v Austria* (1997) 24 EHRR 278, paras 38–47, and the extradition-related judgment in *Aswat v UK* (2014) 58 EHRR 1, paras 48–58. A margin of appreciation may also operate in respect of the proportionality assessment. See D Thym, 'Respect for Private and Family Life under Article 8 ECHR in Immigration Cases: a Human Right to Regularize Illegal Stay?' (2008) 57 *International & Comparative Law Quarterly* 87, 103–04.

[41] *MSS* (n 12). See also *Tarakhel v Switzerland* (2015) 60 EHRR 28.

[42] *MSS*, ibid paras 362–68. Conflicting legal obligations are trumped by the obligation against expulsion under Art 3 – as Wouters highlights, in *Soering* itself, the Court disregarded the 1972 Extradition Agreement between the UK and the USA, thus also 'circumventing the rule of lex posterior derogat legi priori', Wouters (n 11) 319.

7.4. The Specification of the *Non-Refoulement* Duty under Article 3 ECHR

As elaborated in previous chapters, Article 3 is specified in a context-sensitive manner. This raises particular problems in the application of the *non-refoulement* duty, since the Court is often called upon to determine the risk of a prospective breach of Article 3. The ECtHR's test – whether '*substantial grounds* have been shown for believing that an individual would face a *real risk* of being subjected to treatment contrary to Article 3' (emphasis added)[43] – adds further layers of uncertainty and heightens the potential for inconsistent application by State authorities. This is an important overarching issue in relation to the requirement of *ex ante* guidance that is encompassed in the legitimate specification criteria. With this noted as an overarching concern, this section examines thematic areas of significance and contention in the specification of the *non-refoulement* duty as they relate to the legitimate specification requirements of capacity to guide, non-distortion and non-displacement.

7.4.1. Relativism

A recurring issue of contention surrounding Article 3 is the question of 'relativism', particularly in connection with the 'relative' assessment involved in delineating the Article 3 'threshold'. As discussed in Chapter 5, the relative assessment involved in the specification of the Article 3 threshold does not necessarily amount to distortion or displacement of the right, insofar as it *relates* the specification of Article 3 to relevant contextual factors.[44]

However, relativism emerged in a more problematic manner in two ECtHR judgments concerning extradition to the US to face the prospect of grave punishment, notably life imprisonment without parole: *Harkins and Edwards v UK*[45] and *Babar Ahmad v UK*.[46] In its judgments in these cases, the ECtHR sought to clarify a number of distorting distinctions that had been employed by the UK House of Lords in the case of *Wellington*, which concerned Article 3's application to the proposed extradition of a murder suspect to face the prospect of life imprisonment without parole in the US.[47] Yet rather than eliminate the 'relativist' challenge in *Wellington*, the ECtHR in *Harkins* and *Ahmad* seemed, unfortunately, to repackage it.

In addressing the question of whether the extradition of the claimant to the US would violate Article 3 ECHR, the majority of the House of Lords in *Wellington*

[43] *Chahal* (n 19) para 80.

[44] See, further, Cathryn Costello's discussion of 'relativity' in Costello (n 4) 190–91.

[45] *Harkins and Edwards v UK* (2012) 55 EHRR 19.

[46] *Babar Ahmad v UK* (2013) 56 EHRR 1. See, further, N Mavronicola and F Messineo, 'Relatively Absolute? The Undermining of Article 3 ECHR in Ahmad v UK' (2013) 76 *Modern Law Review* 589.

[47] *R (Wellington) v Secretary of State for the Home Department* [2008] UKHL 72, [2009] 1 AC 335.

had appeared to adopt an approach to Article 3's requirements in the context of *extradition* which contradicted the absoluteness starting point. This approach stemmed from a reference to a dictum in the *Soering* judgment, which had clearly been rejected by the ECtHR in *Chahal*.[48] The relevant *Soering* dictum reads:

> [I]nherent in the whole of the Convention is a search for a fair balance between the demands of the general interest of the community and the requirements of the protection of the individual's fundamental rights. As movement about the world becomes easier and crime takes on a larger international dimension, it is increasingly in the interest of all nations that suspected offenders who flee abroad should be brought to justice. Conversely, the establishment of safe havens for fugitives would not only result in danger for the State obliged to harbour the protected person but also tend to undermine the foundations of extradition. These considerations must also be included among the factors to be taken into account in the interpretation and application of the notions of inhuman and degrading treatment or punishment in extradition cases.[49]

The ECtHR judgment in *Saadi*, preceding *Wellington* by a few months,[50] had included a clarification that

> the Court cannot accept the argument … that a distinction must be drawn under Article 3 between treatment inflicted directly by a signatory State and treatment that might be inflicted by the authorities of another State, and that protection against this latter form of ill-treatment should be weighed against the interests of the community as a whole.[51]

Nonetheless, in *Wellington* Lord Hoffmann relied on the ambiguity in *Soering* to suggest that a 'relativist'[52] standard applies in the extradition context, arguing that '[a] relativist approach to the scope of article 3 seems to me essential if extradition is to continue to function'.[53] The implication of this relativism, for Lord Hoffmann, was that

> in cases of *extradition*, article 3 does not apply as if the extraditing state were simply responsible for any punishment likely to be inflicted in the receiving state … [but] applies only in a modified form which takes into account the desirability of arrangements for extradition.[54]

This led Lord Hoffmann, with whom Lady Hale and Lord Carswell agreed, to hold that a 'heightened standard for contravention of article 3 [is applicable] to extradition cases'.[55]

[48] See *Chahal* (n 19) para 81.

[49] *Soering* (n 5) para 89, cited in *Wellington* (n 47) [23] (Lord Hoffmann), [50] (Lady Hale), [57] (Lord Carswell).

[50] *Saadi* (n 32) was decided on 28 February 2008. *Wellington* (n 47) was decided on 10 December 2008.

[51] *Saadi* (n 32) para 138.

[52] *Wellington* (n 47) [27] (Lord Hoffmann).

[53] ibid.

[54] ibid [22] (Lord Hoffmann).

[55] ibid [36] (Lord Hoffmann); *cf* ibid [37]–[47] (Lord Scott), [85]–[89] (Lord Brown).

Lord Hoffmann also reasoned that, while a real risk of *torture* brought about an absolute prohibition on removal, the position in respect of a real risk of inhuman and degrading treatment or punishment was 'more complicated'.[56] According to Lord Hoffmann, it was more complicated because the assessment of what constitutes such treatment must be made by reference to context, *including* the fact that the person might otherwise escape justice: that is, the desirability of extradition.[57] He concluded that '[p]unishment which counts as inhuman and degrading in the domestic context will not necessarily be so regarded when the extradition factor has been taken into account'.[58]

The judges who disagreed with Lord Hoffmann on this point, Lord Brown and Lord Scott, opposed the 'relativist' approach to Article 3. Lord Scott reasoned as follows:

> It is accepted that the absolute nature of the article 3 bar on torture would bar extradition to a country where the extradited person would face torture and that that which would constitute torture for article 3 purposes in Europe would constitute torture for those purposes everywhere. But it is suggested that treatment or punishment that might for article 3 purposes be inhuman or degrading in Europe would not necessarily need to be so categorised if it were treatment or punishment likely to be faced in the requesting country by a person faced with extradition to that country for crimes committed there. But, if that is so, how can it be said that article 3 rights not to be subjected to inhuman or degrading treatment are absolute rights?[59]

Indeed, Lord Hoffmann's relativist approach amounted to an attempt to adjust the substantive scope of proscribed ill-treatment on the basis of considerations which are irrelevant to the character of the ill-treatment at issue: essentially, to distort and effectively to displace the demands of Article 3 insofar as it was considered strongly desirable to do so. As Lord Brown argued, this relativist take on Article 3 was incompatible with the absolute character of the prohibition on *refoulement*, and both *Chahal* and *Saadi* confirmed this.[60]

Lord Scott rightly maintained that 'the standard of treatment or punishment apt to attract the adjectives "inhuman or degrading" for article 3 purposes ought to be a constant', indicating that he could 'not see how otherwise the article 3 prohibition regarding such treatment or punishment can be regarded as an absolute one'.[61] This position coheres with the legitimate specification requirements elaborated in previous chapters. An approach which varies the meaning of Article 3's terms simply on the basis of where the treatment is administered, or which (partly) displaces the prohibition on torture or inhuman or degrading treatment found in Article 3 on the basis of extraneous considerations (such as the desirability of extradition), contradicts the absoluteness starting point.

[56] ibid [23] (Lord Hoffmann).
[57] ibid [24] (Lord Hoffmann).
[58] ibid.
[59] ibid [40] (Lord Scott).
[60] ibid [85]–[87] (Lord Brown).
[61] ibid [41] (Lord Scott).

According to the ECtHR in *Ahmad* and *Harkins*, three distinctions had informed the relativist approach taken by the majority in *Wellington*:

(1) a distinction 'between extradition cases and other cases of removal from the territory of a Contracting State';
(2) a distinction 'between torture and other forms of ill-treatment proscribed by Article 3'; and
(3) a distinction 'between the assessment of the minimum level of severity required in the domestic context and the same assessment in the extra-territorial context'.[62]

In relation to the first distinction, the ECtHR was emphatic that 'the question whether there is a real risk of treatment contrary to Article 3 in another State cannot depend on the legal basis for removal to that State'.[63] Regarding the second distinction, the ECtHR acknowledged that it had 'always distinguished between torture on the one hand and inhuman or degrading punishment on the other',[64] but went on to clarify that, as repeatedly affirmed in relevant case law,[65] the obligation against expulsion did not vary based on whether the prospective treatment would amount to torture or to inhuman or degrading treatment or punishment.[66] Once a substantiated real risk of proscribed ill-treatment had been shown, expulsion would be found to be in breach of Article 3. The ECtHR accordingly appeared to dismiss Lord Hoffmann's relativist approach of adjusting, according to the desirability of extradition, the substantive reach of Article 3 or the degree of risk triggering the *non-refoulement* obligation – an approach which contradicted the absoluteness starting point and resembled the assessment of expulsion in relation to qualified rights such as Article 8 ECHR.[67]

Finally, addressing the third distinction, the ECtHR initially rejected the idea that the assessment of the 'minimum level of severity' test could vary between domestic and extra-territorial contexts. The ECtHR addressed paragraph 89 of *Soering*, which had formed a key premise for the majority's 'relativist' approach in *Wellington*, as follows:

> The Court recalls its statement in *Chahal* … that it was not to be inferred from paragraph 89 of Soering that there was any room for balancing the risk of ill-treatment

[62] *Ahmad* (n 46) para 167; *Harkins* (n 45) para 119.

[63] *Ahmad* (n 46) para 168; *Harkins* (n 45) para 120. In discussing the third distinction, the Court highlighted its unequivocal position in *Chahal* that the basis for seeking the extradition of an individual cannot be a 'balancing point' requiring a greater risk of Art 3 ill-treatment than in other expulsion cases before expulsion would be barred – *Chahal* (n 19) para 81, cited in *Ahmad*, para 172; *Harkins*, para 124.

[64] *Ahmad* (n 46) para 170; *Harkins* (n 45) para 122. While the facts in *Ahmad* and *Harkins* related to the prospect of punishment, it is not clear why the Court referred *only* to 'punishment'.

[65] The Court referred to a body of relevant case law including *Chahal* (n 19) para 80; *Mamatkulov and Askarov v Turkey* (2005) 41 EHRR 25, para 67; *Saadi* (n 32) para 125.

[66] *Ahmad* (n 46) para 171; *Harkins* (n 45) para 123.

[67] See, for instance, *Boultif* (n 40).

> against the reasons for expulsion in determining whether a State's responsibility under Article 3 was engaged. It also recalls that this statement was reaffirmed in *Saadi* … where the Court rejected the argument advanced by the United Kingdom Government that the risk of ill-treatment if a person is returned should be balanced against the danger he or she posed. In *Saadi* the Court also found that the concepts of risk and dangerousness did not lend themselves to a balancing test because they were 'notions that [could] only be assessed independently of each other' … The Court finds that the same approach must be taken to the assessment of whether the minimum level of severity has been met for the purposes of Article 3: this too can only be assessed independently of the reasons for removal or extradition.[68]

The Court thus appeared to reassert the absoluteness starting point by making it clear that any balancing act incorporating considerations of the public interest in, or desirability of, extradition does not pertain to the assessment of real risk or of whether the ill-treatment being risked crosses the Article 3 threshold. Highlighting that 'in the twenty-two years since the *Soering* judgment, in an Article 3 case the Court has never undertaken an examination of the proportionality of a proposed extradition or other form of removal from a Contracting State', it concluded that 'the Court must be taken to have departed from the approach contemplated by paragraphs 89 and 110 of the *Soering* judgment'.[69]

Yet relativism (re)surfaced a few paragraphs later in the ECtHR's reasoning:

> [T]he absolute nature of Article 3 does not mean that any form of ill-treatment will act as a bar to removal from a Contracting State … [T]his Court has repeatedly stated that the Convention does not purport to be a means of requiring the Contracting States to impose Convention standards on other States … This being so, treatment which might violate Article 3 because of an act or omission of a Contracting State might not attain the minimum level of severity which is required for there to be a violation of Article 3 in an expulsion or extradition case.[70]

This reasoning suggests that an act or omission amounting to proscribed ill-treatment in a Contracting State may *not* amount to proscribed ill-treatment when it occurs in a non-Contracting State, such as the US. Such reasoning distorts and partly displaces the obligation against expulsion under Article 3 ECHR.

It is worth reiterating that the obligation against expulsion is borne by a State that is legally subject to the ECHR and concerns a person who at the relevant time is or was within the Contracting State's jurisdiction. Its application therefore involves no legally dubious transfer of treaty obligations to a non-Contracting State, and no basis for adjusting the application of the Convention accordingly. Insofar as the Court's approach involves making the factor of geographic location determinant of the character of the prospective ill-treatment, this constitutes distortion rather than legitimate specification of the relevant wrongs. As Francesco

[68] *Ahmad* (n 46) para 172; *Harkins* (n 45) para 124.
[69] *Ahmad* (n 46) para 173; *Harkins* (n 45) para 125.
[70] *Ahmad* (n 46) para 177; *Harkins* (n 45) para 129.

Messineo and I have argued elsewhere,[71] geographic location is not a relevant factor in delineating torture, inhumanity or degradation: treatment is no more or less inhuman, degrading or torturous because of the colour of the individual's hair, what the perpetrators had for breakfast, or the territory where it occurs.[72] The idea that something that is inhuman or degrading if it takes place in the UK might not be inhuman or degrading if it takes place in the US is unsustainable. There is no scope in the legitimate specification of Article 3 for simultaneously embracing two opposing understandings of whether one and the same situation amounts to inhuman or degrading treatment or punishment. Lord Scott captured the issue aptly in advocating that 'the standard of treatment or punishment apt to attract the adjectives "inhuman or degrading" for article 3 purposes ought to be a constant', given that otherwise the prohibition loses its absolute character.[73]

Alternatively, although couched in rhetorical denial, the Court's reasoning in *Harkins* and *Ahmad* may be read as seeking covertly to (re-)incorporate balancing into extradition cases raising a real risk of proscribed treatment or punishment, effectively resurrecting paragraph 89 of *Soering* and weighing the desirability of extradition against the imperative of Article 3 ECHR.[74] Such a stance by the Court would clearly amount to partial displacement of the obligation at issue. It would also mean that the Court is fundamentally contradicting itself, given its vocal rejection of the 'balancing' argument in paragraph 89 of *Soering* in previous cases as well as in *Harkins* and *Ahmad* themselves.

Ultimately, the ECtHR has tended to avoid adopting the relativist stance that 'treatment which might violate Article 3 because of an act or omission of a Contracting State might not attain the minimum level of severity … in an expulsion or extradition case' in subsequent cases.[75] Moreover, the case law on the subject of irreducible whole life sentences has moved on since *Ahmad*, with the ECtHR in *Vinter v UK*[76] establishing that such sentences are incompatible with Article 3 ECHR upon their imposition and applying this finding in the extradition case of *Trabelsi v Belgium*.[77] In a Concurring Opinion in *Trabelsi*, Judge Yudkivska hailed *Trabelsi* as a 'welcomed departure from *Babar Ahmad and Others v. the United Kingdom*', observing

> that the Court's previous position to the effect that 'treatment which might violate Article 3 because of an act or omission of a Contracting State might not attain the

[71] Mavronicola and Messineo (n 46) 593–94.

[72] ibid 594. See *Saadi* (n 32) para 138, and the discussion below.

[73] *Wellington* (n 47) [41] (Lord Scott).

[74] Battjes suggests that this is a more accurate view of what the ECtHR is in fact doing in the expulsion cases, see Battjes (n 2) 583. See also E Lehto, 'Applicability of Article 3 of the European Convention on Human Rights at the Borders of Europe' (2018) 12 *Helsinki Law Review* 54, 69–70.

[75] Note, however, the mention of this idea in *Yefimova v Russia* App no 39786/09 (ECtHR, 19 February 2013), para 211, and *Aswat* (n 40) para 32; a finding distinct from that in *Ahmad* (n 46) was made in *Aswat* on the basis of the applicant's mental health condition: *Aswat*, para 57.

[76] *Vinter v UK* (2016) 63 EHRR 1.

[77] *Trabelsi v Belgium* (2015) 60 EHRR 21. But note the subsequent refusal of the ECtHR to apply the *Vinter* principles to the applicants in *Harkins*: see *Harkins and Edwards v UK* (2018) 66 EHRR SE5.

> minimum level of severity which is required for there to be a violation of Article 3 in an expulsion or extradition case' is not followed in these particular circumstances.[78]

As I hope the analysis above has demonstrated, the relativism in *Harkins* and *Ahmad* stands fundamentally at odds with the absoluteness starting point and must be explicitly abandoned.

7.4.2. The Challenge of Prospective Assessment

The expulsion context raises the additional challenge of assessing prospectively whether a situation violates Article 3. This is a challenge that is distinct from the speculative assessment of 'real risk' (considered below). It concerns the difficulty in assessing a set of even highly probable prospective circumstances *ex ante*.[79] This difficulty arises chiefly because of the Court's context-specific determination of whether something amounts to treatment proscribed by Article 3. The *ex post facto*, all-relevant-things-considered approach to the assessment of whether the Article 3 threshold has been crossed can be ill-suited to the assessment of a prospective state of affairs.

The issue was prominent in *Ahmad*,[80] which concerned the prospect of not only whole life imprisonment without parole, but also of incarceration in a super-max security prison ('ADX Florence'), and required the Court to assess whether the circumstances of incarceration in the super-max security prison would amount to inhuman or degrading treatment or punishment. The approach adopted by the Court in dealing with the difficulty involved in conducting a prospective assessment is problematic. The ECtHR initially outlined a number of factors that have been 'decisive' in finding breaches of Article 3 in circumstances of imprisonment. These included: duration; premeditation; an intention to debase or humiliate; and others.[81] The Court then stated: 'The Court would observe that all of these elements depend closely upon the facts of the case and so will not be readily established prospectively in an extradition or expulsion context'.[82] This suggests that, rather than erring on the side of caution, the Court is prepared to do the opposite: the margin of error it appears to allow for is one whereby it would be prepared to endorse someone's prospective subjection to inhuman or degrading treatment or punishment rather than too 'readily' to find such ill-treatment to be established prospectively.[83]

This reluctance to arrive at an affirmative conclusion that prospective circumstances are inhuman, degrading or constitutive of torture was reinforced by further problematic reasoning in *Ahmad*:

[78] *Trabelsi* (n 77), Concurring Opinion of Judge Yudkivska.
[79] *Trabelsi*, ibid para 130.
[80] *Ahmad* (n 46).
[81] See *Ahmad* (n 46) para 178. See also *Harkins* (n 45) para 130.
[82] *Ahmad* (n 46) para 178; *Harkins* (n 45) para 130.
[83] See also *Saadi* (n 32) para 142. But see *Paposhvili* (n 13) para 186.

> Finally, the Court reiterates that … it has been very cautious in finding that removal from the territory of a Contracting State would be contrary to Article 3 of the Convention. It has only rarely reached such a conclusion since adopting the *Chahal* judgment … The Court would further add that, save for cases involving the death penalty, it has even more rarely found that there would be a violation of Article 3 if an applicant were to be removed to a State which had a long history of respect of democracy, human rights and the rule of law.[84]

There is a striking presumption in this seemingly factual statement that a treatment or punishment likely to take place in a receiving State with an allegedly 'long history of respect of democracy, human rights and the rule of law' would very rarely cross the Article 3 threshold.[85] This stance does not sit well with the Court's emphasis on the need to ensure effective protection from ill-treatment,[86] given that it appears to enlarge the margin of error the Court signals it is comfortable with, and to do so on the basis of a generalised assessment that elides the context-sensitive approach that the Court otherwise adopts. It relies on a suspect distinction between 'good' States and 'bad' States,[87] along with an empirically dubious reference to the US's human rights record, particularly in relation to torture and ill-treatment.[88]

The uncertainty that might arise in conducting a prospective assessment serves to highlight the significance of guidance-orientated pronouncements by the ECtHR. At the same time, the prospective dimension of the assessment and the potential irreversibility of the act of expulsion and irreparability of what it potentially brings about should attract heightened vigilance and the readiness to err on the side of caution rather than on the side of abandoning individuals to the prospect of grave ill-treatment.[89] Erring on the side of caution aligns with the legitimate specification requirement of non-displacement: a margin of error in the opposite direction is effectively a window allowing for the de facto displacement of protection.

[84] *Ahmad* (n 46) para 179. See, previously, *Harkins* (n 45) para 131; see, subsequently, *Rrapo v Albania* App no 58555/10 (ECtHR, 25 September 2012), para 72; *Čalovskis v Latvia* App no 22205/13 (ECtHR, 24 July 2014), para 134; *Findikoglu v Germany* (Admissibility) App no 20672/15 (ECtHR, 7 June 2016), para 32.

[85] See also its implications for 'real risk' addressed below.

[86] *Soering* (n 5) para 90.

[87] Ralf Alleweldt forcefully dismissed the idea of a legally significant category of 'safe' countries in R Alleweldt, 'Protection Against Expulsion Under Article 3 of the European Convention on Human Rights' (1993) 4 *European Journal of International Law* 360, 372.

[88] See relevant judgments elaborating on the infliction of torture in a Contracting State's territory by agents of the US, as well as direct US involvement in the rendition of individuals, such as *El-Masri v Former Yugoslav Republic of Macedonia* (2013) 57 EHRR 25; *Al Nashiri v Poland* (2015) 60 EHRR 16. See, further, among many, KJ Greenberg and JL Dratel (eds), *The Torture Papers: The Road to Abu Ghraib* (Cambridge University Press 2005); LN Sadat, 'Extraordinary Rendition, Torture, and Other Nightmares from the War on Terror' (2007) 75 *George Washington Law Review* 1200; P Sands, *Torture Team: Deception, Cruelty and the Compromise of Law* (Allen Lane 2008); D Cole (ed), *The Torture Memos: Rationalising the Unthinkable* (The New Press 2009); C Banham, *Liberal Democracies and the Torture of Their Citizens* (Hart Publishing 2017) ch 4. See also, more generally, F de Londras, *Detention in the 'War on Terror': Can Human Rights Fight Back?* (Cambridge University Press 2011).

[89] See Dembour (n 10) 245. See, too, the Concurring Opinion of Judge Zupančič in *Saadi* (n 32), in which he stated that in the assessment of information pertaining to risk of ill-treatment 'the Court

7.4.3. The Prospect of Punishment

The prospect of facing punishment for particular conduct entails that penal proportionality and other penal justificatory reasoning may become live issues in some expulsion cases, and in particular in extradition cases. The application of these criteria to prospective punishment should *not* be equated to or mistaken for balancing the obligation not to expel against broad public interest concerns. Given the 'relativist' stance ultimately adopted in the judgment, and its apparent influence in *Harkins* and *Ahmad*, it is pertinent here briefly to revisit the UK judgment in *Wellington*, where Lady Hale confronted the complexity of assessing (prospective) punishment as follows:

> I agree, of course, that if there is substantial ground for believing that a person who is to be expelled from this country faces a real risk of being subjected to torture or to inhuman or degrading treatment in the country to which he is to be expelled, then his right not to be subjected to such treatment is absolute. It cannot be balanced against other considerations, including the real risk which he poses to the country from which he is to be expelled ... But the particular context of the case is important in assessing whether the treatment which he faces is indeed to be regarded as inhuman or degrading ... The references in *Saadi* ... to the irrelevance of the victim's conduct refer to the absolute nature of the prohibition once it has been determined that there is a real risk of treatment contrary to article 3. They do not cast doubt on the oft-repeated statements that the assessment of the minimum level of severity is relative ... Indeed, if the concept of proportionality in sentencing is relevant to the assessment of severity, then the conduct of which the prospective victim has been found guilty may be central to the assessment of whether the punishment is inhuman or degrading.[90]

Although not put in these terms, at the heart of Lady Hale's reasoning in this passage from *Wellington* is the question of the legitimate specification of inhuman or degrading punishment. As highlighted in Chapter 5, the particular character of 'punishment' brings in considerations which can include the *penal* concept of proportionality.[91] The ECtHR's repeated assertion that '[a]s the prohibition of torture and of inhuman or degrading treatment or punishment is absolute, irrespective of the victim's conduct, the nature of any offence allegedly committed by the applicant is therefore irrelevant for the purposes of Article 3'[92] reflects the applicability parameter of absoluteness. On the other hand, the specification of inhuman and degrading punishment can bring in considerations of proportionality as a penological principle relating to the offence committed by the individual.

must ... favour the security of the person being expelled'; and see *EG v UK* (2012) 54 EHRR 1, Joint Dissenting Opinion of Judges Garlicki and Kalaydjieva, paras 8–9. See, relatedly, Report of the Special Rapporteur on Torture and Other Cruel, Inhuman or Degrading Treatment or Punishment, UN Doc A/73/207, 20 July 2018, para 43.

[90] *Wellington* (n 47) [50]–[51] (Lady Hale).

[91] On proportionality in a penal context, see A Ristroph, 'Proportionality as a Principle of Limited Government' (2005) 55 *Duke Law Journal* 263.

[92] See, for example, *Al Saadoon and Mufdhi v UK* (2010) 51 EHRR 9, para 122.

The ECtHR has made the point that a grossly disproportionate sentence may cross the Article 3 threshold,[93] and has reiterated this in relevant extradition case law such as *Trabelsi*.[94] What is crucial is not to conflate the specific, nuanced determination of whether the sentence faced is grossly disproportionate in a *penal* sense, which amounts to legitimate specification,[95] with balancing writ large, which does not. While Lady Hale's above-quoted remarks about punishment did not engage in such conflation, her endorsement of Lord Hoffmann's relativist reasoning in *Wellington* may be contrasted with the nuance of these particular remarks.

7.4.4. *Non-Refoulement* and 'Naturally Occurring' Suffering: The 'Medical Cases'

The intersection between 'naturally occurring' suffering and the *non-refoulement* duty under Article 3 ECHR raises questions with respect to the absoluteness starting point, and these questions coalesce in what are often termed the 'medical cases'.[96] Battjes has argued: '[Absoluteness] means that no balancing of interests, hence no limitations or interferences, are allowed for in refoulement cases (*Saadi* and *Chahal*). But in medical cases, the absoluteness of the provision does not have this consequence'.[97] The key 'medical cases' Battjes was referring to are *D v UK*[98] and *N v UK*.[99] In brief, the cases concerned the expulsion of seriously ill persons to places where they were likely to face a significant reduction in (quality of) healthcare provision and the consequent health deterioration and suffering that this would entail. In *D v UK* the ECtHR found that the expulsion of a terminally ill person to face circumstances where he would almost completely lack care and support would violate Article 3; in *N v UK* the Court found that the expulsion of a seriously ill person to face a substantially lower standard of care leading to an early death would not violate Article 3. The Grand Chamber's judgment in *N v UK*, in particular, included references to the search for a 'fair balance' in the application of Article 3.[100]

The Grand Chamber's 'fair balance' rhetoric in *N v UK*, to which Battjes was referring, was explicitly linked to the delimitation of positive obligations under Article 3 ECHR:[101]

[93] See, for example, *Vinter* (n 76) para 102.

[94] *Trabelsi* (n 77) para 112; see also the more elaborate discussion – prior to *Vinter* (n 76) – of the gross disproportionality of life sentences in *Ahmad* (n 46) paras 226–44; and *Harkins* (n 45) paras 92–142.

[95] See, further, N Mavronicola, 'Crime, Punishment and Article 3 ECHR: Puzzles and Prospects of Applying an Absolute Right in a Penal Context' (2015) 15 *Human Rights Law Review* 721, 733–34.

[96] See, for example, Battjes (n 2); Greenman (n 2); V Stoyanova, 'How Exceptional Must "Very Exceptional" Be? *Non-Refoulement*, Socio-Economic Deprivation, and *Paposhvili v Belgium*' (2017) 29 *International Journal of Refugee Law* 580.

[97] Battjes (n 2) 598.

[98] *D v UK* (1997) 24 EHRR 423.

[99] *N v UK* (2008) 47 EHRR 39.

[100] ibid para 44.

[101] Battjes acknowledges this in 'In Search of a Fair Balance' (n 2) 600.

> [I]nherent in the whole of the Convention is a search for a fair balance between the demands of the general interest of the community and the requirements of the protection of the individual's fundamental rights … Article 3 does not place an obligation on the Contracting State to [provide] free and unlimited health care to all aliens without a right to stay within its jurisdiction. A finding to the contrary would place too great a burden on the Contracting States.[102]

The fact that in the above-quoted paragraph the Court cited the discredited paragraph 89 of *Soering*[103] and claimed that a search for a 'fair balance' is inherent in the *whole* of the Convention arguably amounts to rhetorical overreach in what might, in part, constitute relevant reasoning in the delimitation of positive obligations. As elaborated in Chapter 6, the delimitation of positive obligations under Article 3 appropriately encompasses considerations of competing claims to limited resources. Article 3 does not place an obligation to provide 'unlimited healthcare' because it requires reasonable rather than unlimited measures of protection. At the same time, it is important to take issue with the ECtHR's emphasis on 'aliens'. Discrimination on the basis of immigration status[104] in determining the substantive scope of positive obligations under Article 3 would run contrary to Article 3's unconditional character and amount to illegitimate specification.[105] As discussed in Chapter 6, 'reasonableness' and 'adequacy' – criteria through which positive obligations are delimited – may admit of a range of considerations. Nonetheless, they are not 'anything goes' criteria. In particular, they should not operate to *displace* protection for those deemed or perceived to be undeserving of protection, and they are constrained by considerations of lawfulness (within the legal framework of the Convention) that militate against exclusion on the basis of discriminatory grounds.[106]

With all of that said in respect of the delimitation of *positive* obligations under Article 3, it is important to revisit the Article 3 *non-refoulement* starting point:

> In so far as any liability under the Convention is or may be incurred, it is liability incurred by the Contracting State, by reason of its having taken action which has as a direct consequence the exposure of an individual to the risk of proscribed ill-treatment.[107]

[102] *N v UK* (n 99) para 44.

[103] *N v UK*, ibid para 44, includes a citation of *Soering* (n 5) para 89: 'inherent in the whole of the Convention is a search for a fair balance between the demands of the general interest of the community and the requirements of the protection of the individual's fundamental rights (see *Soering v. the United Kingdom* … §89)'. This is pointed out in Battjes (n 2) 598–99.

[104] On immigration status as a relevant status under Art 14 ECHR, see *Hode and Abdi v UK* (2013) 56 EHRR 27, paras 46–47.

[105] Note, in this regard, Dembour's argument that 'there is something highly objectionable in the way in which we take for granted that human beings can be treated differently according to the nationality (or lack of nationality) they happen to hold … [which] may one day come to be regarded as itself being inhuman and degrading', Dembour (n 10) 270. Note also the salient analysis in JA Sweeney, 'The Human Rights of Failed Asylum Seekers in the United Kingdom' [2008] *Public Law* 277, 294–96.

[106] Note, with reference to Art 2 ECHR, *Cyprus v Turkey* (2002) 35 EHRR 30, para 219: 'an issue may arise under Article 2 of the Convention where it is shown that the authorities of a Contracting State put an individual's life at risk through the denial of health care which they have undertaken to make available to the population generally'.

[107] *Saadi* (n 32) para 126.

The *non-refoulement* duty under Article 3 encapsulates a negative obligation, and the wrong at issue lies in the act of exposing an individual to the real risk of ill-treatment,[108] with actual or constructive knowledge of such risk. The principled basis for the obligation against expulsion under Article 3 ECHR may therefore be seen to be wider in scope than the expulsion context itself: the overarching duty is a duty not to wrong someone by knowingly exposing them to a real risk of proscribed ill-treatment. The prohibition of expulsion where substantial grounds have been shown that there is a real risk of proscribed ill-treatment in the destination State is just one instantiation of this broader duty. Acknowledging this also allows us to demystify *non-refoulement* under Article 3 ECHR: it is a concrete – and vital – specification of an overarching standard.

Once the act of removal to another State ceases to be exceptionalised, the possible variations of the wrongs at issue can be seen more clearly. A key insight that we may build from this de-exceptionalisation is that the act of expulsion can violate Article 3 by exposing a person to the real risk of torture or inhuman or degrading treatment or punishment *or* that, in some circumstances, expulsion can itself subject a person to inhumanity or degradation or amount to inhuman or degrading treatment.[109] This allows for a conceptual reconsideration of key 'medical cases' and what is at stake in the act of expulsion and its foreseeable and/or indeed inevitable consequences. Consider the facts of *D v UK*: the applicant, who was dying of AIDS-related causes, faced deportation to St Kitts, which would effectively entail coercively removing him from a situation in which he was receiving palliative care and support and placing him in a situation where he would receive neither and endure a particularly painful, and accelerated, end to his life. The Court found that his removal to face a deeply distressing death constituted inhuman treatment.[110]

The central question which arises in facts such as these is whether the coercive act of expulsion, on the basis of immigration status and/or criminality, which removes an ill person's subsisting healthcare, with the direct and foreseeable implication of bringing about grave pain or suffering and/or a serious health deterioration, is an act which subjects that person to inhumanity or degradation. The appropriate answer to that would be 'yes'. The act of expulsion in circumstances such as those in *D v UK* – and, for the dissenting judges in the case, *N v UK*[111] – subjects the individual expelled to inhumanity or degradation. The prohibition on expelling individuals in such circumstances is therefore an instantiation of States'

[108] *Salah Sheekh v Netherlands* (2007) 45 EHRR 50, para 136.

[109] See, further, the nuanced critical account of the (evolution of the) ECtHR's conceptualisation of the *non-refoulement* duty in Stoyanova (n 96).

[110] *D v UK* (n 98) para 53; *Paposhvili* (n 13) para 177.

[111] Judges Tulkens, Bonello and Spielmann in *N v UK* highlighted that 'suffering which flows from naturally occurring illness, physical or mental, may be covered by Article 3, where it is, or risks being, exacerbated by treatment, whether flowing from conditions of detention, *expulsion* or other measures, for which the authorities can be held responsible': *Pretty v UK* (2002) 35 EHRR 1 para 52 (emphasis added), cited in *N v UK* (n 99), Joint Dissenting Opinion of Judges Tulkens, Bonello and Spielmann, para 5.

negative obligations under Article 3. On this basis, the dissenting judges in *N v UK* were deeply critical of the balancing rhetoric and pragmatism that they identified as underpinning the majority judgment.[112] It is worth noting, in this regard, that the ECtHR rightly focused on the act of removal causing a deterioration in health in the extradition case of *Aswat v UK*. Haroon Aswat was able to show that he faced a prospect of a severe deterioration in his mental health following extradition to the US. On this basis, the act of coercively placing him in such circumstances would violate Article 3 ECHR.[113]

More recently, in *Paposhvili v Belgium*,[114] the Court revisited the 'medical cases' under Article 3 ECHR and, with a nod to *Aswat*, appeared to adopt a position of principle that acknowledges the act of expulsion as central to the wrong at issue. It affirmed that what is in issue is the expelling State's '*negative* obligation' (emphasis added)[115] and that central to delineating the wrong is 'the [health] impact of removal on the person concerned'.[116] It clarified that the inhuman or degrading treatment in such cases is not located in the 'lack of medical infrastructure in the receiving State', or in the failure to provide 'free and unlimited health care' by the returning State.[117] It is therefore *not* a matter of specifying States' positive obligations and the more wide-ranging criteria that this specification encompasses (to which the 'fair balance' rhetoric may be applicable).[118] Rather, according to the Court:

> The responsibility that is engaged under the Convention in cases of this type is that of the returning State, on account of an act – in this instance, expulsion – which would result in an individual being exposed to a risk of treatment prohibited by Article 3.[119]

Unfortunately, however, the Court's line-drawing in delimiting the *non-refoulement* duty in this area continues to encompass a tendency towards arbitrariness. *D v UK* sowed the seeds for this potential for arbitrariness in the determination of such cases. With much emphasis placed on States' right to control the 'entry, residence and expulsion of aliens' and the idea that 'aliens' who have served prison sentences and are subject to expulsion cannot claim an entitlement to remain in a Contracting State to continue to benefit from medical or social assistance,[120] the Court in *D v UK* repeatedly highlighted the 'exceptional' or '*very* exceptional' (emphasis added) circumstances of the case.[121] It found that 'in the very exceptional circumstances of this case and given the compelling humanitarian

[112] *N v UK* (n 99), Joint Dissenting Opinion of Judges Tulkens, Bonello and Spielmann, para 8.
[113] *Aswat* (n 40) para 57.
[114] *Paposhvili* (n 13).
[115] ibid para 188.
[116] ibid.
[117] ibid para 192.
[118] See Ch 6.
[119] *Paposhvili* (n 13) para 192.
[120] *D v UK* (n 98) para 53.
[121] ibid paras 53–54.

considerations at stake, it must be concluded that the implementation of the decision to remove the applicant would be a violation of Article 3'.[122] In *N v UK* the Court reasoned that there is a 'high threshold' set for Article 3 to apply in such cases[123] and cemented the exceptionality filter, indicating that

> the decision to remove an alien who is suffering from a serious mental or physical illness to a country where the facilities for the treatment of that illness are inferior to those available in the contracting state may raise an issue under Art.3, but only in a very exceptional case, where the humanitarian grounds against the removal are compelling.[124]

The 'very exceptional case' filter was applied in *N v UK* to conclude that the circumstances prevailing in the destination State for the applicant, who faced a real prospect of acute suffering and a rapid health deterioration in the destination State but was not as gravely ill as the applicant in *D v UK* at the time of the (proposed) expulsion, did not disclose 'very exceptional circumstances' of the kind present in the *D* case.[125] The exceptionality filter subsequently led to the dismissal, in admissibility decisions and judgments on the merits, of a range of applications to the Court.[126]

The Grand Chamber judgment in *Paposhvili v Belgium*[127] gave a slightly more expansive interpretation than the cases that preceded it had given to the elusive window of 'very exceptional cases' that might bar removal. The Court revisited the position in *N v UK* that

> in addition to situations of the kind addressed in *D*… in which death was imminent, there might be other very exceptional cases where the humanitarian considerations weighing against removal were equally compelling,[128]

and indicated that

> the 'other very exceptional cases' … which may raise an issue under Article 3 should be understood to refer to situations involving the removal of a seriously ill person in which substantial grounds have been shown for believing that he or she, although not at imminent risk of dying, would face a real risk, on account of the absence of appropriate treatment in the receiving country or the lack of access to such treatment, of being exposed to a serious, rapid and irreversible decline in his or her state of health resulting in intense suffering or to a significant reduction in life expectancy.[129]

[122] ibid para 54.
[123] *N v UK* (n 99) para 43.
[124] ibid para 42.
[125] ibid para 51.
[126] See, for example, *Tatar v Switzerland* (2016) 62 EHRR 11, paras 43, 50. Many more of these cases are cited in Stoyanova (n 96) 582, fn 10.
[127] *Paposhvili* (n 13).
[128] ibid para 178, referring to *N v UK* (n 99) para 43.
[129] ibid para 183.

The Grand Chamber in *Paposhvili* also demanded that States provide the procedural means to conduct the necessary assessment to determine such risk[130] and offered guidance on the criteria that should inform this assessment. It established that the sending State's authorities

> must verify on a case-by-case basis whether the care generally available in the receiving State is sufficient and appropriate in practice for the treatment of the applicant's illness so as to prevent him or her being exposed to treatment contrary to Article 3.[131]

They must also determine 'the extent to which the individual in question will actually have access to this care and these facilities in the receiving State',[132] with relevant criteria in this assessment including the cost of medication and treatment, the existence of a social and family network, and the distance to be travelled in order to have access to the required care.[133] If doubt persists, according to the Court, sending States must obtain 'individual and sufficient assurances' that the requisite healthcare will be available and accessible to the individual facing removal.[134] These principles have subsequently been applied to bar the removal from Denmark to Turkey, absent individual and reliable assurances, of a mentally ill person facing the prospect of gravely inadequate medical care and support and a consequent deterioration in his mental health in *Savran v Denmark*.[135]

Caution must be employed in hailing *Paposhvili* as a significant positive departure from the restrictive case law that preceded it.[136] It certainly extends the pre-existing understanding of 'very exceptional cases' and, crucially, places an onus on the sending State to ensure that the circumstances in which a person finds themselves in the receiving State are not inhuman or degrading. But the Court in *Paposhvili* did not wholly re-examine the doctrine's (problematic) focal points, notably the idea that a 'high threshold'[137] must be applied in the 'medical cases' on the expulsion of non-citizens, and the use of the exceptionality filter to delimit the duty not to expel.

130 ibid paras 185–87.

131 ibid para 189.

132 ibid para 190.

133 ibid.

134 ibid para 191.

135 *Savran v Denmark* App no 57467/15 (ECtHR, 1 October 2019). For an analysis of the significance of *Savran*, see M Klaassen, 'A new chapter on the deportation of ill persons and Article 3 ECHR: the European Court of Human Rights judgment in Savran v. Denmark', *Strasbourg Observers*, 17 October 2019, available at: https://strasbourgobservers.com/2019/10/17/a-new-chapter-on-the-deportation-of-ill-persons-and-article-3-echr-the-european-court-of-human-rights-judgment-in-savran-v-denmark/ (accessed 3 January 2020). See also, on the application of the procedural elements of *Paposhvili* in relation to the prospect of chain *refoulement*, *Ilias and Ahmed v Hungary* App no 47287/15 (ECtHR, 21 November 2019).

136 See Stoyanova (n 96).

137 *Paposhvili* (n 13) para 183. See also *Savran* (n 135) para 65, and the Joint Dissenting Opinion of Judges Kjølbro, Motoc and Mourou-Vikström.

The doctrine raises significant substantive concerns as well as uncertainty. In respect of the doctrine's capacity to guide, the 'standard' of exceptionality which characterised the case law until *Paposhvili* offered little by way of guidance, allowing case after case to be dismissed as being insufficiently 'exceptional', with the main benchmark being that it had to be more compelling from a humanitarian perspective than *N v UK*,[138] and preferably as compelling as the circumstances in *D v UK*.[139] The *Paposhvili* specification offers some further guidance in this regard, but retains the obscure exceptionality filter and associated 'high threshold' idea.

Substantively, the exceptionality filter does not align well with the legitimate specification criteria. Exceptionality appears simply to add an ill-defined layer to the 'minimum level of severity' threshold. As argued in Chapter 6, the reasoning of the ECtHR in determining whether positive obligations arise in relation to 'suffering which flows from a naturally occurring illness', to the effect that 'the threshold in such situations is high, because the alleged harm emanates not from acts or omissions of the authorities but from the illness itself',[140] is substantively suspect, indicative of a distortion or displacement of the right in its socio-economic application. After all, the same argument – that the harm did not emanate (directly) from acts or omissions of the authorities – could be made about ill-treatment at the hands of non-State actors, which clearly attracts positive obligations. In the context of the *refoulement* 'medical cases', the Court has justified the 'high threshold' in similar terms,[141] but put the issue more curtly in *Paposhivili*, speaking simply of 'a high threshold for the application of Article 3 of the Convention in cases concerning the removal of aliens suffering from serious illness'.[142] An important contextual factor therefore informs the exceptionality filter in the 'medical cases': the status of 'aliens'. There is an exclusionary dynamic to the setting apart of 'aliens suffering from serious illness': a heightened threshold whose rationale attaches to one's status as 'alien' entails a readiness to refuse 'aliens' a certain degree of protection under Article 3. Such othering can be viewed as fundamentally distorting and potentially partly displacing the protection of the right, and accordingly as running counter to the right's absolute character.

The fundamental wrong involved in the 'medical cases' warrants restatement. It is the wrong of taking coercive action (on the basis of immigration status and/or criminality) which removes an ill person's subsisting access to healthcare with the direct and foreseeable consequence of causing them grave pain or suffering and/or a serious health deterioration, with actual or constructive knowledge of this prospect, that violates Article 3. Relevant ECtHR case law on exposing persons to inhuman or degrading living conditions upon expulsion contains reasoning that acknowledges

[138] *N v UK* (n 99).

[139] *D v UK* (n 98).

[140] *Hristozov and others v Bulgaria* App nos 47039/11 and 358/12 (ECtHR, 13 November 2012), para 111.

[141] *N v UK* (n 99) para 43.

[142] *Paposhvili* (n 13) para 183.

that the wrong lies in the act of knowingly subjecting someone to (the prospect of) inhumanity or degradation. The delineation of the duty not to expel in cases such as *MSS v Belgium and Greece*[143] and *Tarakhel v Switzerland*[144] involved a more typical Article 3 severity assessment, with sensitivity to context and with some attention paid to the vulnerability experienced by asylum seekers and especially asylum-seeking children and their families.[145] The Court in *MSS* found Belgium to have violated Article 3 by knowingly exposing the applicant, through expelling him to Greece, to degrading conditions of detention and degrading living conditions; and found Greece to have subjected the applicant to degrading conditions of detention and to have exposed him to degrading living conditions.[146] The Court in *Tarakhel* found that the applicants' prospective removal to Italy risked exposing them to living conditions contrary to Article 3 ECHR.[147] As the Court put it in *Tarakhel*, 'the source of the risk does nothing to alter the level of protection guaranteed by the Convention or the Convention obligations of the state ordering the person's removal'.[148]

Ultimately, therefore, the Court is not grappling with what is demanded of the receiving State by way of positive or negative obligations (except in cases where the receiving State is also a Contracting State that the applicant argues has violated their rights). As the Court underlined in *Paposhvili*, what is at issue 'is the negative obligation not to expose persons to a risk of ill-treatment proscribed by Article 3'.[149] There should be no room for distorting or displacing this obligation through implicit or explicit balancing considerations or through the othering of its potential beneficiaries. The wrongful act is that of expulsion, which forcibly subjects or exposes the person expelled to (the prospect of) torture, inhumanity or degradation; and the ECtHR's doctrine in *refoulement* cases concerning 'naturally occurring' suffering ought to reflect that.

7.5. Real Risk

The Court has stipulated that expulsion is proscribed 'where substantial grounds have been shown for believing that the person concerned faces a real risk' of Article 3 ill-treatment in the destination State.[150] In broad terms, the 'substantial grounds' element may be taken to relate to matters of proof and process, while the 'real risk' element is the substantive standard at issue.

143 *MSS* (n 12).

144 *Tarakhel* (n 41).

145 See ibid paras 118–19; *MSS* (n 12) paras 251, 259, 263 (referred to in the Court's assessment of the act of expulsion at paras 366–67).

146 *MSS* (n 12) paras 362–68 and paras 205–264 respectively.

147 *Tarakhel* (n 41) paras 93–122.

148 ibid para 104. But see the dubious distinction drawn in *Sufi and Elmi v UK* (2012) 54 EHRR 9, paras 280–83, and *SHH v UK* (2013) 57 EHRR 18, paras 88–95, discussed in Costello (n 4) 188–90, 217–18.

149 *Paposhvili* (n 13) para 188.

150 *MSS* (n 12) para 365. See also *Hirsi Jamaa* (n 12) para 114.

7.5.1. Substantial Grounds, Knowledge and Process

The terminology of 'substantial grounds' appears at first sight to impose a significant burden on the person seeking to be spared from expulsion, and the Court has indicated that

> [i]t is in principle for the applicant to adduce evidence capable of proving that there are substantial grounds for believing that, if the measure complained of were to be implemented, he would be exposed to a real risk of being subjected to treatment contrary to Article 3.[151]

Nonetheless, in spite of this starting point, in many cases the Court tends to espouse and expect an approach of rigorous scrutiny, which encompasses the open, *ex nunc*[152] assessment of relevant information, including material obtained *ex proprio motu*.[153] As the Court put it in *Hirsi Jamaa v Italy*, '[i]n determining whether it has been shown that the applicant runs a real risk of suffering treatment proscribed by art.3, the Court will assess the issue in the light of all the material placed before it, or, if necessary, material obtained *proprio motu*', and its 'examination of the existence of a real risk of ill-treatment must necessarily be a rigorous one'.[154]

In *Paposhvili* the Court affirmed that, while 'it is for the applicants to adduce evidence *capable of demonstrating* that there are substantial grounds for believing that … they would be exposed to a real risk of being subjected to treatment contrary to Article 3' (emphasis added), this is 'not a matter of requiring the persons concerned to provide clear proof of their claim that they would be exposed to proscribed treatment'.[155] Moreover, where they adduce such evidence (that is, evidence capable of demonstrating substantial grounds), 'it is for the authorities of the returning State, in the context of domestic procedures, to dispel any doubts raised by it'.[156] This means that the risk alleged

> must be subjected to close scrutiny in the course of which the authorities in the returning State must consider the foreseeable consequences of removal for the individual concerned in the receiving State, in the light of the general situation there and the individual's personal circumstances,

and this close scrutiny must include a review of general sources of intergovernmental and 'reputable' non-governmental organisations.[157]

[151] *H and B v UK* App nos 70073/10 and 44539/11 (ECtHR, 9 April 2013), para 91.
[152] *JK v Sweden* (2017) 64 EHRR 15, para 83.
[153] See, for example, *Cruz Varas v Sweden* (1992) 14 EHRR 1, para 75.
[154] *Hirsi Jamaa* (n 12) para 116 (citations omitted).
[155] *Paposhvili* (n 13) para 186.
[156] ibid para 187.
[157] ibid.

As outlined above, the wrong involved in Article 3-incompatible expulsion encompasses actual or constructive knowledge of (or indifference towards ascertaining) the prospect, or real risk, of ill-treatment. The procedural demands made of Contracting States by the ECtHR in ascertaining risk draw a vital link between the element of *knowing* the real risk and enabling such real risk to be (made) known. The case law clearly establishes that 'no questions asked' practices of expulsion – whether they amount to mass or indiscriminate expulsion or summary processes – do the opposite of absolving States of the wrong of *refoulement*.[158] Rather, the Court requires there to be a process involving a 'thorough and individualised examination of the situation of the person concerned'.[159] The link between knowing the risk and enabling the risk to be made known translates into a robust procedural duty, which demands that the applicant be given the opportunity to adduce relevant evidence and that a thorough and individualised risk assessment be conducted. Moreover, the evidentiary burden can vary according to what is being alleged and the information available:

> [In] relation to asylum claims based on a well-known general risk, when information about such a risk is freely ascertainable from a wide number of sources, the obligations incumbent on the States under Articles 2 and 3 of the Convention in expulsion cases entail that the authorities carry out an assessment of that risk of their own motion …
>
> By contrast, in relation to asylum claims based on an individual risk, it must be for the person seeking asylum to rely on and to substantiate such a risk. Accordingly, if an applicant chooses not to rely on or disclose a specific individual ground for asylum by deliberately refraining from mentioning it, be it religious or political beliefs, sexual orientation or other grounds, the State concerned cannot be expected to discover this ground by itself. However, considering the absolute nature of the rights guaranteed under Articles 2 and 3 of the Convention, and having regard to the position of vulnerability that asylum seekers often find themselves in, if a Contracting State is made aware of facts, relating to a specific individual, that could expose him to a risk of ill-treatment in breach of the said provisions upon returning to the country in question, the obligations incumbent on the States under Articles 2 and 3 of the Convention entail that the authorities carry out an assessment of that risk of their own motion. This applies in particular to situations where the national authorities have been made aware of the fact that the asylum seeker may, plausibly, be a member of a group systematically exposed to a practice of ill-treatment and there are serious reasons to believe in the existence of the practice in question and in his or her membership of the group concerned …[160]

Accordingly, the Court's context-sensitive approach operates to distribute evidentiary burdens with due consideration of relevant circumstances, including the particular vulnerabilities at play. Further, the Court has stipulated, often applying Article 13 in conjunction with Article 3 ECHR, that allegations of a real risk

[158] See, notably, *MA v Lithuania* (n 15) paras 103, 113–15; *Amerkhanov* (n 15) paras 57–58. Note also Art 4 of Protocol 4 to the ECHR and the (qualified) safeguards in Art 1 of Protocol 7 to the ECHR.

[159] *Tarakhel* (n 41) para 104.

[160] *FG v Sweden* App no 43611/11 (ECtHR, 23 March 2016), paras 126–27 (citations omitted).

of ill-treatment 'must imperatively be subject to close scrutiny by a "national authority"'[161] that is capable of triggering suspensive measures: that is, measures suspending enforcement of any expulsion decision where the real risk of inhuman or degrading treatment is established.[162]

In assessing relevant country reports, the Court has refused to consider that the mere existence of domestic laws or the ratification of human rights treaties can refute the reality depicted by overwhelmingly damning reports.[163] This is a manifestation of the Court's awareness of the real limitations of law's promise of protection in view of poor enforcement in practice.[164]

On this brief and necessarily non-exhaustive account, a few observations may be made. The context-sensitive, nuanced demands being made of States in the evidential context are, in principle, appropriately tied to the character of the wrong at issue. The specification of a procedural assessment for establishing substantial grounds of real risk rightly views ascertaining risk as a *sine qua non* of discharging the overarching duty. The Court accordingly compels States to deliver procedures which engage with all the relevant factors in assessing the prospect of ill-treatment. Moreover, the Court's adjustment of evidentiary expectations and burdens in recognition of applicants' vulnerability and the fundamental asymmetry of power between State authorities and persons facing expulsion suggests a recognition – though, arguably, not a perfectly concretised one – of the asymmetrical relationships and contexts of othering in which violations of human dignity tend to occur.[165] With this said, it is important to note, and endorse, Vladislava Stoyanova's concern that the procedural requirements outlined in judgments such as *Paposhvili* can operate as a means of sidelining the Court's substantive oversight of expulsion decisions,[166] and Marie-Benedicte Dembour's indictment of the way the Court has often apportioned credibility in a way disproportionately favourable to State authorities and unfavourable to applicants.[167]

7.5.2. Determining 'Real Risk'

There is no simple determinant of 'real risk'. Some principles informing this standard have, nonetheless, emerged. For example, despite some initial doctrine to that

[161] *Tarakhel* (n 41) para 126; *Hirsi Jamaa* (n 12) para 198.

[162] See, for example, *Tarakhel* (n 41) para 104.

[163] *Hirsi Jamaa* (n 12) para 128.

[164] Note, in this regard, N Grief and M Addo, 'Some Practical Issues Affecting the Notion of Absolute Right in Article 3 ECHR' (1998) 23 *European Law Review* 17.

[165] See Ch 3.

[166] Stoyanova (n 96) 610–14. See also V Stoyanova, 'The Grand Chamber Judgment in Ilias and Ahmed v Hungary: Immigration Detention and how the Ground beneath our Feet Continues to Erode', *Strasbourg Observers*, 23 December 2019, available at: https://strasbourgobservers.com/2019/12/23/the-grand-chamber-judgment-in-ilias-and-ahmed-v-hungary-immigration-detention-and-how-the-ground-beneath-our-feet-continues-to-erode/ (accessed 3 January 2020).

[167] Dembour (n 10) ch 7; but note her discussion of the Court's approach in *MSS* (n 12) in ch 12. *Cf* M Bossuyt, 'Judges on Thin Ice: The European Court of Human Rights and the Treatment of Asylum Seekers' (2010) 3 *Inter-American and European Human Rights Journal* 3.

effect,[168] the ECtHR has made it clear that 'real risk' does not always necessitate a risk particular to the individual that exceeds even a substantial risk stemming from a general situation of violence, inhumanity or degradation.[169] The Court clarified this in *Sufi and Elmi v UK*, affirming that a previous decision in *Vilvarajah v UK*[170]

> should not be interpreted so as to require an applicant to show the existence of special distinguishing features if he could otherwise show that the general situation of violence in the country of destination was of a sufficient level of intensity to create a real risk that any removal to that country would violate art.3 of the Convention.[171]

The Court rightly considered that to insist in such cases that the applicant show special distinguishing features would render Article 3's protection 'illusory' and call into question its absolute character.[172] Accordingly, a general situation of violence, inhumanity or degradation can fulfil the 'real risk' criterion.[173] The Court has also clarified that membership of a (vulnerable) group of persons that faces a systemic or constant risk of Article 3 ill-treatment in the relevant State can satisfy the 'real risk' requirement.[174]

The ECtHR also recognises that chain *refoulement*, that is, expulsion to a place where there is a real risk of expulsion to face a real risk of ill-treatment, violates Article 3.[175] In *MSS*, for example, the Court found a real risk of chain *refoulement* on the return of the applicant by Belgium to Greece, based on the systemic inadequacy of asylum claim procedures in Greece, which entailed that 'at the time of the applicant's expulsion the Belgian authorities knew or ought to have known that he had no guarantee that his asylum application would be seriously examined by the Greek authorities'.[176] In response to the Belgian government's argument that the applicant had not sufficiently individualised the risk of having no access to the asylum procedure and of being sent back to Afghanistan by the Greek authorities, the Court indicated that the onus was on the Belgian authorities, in light of the systemically problematic circumstances prevailing in Greece, 'not merely to assume that the applicant would be treated in conformity with the Convention standards but, on the contrary, to first verify how the Greek authorities applied their legislation on asylum in practice'.[177] Again, it is evident that the plight of the individual at issue does not have to be 'special' in the sense of being

[168] See, for instance, *Vilvarajah v UK* (1992) 14 EHRR 248, para 111.

[169] See, for instance, *Sufi and Elmi* (n 148). See also *MSS* (n 12) para 359.

[170] *Vilvarajah* (n 168).

[171] *Sufi and Elmi* (n 148) para 217 (citations omitted), citing *Vilvarajah* (n 168) and *NA v UK* (2009) 48 EHRR 15. But note *JK v Sweden* (n 152) para 94.

[172] *Sufi and Elmi*, ibid para 217. See, further, N Mole and C Meredith, *Asylum and the European Convention on Human Rights* (Council of Europe 2010) 42–46.

[173] See, too, *MSS* (n 12) para 359. See the nuanced discussion in Costello (n 4) 193–94.

[174] See, for instance, *Ergashev v Russia* App no 49747/11 (ECtHR, 16 October 2012); *FG v Sweden* (n 160), especially paras 120, 156–58.

[175] *MSS* (n 12).

[176] ibid para 358.

[177] ibid para 359.

both particular to the individuals and heightened vis-à-vis other people placed in similar circumstances. As the Court clarified in *MSS*: 'The fact that a large number of asylum seekers in Greece find themselves in the same situation as the applicant does not make the risk concerned any less individual where it is sufficiently real and probable ….'[178] It is the reality of the danger, rather than its uniqueness, which is key to the 'real risk' requirement.

Furthermore, the Court has reasoned that a real risk of ill-treatment at the hands of non-State actors will be taken to subsist where 'the authorities of the receiving state are not able to obviate the risk by providing appropriate protection'.[179] It follows that this would also apply when the receiving State's authorities have been shown not to be willing[180] to obviate the risk in question by providing appropriate protection. The focal point remains the reality of the risk and how far it is likely to be alleviated.

While it is not clear what level of probability is represented by 'real risk', it can be extrapolated from the case law that it is more than 'mere possibility',[181] but less than the balance of probabilities (or 'more likely than not'), given that an attempt by the UK government to argue for the latter was not accepted in *Saadi*.[182] It may also be assumed that a level of risk which is (virtually) identical to that subsisting in the sending State will generally not be sufficient to bar expulsion, except in certain circumstances involving chain *refoulement*.[183]

Mark Elliott has suggested that the 'real risk' requirement represents an offsetting of the interest in not being ill-treated:

> Not all risks of ill-treatment will prevent deportation; only real risks will have such an effect – a distinction that implies the Court is prepared to countenance a degree of offsetting of the individual's interest in not being ill-treated against the state's interest in removing non-nationals from its territory.[184]

It is correct that the individual's 'interest' in not being ill-treated is not expected to be secured *exhaustively* under Article 3, or under Article 3's obligations on expulsion – Article 3's absolute character does not entail a factual guarantee that no one will be subjected to torture or to inhuman or degrading treatment or punishment, and this is the case in respect of exposure to risk (including through acts other than expulsion). The wrong at issue in *refoulement* cases is that of taking action which exposes persons to an amplified risk of ill-treatment compared to the

[178] ibid para 359.

[179] *Hirsi Jamaa* (n 12) para 120. See also *HLR* (n 10) para 40; *Sufi and Elmi* (n 148) para 213; *NA v UK* (n 171) para 110; *JK v Sweden* (n 152) para 80; *SHH v UK* (2013) 57 EHRR 18, para 70; *JH v UK* (2012) 55 EHRR 27, para 51; *AA and others v Sweden* App no 14499/09 (ECtHR, 28 June 2012), para 72.

[180] See *JK v Sweden* (n 152), Concurring Opinion of Judge O'Leary, para 8.

[181] *Vilvarajah* (n 168) para 111.

[182] *Saadi* (n 32) paras 122, 130–31.

[183] See the two layers of risk in relation to Greece in *MSS* (n 12).

[184] M Elliott, 'The "War on Terror", UK-style – The Detention and Deportation of Suspected Terrorists' (2010) 8 *International Journal of Constitutional Law* 131, 139.

one subsisting prior to such action. The specification of the wrong at issue in these terms delineates circumstances in which individuals are wronged by forcible exposure to augmented risk, and does not thereby amount to a partial displacement of the right. This, of course, by no means entails that we should refrain from critically interrogating the quality of the Court's concrete assessments of real risk and the potentially flawed assumptions, reasoning or outcomes involved therein.[185]

7.5.3. Balancing Risk Against Extraneous Considerations

The need to distinguish between relevant and irrelevant reasoning becomes particularly pronounced in the ECtHR's response to States' attempts to introduce a 'balancing' or trade-off between extraneous considerations militating in favour of expulsion and the degree of risk that operates to bar expulsion. For example, in *Saadi v Italy* the Court rejected the UK government's argument that greater risk should be required where there is a threat to national security associated with the individual's presence in the expelling State.[186] In doing so, the ECtHR underlined that public interest considerations (purportedly) militating in favour of expulsion did not pertain to the question of risk of ill-treatment and were therefore not relevant to the specification and application of 'real risk':

> The Court considers that the argument based on the balancing of the risk of harm if the person is sent back against the dangerousness he or she represents to the community if not sent back is misconceived. The concepts of 'risk' and 'dangerousness' in this context do not lend themselves to a balancing test because they are notions that can only be assessed independently of each other. Either the evidence adduced before the Court reveals that there is a substantial risk if the person is sent back or it does not. The prospect that he may pose a serious threat to the community if not returned does not reduce in any way the degree of risk of ill treatment that the person may be subject to on return. For that reason it would be incorrect to require a higher standard of proof ... where the person is considered to represent a serious danger to the community, since assessment of the level of risk is independent of such a test ... With regard to the second branch of the UK Government's arguments, to the effect that where an applicant presents a threat to national security, stronger evidence must be adduced to prove that there is a risk of ill-treatment, the Court observes that such an approach is not compatible with the absolute nature of the protection afforded by art.3 either.[187]

The Court has accordingly affirmed that the question of real risk is not properly addressed by reasoning which is in reality orientated at denting or displacing the

[185] See, for example, F Vogelaar, 'Principles Corroborated by Practice? The Use of Country of Origin Information by the European Court of Human Rights in the Assessment of a Real Risk of a Violation of the Prohibition of Torture, Inhuman and Degrading Treatment' (2016) 18 *European Journal of Migration and Law* 302.

[186] See *Saadi* (n 32) para 122.

[187] ibid paras 139–40.

obligation against expulsion.[188] There is no room for balancing either the severity of the prospective treatment[189] *or* the degree of risk of such ill-treatment on the one hand, with the desirability of expulsion on the other. This clarification coheres with the legitimate specification requirements of relevant reasoning and non-displacement. Even while in some case law the application of Article 3 to concrete scenarios in the context of expulsion may have followed dubious reasoning or indeed come to the wrong conclusions,[190] the rejection of balancing in the assessment of risk coheres with the requirements of non-displacement and relevant reasoning.[191] Nonetheless, it is important to acknowledge that the case law does not necessarily provide optimal guidance as to what will make out real risk, or disclose an entirely transparent and consistent approach to assessing real risk from case to case.[192]

7.5.4. Diplomatic Assurances

Diplomatic assurances are a mechanism used to alleviate a substantiated real risk, through an undertaking by the receiving State's authorities to refrain from torture or inhuman or degrading treatment or punishment and/or to take steps to protect the individual from torture, inhumanity or degradation. Diplomatic assurances are often provided in the form of Memoranda of Understanding (MoUs) or similar diplomatic agreements.[193] Colin Warbrick has pointed out that such non-binding agreements tend to be negotiated with States which also have treaty obligations in relation to torture and ill-treatment; but, he highlights, they are clearly needed only where there is a significant risk, based on concrete evidence, that the relevant State will not comply, and most likely *is not* complying, with its treaty obligations.[194] Accordingly, as Warbrick sees it, '[i]t is hard to understand why a non-binding obligation might assure more faithful discharge of the State's duties'.[195] Reflecting

[188] See, further, Gentili (n 32).

[189] But see the clarification/contradiction dynamic in *Harkins* (n 45) and *Ahmad* (n 46), discussed above.

[190] Besides *Harkins* (n 45) and *Ahmad* (n 46), see also the critical account of the Court's reasoning and findings in its rejection of a number of Art 3 asylum claims by gay and lesbian persons in P Johnson and S Falcetta, 'Sexual Orientation Discrimination and Article 3 of the European Convention on Human Rights: Developing the Protection of Sexual Minorities' (2018) 43 *European Law Review* 167, 178–81; see also S Falcetta and P Johnson, 'Migration, Sexual Orientation, and the European Convention on Human Rights' (2018) 32 *Journal of Immigration, Asylum and Nationality Law* 210, 220–30. For a more wide-ranging critical commentary, see Dembour (n 10) chs 7 and 12.

[191] See the analysis above. See also, for example, *Muminov v Russia* (2011) 52 EHRR 23, para 89.

[192] See, for example, Vogelaar (n 185). But note the systematic analysis of the factors considered in assessments of real risk in EK Blöndal and OM Arnardóttir, 'Non-Refoulement in Strasbourg: Making Sense of the Assessment of Individual Circumstances' (2018) 5 *Oslo Law Review* 147.

[193] See commentary by Colin Warbrick in C Warbrick, 'Diplomatic Assurances and the Removal of Terrorist Suspects from the UK' (2006) 4 *Archbold News* 6, 7–9. See also R Grozdanova, 'The United Kingdom and Diplomatic Assurances: A Minimalist Approach towards the Anti-Torture Norm' (2015) 15 *International Criminal Law Review* 369, 370–71.

[194] Warbrick (n 193) 8.

[195] ibid. See also M Giuffré, 'Deportation with Assurances and Human Rights: The Case of Persons Suspected or Convicted of Serious Crimes' (2017) 15 *Journal of International Criminal Justice* 75.

on the use of diplomatic assurances in practice, former UN Special Rapporteur on Torture Manfred Nowak concluded that they are 'nothing but an attempt by European and other States to circumvent their obligation to respect the principle of *non-refoulement*'.[196] These are robust criticisms which highlight that, if diplomatic assurances are meant to alleviate a real risk of ill-treatment, they may at best be a blunt tool, and at worst a bad faith manoeuvre to avoid discharging the *non-refoulement* duty.[197]

The ECtHR has retained a degree of faith in diplomatic assurances as capable of being potent tools of protection in spite of these concerns. This may be linked, in part, to its focus on determining the cases before it on an individualised, case-by-case basis,[198] rather than passing judgement more generally on the practice of diplomatic assurances. It has suggested that it is

> not for this Court to rule upon the propriety of seeking assurances, or to assess the long term consequences of doing so; its only task is to examine whether the assurances obtained in a particular case are sufficient to remove any real risk of ill-treatment.[199]

Nonetheless, because diplomatic assurances tend to enter the equation at the point where a real risk has been substantiated, they should in principle be examined with the burden of proof being placed squarely on the expelling State's government to disprove the real risk. A default position of scepticism towards such undertakings is surely right. Indeed, diplomatic assurances are not generally taken at face value by the Court,[200] but are rather assessed in light of an array of evidence regarding the reality to be faced by the individual in the destination State. The Court has indicated that 'diplomatic assurances are not in themselves sufficient to ensure adequate protection against the risk of ill-treatment where reliable sources have reported practices resorted to or tolerated by the authorities which are manifestly contrary to the principles of the Convention'.[201]

For further critical commentary, see M Jones, 'Lies, Damned Lies and Diplomatic Assurances: The Misuse of Diplomatic Assurances in Removal Proceedings' (2006) 8 *European Journal of Migration and Law* 9; T Prasanna, 'Taking Remedies Seriously: The Normative Implications of Risking Torture' (2012) 50 *Columbia Journal of Transnational Law* 370; L Skoglund, 'Diplomatic Assurances Against Torture – An Effective Strategy? A Review of Jurisprudence and Examination of the Arguments' (2008) 77 *Nordic Journal of International Law* 319.

[196] M Nowak, 'Challenges to the Absolute Nature of the Prohibition of Torture and Ill-treatment' (2005) 23 *Netherlands Quarterly of Human Rights* 674, 687.

[197] To these can be added the current Special Rapporteur's criticism that 'even if diplomatic assurances were to be faithfully implemented by the receiving State, they reflect the expectation that the receiving State will comply only selectively with the prohibition of torture and ill-treatment', with expelling States effectively sanctioning 'a two-tier system of protection against torture and ill-treatment', Report of the Special Rapporteur on Torture and Other Cruel, Inhuman or Degrading Treatment or Punishment, UN Doc A/HRC/37/50, 23 November 2018, para 47. See also Nowak (n 196) 687.

[198] Giuffré (n 195) 84.

[199] *Othman (Abu Qatada) v UK* (2012) 55 EHRR 1, para 186.

[200] Judge Sicilianos has put it as follows: 'It is extremely rare for the Court to rely mainly on diplomatic assurances. It usually remains cautious'. See L-A Sicilianos, 'The European Court of Human Rights at a Time of Crisis in Europe' (2016) 2 *European Human Rights Law Review* 121, 128.

[201] *Ryabikin v Russia* (2009) 48 EHRR 55, para 121. See also *Saadi* (n 32) paras 147–48. But see *Othman (Abu Qatada)* (n 199) paras 188–89.

The ECtHR Grand Chamber in *Othman (Abu Qatada) v UK* provided a set of considerations that the Court deems relevant in assessing diplomatic assurances' quality and reliability:

> (i) whether the terms of the assurances have been disclosed to the Court;
> (ii) whether the assurances are specific or are general and vague;
> (iii) who has given the assurances and whether that person can bind the receiving State;
> (iv) if the assurances have been issued by the central government of the receiving State, whether local authorities can be expected to abide by them;
> (v) whether the assurances concerns treatment which is legal or illegal in the receiving State;
> (vi) whether they have been given by a Contracting State;
> (vii) the length and strength of bilateral relations between the sending and receiving States, including the receiving State's record in abiding by similar assurances;
> (viii) whether compliance with the assurances can be objectively verified through diplomatic or other monitoring mechanisms, including providing unfettered access to the applicant's lawyers;
> (ix) whether there is an effective system of protection against torture in the receiving State, including whether it is willing to cooperate with international monitoring mechanisms (including international human rights NGOs), and whether it is willing to investigate allegations of torture and to punish those responsible;
> (x) whether the applicant has previously been ill-treated in the receiving State; and
> (xi) whether the reliability of the assurances has been examined by the domestic courts of the sending/Contracting State.[202]

Through considerations such as the above, the ECtHR seeks to conduct, and to provide the tools for conducting, a fact-sensitive assessment of whether the real risk substantiated by the applicant has been alleviated through a combination of factors rendering assurances and associated undertakings likely to be enforced and subject to effective verifiability and accountability mechanisms.[203] As Mariagiulia Giuffré observes, the ECtHR has tended to look 'beyond the subjective affirmation of the receiving state by also examining its actions and human rights track record in practice'.[204] The Court has been 'frequently unpersuaded' that diplomatic assurances alleviate real risk, especially where the receiving country exhibits patterns of 'endemic or persistent' abuses.[205] This discloses *some* critical consideration both of the credibility of assurances on their face and of the practical likelihood that the undertakings 'assured' will materialise in an effective and sustainable way after expulsion.[206]

[202] *Othman (Abu Qatada)* (n 199) para 189 (citations omitted).

[203] On the pragmatic character of this approach, see ME Salerno, 'Can Diplomatic Assurances, in Their Practical Application, Provide Effective Protection Against the Risk of Torture and Ill Treatment? A Focus on the Evolution of the Pragmatic Approach of the European Court of Human Rights in Removal Cases of Suspected Terrorists' (2017) 8 *New Journal of European Criminal Law* 453.

[204] Giuffré (n 195) 83.

[205] ibid 84. See also Blöndal and Arnardóttir (n 192) 153.

[206] But for a robust critique of credibility dynamics in expulsion decisions, see Dembour (n 10) ch 7.

The Court is also particularly sceptical of generic undertakings. For example, in *MSS* it found that the diplomatic assurances given by Greece to the Belgian authorities in respect of the applicant did not amount to a sufficient guarantee, noting that the relevant documentation had been 'worded in stereotyped terms ... [containing] no guarantee concerning the applicant in person' or 'merely referred to the applicable legislation, with no relevant information about the situation in practice'.[207] Similar dismissals of generic, broad-brush or vague assurances can be found in other case law.[208] On the other hand, the Court has given weight to assurances where they have been 'specific, clear and unequivocal'.[209]

Nonetheless, the default position of scepticism towards diplomatic assurances is challenged in judgments such as *Paposhvili*, where the Court has indicated that

> [w]here serious doubts persist regarding the impact of removal on the persons concerned – on account of the general situation in the receiving country and/or their individual situation – the returning State must obtain individual and sufficient assurances from the receiving State, as a precondition for removal, that appropriate treatment will be available and accessible to the persons concerned so that they do not find themselves in a situation contrary to Article 3.[210]

This position, shaped by a focus on securing individual protection for persons facing expulsion, appears to give considerable weight or even primacy to diplomatic assurances as tools of risk alleviation and effective protection. In order for the Court's doctrine to cohere with the need for a rigorous and fact-sensitive assessment of real risk, the question of the 'sufficiency' of diplomatic assurances in securing protection should be closely examined, and a default position of scepticism towards diplomatic assurances should be maintained.

7.5.5. Safe Destination States?

In assessing risk, the idea of 'safe' States, presumed to be destinations where a real risk of ill-treatment or of *refoulement* does not prevail, is problematic, both as a general matter and in eliding the rigorous, fact-sensitive assessment that is required in discharging the *non-refoulement* duty under Article 3 ECHR. *MSS*, decided in 2011, confirms that the ECtHR does not consider the fact that a State is bound by the ECHR and by EU norms and subject to Council of Europe and EU legal and monitoring mechanisms to be sufficient guarantee against the real risk of ill-treatment.[211] Moreover, the ECtHR has demanded fact-sensitive assessments

[207] *MSS* (n 12) para 354.
[208] See, for example, *Saadi* (n 32) paras 147–48; *Klein v Russia* App no 24268/08 (ECtHR, 1 April 2010), para 55; *Khaydarov v Russia* App no 21055/09 (ECtHR, 20 May 2010), para 111; *Trabelsi* (n 77) para 135.
[209] See, for example, *Rrapo v Albania* App no 58555/10 (ECtHR, 25 September 2012), para 73.
[210] *Paposhvili* (n 13) para 191; see also *Tarakhel* (n 41) paras 120–21; and *Savran* (n 135) paras 48, 66–67.
[211] *MSS* (n 12) paras 359–60; see also *Paposhvili* (n 13) para 193.

in respect of the concept of 'safe third countries', the basis of such a categorisation, and the extent to which 'safety' can be assumed in respect of the particular applicant(s).[212]

Nonetheless, the idea that the ECtHR would rarely find a prospective violation of Article 3 in circumstances of expulsion to a State with 'a long history of respect of democracy, human rights and the rule of law', put forward in cases like *Harkins* and *Ahmad*,[213] is deeply problematic. Insofar as such a stance purports to create an evidentiary presumption against a finding of real risk, it opens up a doctrinally ordained margin of error which is inconsistent with the basis of the duty against expulsion and can practically operate to displace it; it bases this margin on an open-ended and inherently problematic distinction between 'good' and 'bad' States;[214] and, in the cases mentioned, it applies this margin in relation to a State with at best a questionable record in relation to torture and inhuman and degrading treatment and punishment.[215] Such an approach distorts the fact-focused assessment demanded by the *non-refoulement* duty under Article 3 ECHR and is capable of effectively displacing its protection. It is therefore incompatible with the absoluteness starting point.

7.6. Conclusion

The account offered of Article 3's application to expulsion decisions in this chapter has sought to elucidate the negative obligation against expulsion and the way the wrong(s) involved can be understood. The fundamental wrong at issue involves coercively subjecting or exposing persons to (a real risk of) torture or inhuman or degrading treatment or punishment; doing so by way of expulsion is only one – if particularly contentious – manifestation of such a wrong. Given the contours of the obligation against expulsion, its specification requires even more sensitivity to context than is the norm in cases concerning Article 3 ill-treatment, as a context-sensitive assessment is required not only in determining the character of the relevant (prospective) treatment or punishment, but also in ascertaining the risk involved.

[212] *Ilias and Ahmed* (n 135) paras 142–64; European Court of Human Rights, Research Division, *Articles 2, 3, 8 and 13: The concept of a "safe third country" in the case-law of the Court* (Council of Europe 2018), available at: www.echr.coe.int/Documents/Research_report_safe_third_country_ENG.pdf (accessed 3 January 2020). See the critical appraisal in M-T Gil-Bazo, 'The Safe Third Country Concept in International Agreements on Refugee Protection: Assessing State Practice' (2015) 33 *Netherlands Quarterly of Human Rights* 42; AEDH, FIDH and EuroMed Rights, *"Safe" countries: A denial of the right of asylum* (2016), available at: www.ohchr.org/Documents/Issues/MHR/ReportLargeMovements/FIDH2%20.pdf (accessed 3 January 2020).

[213] *Harkins* (n 45) para 131; *Ahmad* (n 46) para 179. See, too, *Čalovskis* (n 84) para 134. See also, in relation to diplomatic assurances, *Rrapo* (n 84) para 72.

[214] See Mavronicola and Messineo (n 46) 602.

[215] See the materials cited in n 88.

An examination of some of the key substantive parameters of the *non-refoulement* duty under Article 3 suggests that, while the Court often sets up robust starting points in delineating the obligation, which tend to cohere in principle with the requirements of non-displacement and relevant reasoning, it sometimes unduly deviates from these. In this respect, *Harkins* and *Ahmad* represent significant departures from the absoluteness starting point, and the 'relativist' approach adopted therein should be explicitly abandoned. Furthermore, as argued in this chapter, adherence to the absoluteness starting point and notably to the imperative of non-displacement in the prospective assessment involved in applying the *non-refoulement* duty entails that the Court – and other norm-appliers – should err on the side of caution, rather than the opposite, where doubt persists in respect of the nature of the treatment faced or the degree of risk involved. The requirement of certainty, moreover, calls for further generalisable pronouncements on Article 3's demands in the context of expulsion decisions. These pronouncements should at the same time be principled rather than arbitrary (an example of the latter being the 'exceptionality' filter in medical cases), and uphold rather than elide the fact-sensitive assessment required in respect of any person claiming that expulsion will violate their right not to be subjected to torture or to inhuman or degrading treatment or punishment under Article 3 ECHR.

8

Conclusion

Throughout this book, I have tried to make sense of the concept of absolute rights and, by focusing more closely on State duties, of absolute *wrongs* as a matter of human rights law. This endeavour has been anchored in a wide-ranging examination of the contours of the right not to be subjected to torture or inhuman or degrading treatment or punishment, enshrined in Article 3 ECHR. The substantial body of jurisprudence that has emerged on the right's application in a vast variety of circumstances makes for a rich and complex landscape, which I have sought to navigate with reference to the right's absolute character and the specification requirements emerging therefrom. While I do not offer an exhaustive account of the circumstances which may lead to a finding of a breach of Article 3 – nor could I – I hope that this book provides conceptual tools that may be employed to understand, critique and progress the specification of Article 3 ECHR in light of the right's absolute character. To conclude, rather than summarise, I want briefly to reflect on and draw out certain strands of analysis from the preceding chapters and contemplate some of their implications for rights reasoning in general, and for the right not to be subjected to torture or inhuman or degrading treatment or punishment in particular.

8.1. What Are (the Implications of) Absolute Rights?

As this study supports, there *are* absolute rights at law, and the significance of attributing the character of absoluteness to rights endures. However, to do justice to the concept, we must be clear about what it entails and, crucially, what it does not entail. Appreciating the implications of absoluteness allows us to sharpen our understanding of human rights provisions and human rights reasoning. This elucidation is critical given that uncertainty has been, and continues to be, exploited to undermine and dilute human rights.

The absolute character of a right entails that it is non-displaceable – that it cannot be overridden by extraneous concerns. As argued in this study, if the right's absolute character is to be respected, the obligations that flow from the right must be specified in a way that coheres with that absoluteness. They must not be interpreted in a way that displaces the right or otherwise undermines its absolute character. Achieving this is the unenviable and complex task of those who apply absolute rights, including, ultimately, the courts that pronounce on them. In the context of Article 3 ECHR this means it is the task of the ECtHR to specify the right's correlative obligations by relying on *relevant* reasoning, which interprets rather than distorts the wrongs at issue, and without displacing the right through the back door. This specification may quite rightly show sensitivity to relevant context, and a readiness to rethink or reimagine the wrongs corresponding to the right – but it should also attend to the importance of providing a degree of guidance so that the right may be understood and applied effectively and in accordance with its absolute character by rights-holders, duty-bearers and other norm-appliers. These are the requirements – encompassing a capacity to guide, delimitation through relevant reasoning, and non-displacement – that the specification of an absolute right should fulfil.

At the same time, it is important to appreciate what the absolute character of a right does *not* entail. The absolute character of a right does not guarantee that it is never disputed, contested or violated *as a matter of fact*. It does not entail that its interpretation should be originalist, minimalist or detached from relevant context. It does not necessitate that the right's substantive scope should be narrow, nor that it should be broad; arguments that push in either direction without engaging substantively with the wrongs at issue are misplaced. In this regard, it is important to underline that the prevalence of particular forms of ill-treatment – for instance, police violence – does not vitiate or otherwise 'dent' their absolute wrongfulness: an act need not be aberrant in fact for its prohibition to be absolute.

The absolute character of a right also does not entail that the positive obligations it gives rise to are boundless: rather, these are appropriately circumscribed by criteria that delineate wrongful omissions, including the criterion of intra-Convention lawfulness. The latter point is, of course, fundamental to unravelling arguments that torturing or ill-treating 'terrorist' suspects or other suspected wrong-doers is warranted or even compelled on the basis of positive obligations to protect other persons. There is no positive obligation to torture or ill-treat someone as a means of safeguarding an absolute right against torture or ill-treatment.[1]

Across the book I have sought to respond to strands of scepticism about absolute rights in general, and the absolute right enshrined in Article 3 ECHR in particular, and to offer conceptual clarity on how an absolute right may be understood and delimited, providing a theoretically informed assessment of the ECtHR's specification of the absolute right not to be subjected to torture or inhuman or degrading treatment or punishment in the face of the continued contestation surrounding it. In pursuing its dual function of elucidating the concept of an absolute right and concretising it in Article 3 ECHR, I hope that this book has illustrated why and how delimiting the absolute matters, and how this delimitation may be coherently pursued.

[1] See Chs 2, 3 and 6; see, further, N Mavronicola, 'Is the Prohibition against Torture and Cruel, Inhuman and Degrading Treatment Absolute in International Human Rights Law? A Reply to Steven Greer' (2017) 17 *Human Rights Law Review* 479, 483–85.

8.2. Context, Justificatory Reasoning and the Legitimate Specification of Article 3 ECHR

As the analysis in much of the book demonstrates, the delimitation of the wrongs of torture, inhumanity and degradation proscribed by Article 3 ECHR can and indeed must operate in a context-sensitive manner: attention to relevant context can help locate the boundaries between intimacy and violence, between self-defence and brutality, between the protection of a person and the violation of one's person. Context may be relevant in delineating the wrongs at issue even in respect of the infliction of substantial suffering: there are circumstances in which someone might inflict considerable suffering on another person without this amounting to inhuman or degrading treatment or punishment or torture. Consider, for example, a doctor informing someone of a loved one's death; no matter how kind and respectful they may be, they are nonetheless bringing about significant suffering. To illustrate the way in which the character of an act inflicting suffering may vary from one context to another, we may contrast that scenario with one in which the same words are uttered by a lying interrogator, with the intent of driving someone to desperation and a useful revelation.

Sometimes the factors that distinguish an act that falls within the 'torture continuum' from one that does not may be seen to bear the hallmarks of justificatory reasoning. A classic context in which this occurs is the use of force by law enforcement officials, in the context of policing a demonstration, for example. The ECtHR has found that the use of force against someone is not prohibited by Article 3 ECHR where it is strictly necessary to repel a threat to life or limb that is immediately posed by the person against whom such force is used.[2] As argued in this book, this is not a case of justifying and accordingly legalising certain forms of inhuman, degrading or torturous treatment. Rather, it involves distinguishing uses of force that are inhuman, degrading or torturous from those that are not. Article 3 does not proscribe the use of force per se – it proscribes torture as well as inhuman or degrading treatment or punishment, including uses of force that *wrong* someone in a way that is inhuman, degrading or torturous. Rather than displacing the prohibition, the Court's application of a strict necessity test in determining whether the use of force by State agents in defence of self or others violates Article 3 can serve to distinguish uses of force that are disrespectful of human dignity, and are thereby inhuman or degrading, from those that are not.[3] Accordingly, the Court's use of justificatory reasoning in this context seeks, in principle, to interpret

[2] See, for example, *Güler and Öngel v Turkey* App nos 29612/05 and 30668/05 (ECtHR, 4 October 2011), discussed in N Mavronicola, '*Güler and Öngel v Turkey*: Article 3 of the European Convention on Human Rights and Strasbourg's Discourse on the Justified Use of Force' (2013) 76 *Modern Law Review* 370; see, further, Report of the Special Rapporteur on Torture and Other Cruel, Inhuman or Degrading Treatment or Punishment, UN Doc A/72/178, 20 July 2017.

[3] See the discussion in Ch 5.

rather than to distort or displace the right not to be subjected to torture or inhuman or degrading treatment or punishment, a right which is 'closely bound up with respect for human dignity'.[4] There is a critical difference between a relevant circumstance that distinguishes human dignity-respecting from human dignity-disrespecting action – consider consent in a sexual context, for example[5] – and the *displacement* of the right not to be treated in an inhuman or degrading manner.

This clarification is part of a broader argument, central to the book, that 'delimiting the absolute' as concretised in Article 3 ECHR requires us to focus on the wrongs at issue, and not purely on the harms with which they tend to be associated. Thus, the 'minimum level of severity' criterion may be understood in relational and qualitative terms, and as attaching to the character of the treatment, rather than relating solely to its repercussions on the victim – although the latter will often play a significant role in shaping the wrong in question. Reframing the delimitation of Article 3 ECHR by focusing on the wrongs at issue is critical if we are to avoid misreading the right and the role of contextual and sometimes justificatory reasoning in delimiting it, particularly insofar as such misreading may lead to suggestions that the right is not absolute.[6] The book accordingly counters arguments suggesting that justificatory reasoning or sensitivity to context *necessarily* undermine absoluteness and offers some reflections on when such reasoning may appropriately specify rather than distort or displace the right.

While rationalising the relevance of context and certain justificatory reasoning is an important element of this study, much of the book is also dedicated to probing and challenging elements of the ECtHR's specification of Article 3 that raise concerns in relation to absoluteness and the legitimate specification requirements. Such elements include an undue focus on tangible injuries in delineating torture or other ill-treatment,[7] the spectre of relativism in extradition case law,[8] and pockets of uncertainty within the doctrine.[9] In engaging in this critical endeavour I have sought affirmatively to follow the legitimate specification requirements developed in this study and to reason coherently through the doctrine in light of Article 3's letter and spirit. While my critical exercise, in the context of a vast body of case law and a myriad of morally loaded legal issues, has necessarily been incomplete, I hope nonetheless to have planted 'seeds' out of which further critical engagement

[4] *Bouyid v Belgium* (2016) 62 EHRR 32, para 81.

[5] For a nuanced account on consent and sexual violence, see E Dowds, *Feminist Engagement with International Criminal Law: Norm Transfer, Complementarity, Rape and Consent* (Hart Publishing 2020) chs 4–6.

[6] See, for example, DJ Harris, M O'Boyle, EP Bates and CM Buckley, *Harris, O'Boyle and Warbrick: Law of the European Convention on Human Rights* (4th edn, Oxford University Press 2018) 237; S Greer, 'Is the Prohibition against Torture, Cruel, Inhuman and Degrading Treatment Really "Absolute" in International Human Rights Law?' (2015) 15 *Human Rights Law Review* 101.

[7] See Chs 4 and 5.

[8] See Ch 7.

[9] These are considered throughout the book, see, for example, Ch 6.

with the rich contours of the right not to be subjected to torture or inhuman or degrading treatment or punishment may grow.[10]

8.3. Positive Duties to Protect – And Their Limits

As acknowledged in Chapter 6, the challenges surrounding the specification of an absolute right are amplified in the arena of positive obligations. Three aspects of positive obligations under the absolute right not to be subjected to torture or inhuman or degrading treatment or punishment are worth stressing. The first is that, while obligations to protect operate in respect of both the general and particular incidence and risks of ill-treatment, their substantive scope is, as mentioned above, not boundless. What they may demand of States is appropriately shaped by both rigid and fluid constraints, including intra-Convention legality and resource availability, but subject to a criterion of adequacy. The ECtHR's specification of positive obligations under Article 3 through considerations of reasonableness and adequacy therefore does not amount to displacement but rather amounts to a specification whose criteria, at least in principle, can serve to delineate what constitutes a wrongful omission by the State.

Second, in respect of the capacity to guide, the specification of positive obligations combines the certainty challenges associated with the specification of torture and inhuman or degrading treatment or punishment with those surrounding the inevitably varied operation of the criteria of reasonableness and adequacy in delineating the context-sensitive measures demanded from case to case. Nonetheless, the reasoned elaboration of particular types of measures – such as investigations – required in particular contexts contributes to providing *ex ante* guidance. At the same time, more clarity is warranted in respect of Article 3's socio-economic application, not least in relation to duties to alleviate (risks of) acute hardship and related suffering. The Court's increasing acknowledgement that official indifference – understood as inaction – in the face of (a risk of) acute hardship violates Article 3 ECHR can be further elucidated towards demanding reasonable and adequate positive measures, tailored to the circumstances, to alleviate such hardship.

Lastly, the orientation of positive obligations is meant to be *protective*, not coercive.[11] This means that the specification of positive obligations under Article 3 ECHR must be orientated at effectively protecting persons from torture, inhumanity or degradation, rather than at criminalising these wrongs or pursuing

[10] It is worth noting that, while the book tackles various elements of substance in the specification of Article 3 ECHR, a systematic mapping of the function of the margin of appreciation and of consensus reasoning in shaping the right and its application remains to be undertaken in another study.

[11] See the critical analysis in L Lazarus, 'Positive Obligations and Criminal Justice: Duties to Protect or Coerce?' in L Zedner and J Roberts (eds), *Principles and Values in Criminal Law and Criminal Justice* (Oxford University Press 2012).

punishment per se.[12] This clarification goes to the heart of Article 3, given the profound tension between the interventions made on the basis of Article 3 and human dignity to soften the edge of State penality, and the coercive push, in positive obligations doctrine, to sharpen it. This calls for a reconsideration of the ECtHR's coercive focus in delimiting positive obligations under Article 3 ECHR – primarily through duties to criminalise, police, prosecute and punish – and a protective reorientation that embraces non-carceral pathways to protection and prevention.

Understanding positive obligations as arising in respect of a variety of general and particular risks and as having a *protective* rather than coercive character entails envisioning the prospect of a recalibration in how positive obligations corresponding to an absolute right such as Article 3 ECHR are conceptualised and delimited. It invites us to contemplate a shift from focusing on the mobilisation of criminal law (enforcement) to secure the right, towards demanding the multi-layered mobilisation of State resources to provide meaningful protection to (potential) victims and to address the structural conditions that drive, enable or otherwise sustain these wrongs. Such a shift is by no means a simple or straightforward endeavour and there is considerable scope for systematic investigation of how it may be pursued and achieved.

8.4. Between the Certain and the Right

Another key theme running – perhaps in understated fashion – across the book is the tension between the imperative of certainty and the rejection of complacency in the specification of torture, inhumanity and degradation. Given the non-displaceable nature of the right enshrined in Article 3 ECHR, the specification of its content is decisive of the lawfulness of State action or inaction (and, of course, conclusively determines the substantive scope of the relevant entitlement). Accordingly, as argued in this book, transparent reasoning which is authoritative and 'teachable' is vital towards securing respect for Article 3 but also in upholding the rule of law under the Convention. At the same time, the study acknowledges and underlines that, in the specification of Article 3 ECHR, the ECtHR must remain attentive to the relevant context and circumstances that shape whether something amounts to torture, inhumanity and degradation, and prepared to refine its understanding

[12] On the insufficiency of criminal law tools in preventing torture, see generally D Celermajer, *The Prevention of Torture: An Ecological Approach* (Cambridge University Press 2018). For critical perspectives on anti-impunity within human rights, see K Engle, Z Miller and DM Davis (eds), *Anti-Impunity and the Human Rights Agenda* (Cambridge University Press 2016). See, further, L Lavrysen and N Mavronicola (eds), *Coercive Human Rights: Positive Duties to Mobilise the Criminal Law under the ECHR* (Hart Publishing 2020).

of the wrongs at issue, not least by recognising the 'egregious in the everyday'.[13] In mediating between the imperative of certainty and the imperative of getting it right, the ECtHR is called upon to deliver clear and coherent pronouncements on Article 3 ECHR that are capable of offering some *ex ante* guidance, while at the same time neither abandoning its open-minded consideration of (relevant) contextual factors nor refusing to reconsider problematic 'precedent' or egregious but entrenched aspects of the status quo.

While there are many elements of Article 3 ECHR that warrant a greater attention to certainty and further *ex ante* guidance, as is frequently suggested throughout the book, it is both impossible and ill-advised to seek to provide complete certainty on any legal norm, including an absolute right. This is especially so in relation to wrongs which have infinitely varied manifestations, and in respect of a norm whose *circumvention* has often involved the deployment of substantial expertise and imagination in the face of (perceived) rigidity. The latter point refers, of course, to practices that have sought to exploit the perceived boundaries of 'torture'.

Nonetheless, the element of uncertainty we have to accept in the specification of Article 3 ECHR should not operate to *reduce* protection, whether as a basis for judicial reluctance to make a finding of violation or as a licence for other norm-appliers to err on the side of recklessness. It is deeply concerning when an inevitable degree of uncertainty in Article 3's specification – for example, in conducting prospective assessments of circumstances likely to be faced upon removal to another country – produces a reluctance to find an Article 3 violation at ECtHR level, and a window for reckless or bad faith conduct on the part of States. As argued in this book, the appropriate approach in circumstances of uncertainty is to err on the side of caution and thus 'risk' surpassing the protection required rather than crossing what is meant to be a red line.

8.5. Defending and Upholding the Right Not to Be Subjected to Torture or Inhuman or Degrading Treatment or Punishment: The Future

This book's defence of the absolute right not to be subjected to torture or inhuman or degrading treatment or punishment rests chiefly on conceptual clarification. While I do not claim to offer a complete moral defence of this, or any other, absolute right, I hope that I have nonetheless provided a robust line of defence for Article 3's increasingly contested claim to absoluteness amidst the ebb and flow of political appetite for (supporting) torture or for diluting or circumventing the

[13] Rhonda Copelon called for recognising the 'egregious in the everyday': R Copelon, 'Recognizing the Egregious in the Everyday: Domestic Violence as Torture' (1994) 25 *Columbia Human Rights Law Review* 291.

right not to be subjected to such abuse. I hope too that the imagination and creativity of many (critical) friends of human rights may be mobilised in defending and shaping (the future of) this right.

There is no room for complacency in respect of the future of the right not to be subjected to torture or inhuman or degrading treatment or punishment. Not only must the right and its absolute character be defended with vigour, it must also be interpreted both coherently and dynamically, and with a readiness to reason rigorously through its thorniest aspects, on the basis of the egalitarian commitment to human dignity that underpins it. Defending and upholding the right not to be subjected to torture or inhuman or degrading treatment or punishment requires us to acknowledge how the wrongs it proscribes and the modalities of its violation are linked to othering – notably the setting apart of those considered undeserving of basic respect and protection. It therefore requires a dedication to confronting and resisting such exclusionary dynamics, not least in the specification of the right, and to not only acknowledging but foregrounding those pervasively marginalised and dehumanised through systematic or systemic othering.

Substantively, the future of the right calls for a redistribution in focus as well as resources. From a shift out of varying 'all-things-considered' conclusions towards principled, standard-setting reasoning on the contours of torture, inhumanity and degradation and their manifestation in the banal-ised everyday,[14] to rescuing positive obligations from being captured by carceral tools,[15] there is considerable scope for coherently (re)thinking and (re)shaping the specification of the right. Substantial attention should continue to be directed to the right's contested contours and perceived 'edges', with a readiness to grapple abstractly and concretely with the demands of human dignity.[16] It is to be hoped that, in this process, the right's demands can be ever more cogently elaborated, moving beyond fragmented findings and under-reasoned distinctions.

The interpretive endeavour that the absolute right not to be subjected to torture or inhuman or degrading treatment or punishment calls for brims with both possibilities and pitfalls. It demands that we probe familiar and less familiar terrain and that we navigate between specification and abstraction with a preparedness to reason meaningfully and transparently through what makes up the absolute wrongs at issue. I hope that this book provides a groundwork for transparently and coherently (re)interpreting – or even reimagining – the right's contours, while affirming its absolute character.

[14] Susan Marks has called on the human rights movement to turn its 'gaze' to what is 'hidden in plain sight' (S Marks, 'Four Human Rights Myths' in D Kinley, W Sadurski and K Walton (eds), *Human Rights: Old Problems, New Possibilities* (Edward Elgar 2013) 235) and criticised a language of 'exceptionalism' regarding torture that 'obscures the normality of abuses' (S Marks, 'Apologising for Torture' (2004) 73(3) *Nordic Journal of International Law* 365, 378). See also Copelon (n 13).

[15] See some of the critical discussions in Lavrysen and Mavronicola (eds) (n 12).

[16] See, in this regard, E Webster, *Dignity, Degrading Treatment and Torture in Human Rights Law: The Ends of Article 3 of the European Convention on Human Rights* (Routledge 2018).

INDEX

Note on the index:
The index includes authors mentioned in the body of the text, and those quoted in the footnotes or mentioned there in in a substantive way. All joint authors are given their own entries. Cases have been included where discussed in the body of the text or substantively in the footnotes.

Lightning Source UK Ltd.
Milton Keynes UK
UKHW021208140422
401552UK00003B/122

9 781509 902996